MEDIA LITERACY EDUCATION IN ACTION

Media Literacy Education in Action brings together the field's leading scholars and advocates to present a snapshot of the theoretical and conceptual development of media literacy education—what has influenced it, current trends, and ideas about its future. Featuring a mix of perspectives, it explores the divergent ways in which media literacy is connected to educational communities and academic areas in both local and global contexts. The volume is structured around seven themes:

- Media Literacy—Past and Present
- Digital Media and Learning
- Global Perspectives
- Public Spaces
- Civic Activism
- Policy and Digital Citizenship
- Future Connections

Compelling, well-organized, and authoritative, this one-stop resource for understanding more about media literacy education across disciplines, cultures, and divides offers the fresh outlook that is needed at this point in time. Globally, as more and more states and countries call for media literacy education more explicitly in their curriculum guidelines, educators are being required to teach media literacy in both elementary and secondary education contexts. This book serves both as a valuable primer for media and information literacy courses and to give elementary and secondary teachers an essential pedagogical framework for teaching students about the media and mediated environments in their classrooms.

Belinha S. De Abreu is Assistant Professor of Educational Technology at Fairfield University, USA.

Paul Mihailidis is Assistant Professor in the School of Communication at Emerson College, USA.

MEDIA LITERACY EDUCATION IN ACTION

Theoretical and Pedagogical Perspectives

Edited by
Belinha S. De Abreu
and Paul Mihailidis

Routledge
Taylor & Francis Group

NEW YORK AND LONDON

First published 2014
by Routledge
711 Third Avenue, New York, NY 10017

and by Routledge
2 Park Square, Milton Park, Abingdon, Oxon OX14 4RN

Routledge is an imprint of the Taylor & Francis Group, an informa business

Library of Congress Cataloging-in-Publication Data

Media literacy education in action : theoretical and pedagogical perspectives /
edited by Belinha S. De Abreu & Paul Mihailidis. — First edition.
    pages cm
  Includes bibliographical references and index.
  1. Media literacy—Study and teaching. 2. Educational technology.
I. De Abreu, Belinha S. II. Mihailidis, Paul, 1978–
P96.M4M464   2014
302.23071—dc23   2013024957

ISBN: 978-0-415-65834-8 (hbk)
ISBN: 978-0-415-65837-9 (pbk)
ISBN: 978-0-203-07612-5 (ebk)

Typeset in Bembo
by Apex CoVantage, LLC

Printed and bound in the United States of America by Publishers Graphics,
LLC on sustainably sourced paper.

To my husband, parents, sister, and brother-in-law, and my personal learning community that includes both friends and colleagues.

Belinha

This book is dedicated to Valerie Diggs, who has shown to me the strength, dedication, and passion needed to succeed in the classroom, and in life.

Paul

CONTENTS

FOREWORD

Like the field it describes, *Media Literacy Education in Action* is nothing if not diverse. The book contains a wide range of conceptual arguments and rationales; overviews of the history of the field and the current state of play in different national contexts; competing definitions, recommendations, and manifestos; curriculum proposals, both for media education as a distinct subject field and as an element of other fields, including technology, citizenship, information literacy, rhetoric, and arts education; accounts of practice in classrooms and in other public spaces, such as libraries, community settings, and social movements; and discussions of wider policy developments in the fields of communication and education. There are also signs of the emerging international dialogue in media literacy education and indications of what we can learn from studying the politics of educational and media systems in different contexts around the world—although there is undoubtedly scope for further engagement here with colleagues from non-Western and non-English-speaking countries.

Across these diverse contributions, several key themes emerge, but perhaps the most significant is to do with the changing nature of contemporary media—and particularly the impact of digital technology. As the wider media landscape has "gone digital," so too has education. The past twenty years has seen a massive push—on the part of governments, but also of technology corporations—to insert digital media in schools. This has been accompanied by a veritable explosion of hype about the wonders of technology and its uniformly beneficial effects on learning, on society and on the mind. In the process, it has often seemed as though media literacy education, and the critical perspectives it entails, have been left behind.

In this context, it still bears repeating that media education (teaching about media) is not the same thing as educational technology (teaching through media)—although clearly there can and should be a relationship between them. Yet the advent of so-called "participatory" media and the euphoric business rhetoric of "media 2.0" seems to have resulted in a further confusion: some of us seem to have abandoned what Neil Postman many years ago called our "crap detectors." It is obviously imperative for media educators to engage with these technological developments, and with their considerable potential for promoting more engaging, student-centered learning. Yet it is also increasingly important to insist on the civic and public dimensions of media education, and on the need for critical analysis and evaluation, if it is not to degenerate into a superficial celebration of media fandom or a vacuous notion of creativity.

The new metaphors and buzzwords that are employed by many of the contributors here—curation, remix, participation, and others—do help to identify and explain what some young people can now do with media outside school. They also help to move the debate further beyond the protectionist approach that is still very apparent in some contexts (and perhaps particularly in the United States). Thankfully, very few of the contributors here seem to conceive of their role in terms of defending children against morally harmful influences—although perhaps it also bears repeating that media education is not about Internet safety, even if this is an issue that it might briefly address.

However, these new '2.0' arguments tend to accentuate the positive and to neglect issues of inequality and the political economy of media, and they also overestimate the novelty of these developments. Perhaps more significantly in this context, they don't tell us much about pedagogy in classrooms—about what and how we might teach about new media, and how students might actually learn. There is a continuing need here, not so much for recommendations and proposals about how to do media literacy education, but for detailed, honest and reflexive accounts of what it looks like in classrooms—in real classrooms, without all the state-of-the-art, high-tech gadgets—and of what learners actually make of it all. Because whatever else it may be, media literacy education certainly isn't easy or straightforward.

Of course, the diversity of these issues and perspectives might be seen to reflect a troubling lack of coherence and consensus. But we might equally see this proliferation as a positive sign. As an old-timer in the field, I know that we are unlikely ever to arrive at a point where we can all sign up to a single definition and prescription for media literacy education. This is the case in most other areas of education, and it's a healthy phenomenon: We should let the thousand flowers bloom.

In his opening chapter, Julian McDougall describes media literacy education as an "unfinished project," and looks forward to the point at which it will be completed. Personally, I doubt that this will ever happen, and I'm not sure I would like it to do so either. As the media and education change, the field will continue to evolve; and it will do so both through abstract debate and through reflection on the concrete difficulties of practice. At the risk of ending on a gnomic and mystical note, let us accept and even celebrate the fact that the project will forever be unfinished. . .

David Buckingham
Loughborough University, London, May 2013

PREFACE

Today's digital media culture presents numerous opportunities and challenges for how we prepare the next generation of citizens. From public schools, libraries, and museums, to home, church, and work, digital media are fundamentally changing the way we go about our daily lives. With this comes a host of interesting new questions about how new social platforms and mobile technologies are changing the way in which communicate with our friends, family, and acquaintances. How we hear about what's going on in the world. And how we choose to express our opinions, share interesting things, and feel part of communities large and small.

This culture is also affecting how we teach and learn about the world. Our ability to memorize and recall information is now challenged by an endless sea of information at our fingertips. Our ability to concentrate on a single task for an extended period of time is now challenged by our social networks that tether us to our peers from the minute we wake to the minute we sleep. Our ability to think critically about our local, national, and global communities is challenged by the ever fast pace of information and communication that gives little time for breadth, scope, and reflection.

How we build core competencies to thrive in this new information age are at the core of *Media Literacy Education in Action: Theoretical and Pedagogical Perspectives*. We both come to this project in the middle of careers that take us around the world looking at the ways in which teachers, parents, citizens, students, journalists, public officials, curators, librarians, and youth are learning to engage with media to become more mindful, critical, and expressive thinkers. This book grew out of a need to cement some of these experiences in a concrete and holistic way and make them available for others to see.

We see so many fascinating media literacy projects, initiatives, and movements happening across public spaces—libraries, parks, museums, community centers—and in the home, school, city, and countryside. At the same time, our field is so encompassing that we have trouble finding a coherent and unified set of works around which we can show scholars, teachers, parents, and policy makers all the diverse and unique ways media literacy education is working to prepare young people for lives of active inquiry and inclusive citizenship.

This book was put together to offer a state of the field perspective for media literacy. It's meant to be inclusive, offering perspectives for teachers, parents, local and national policy makers, librarians, civic activists, and media scholars interested in exploring the myriad of ways that media literacy is responding to the digital media age. The book incorporates 36 scholars of media, education, and communication, who share their experiences, ideas, and scholarship across 26 chapters divided into 7 parts. Seminal media education scholar David Buckingham provides a foreword that grounds the work of these scholars in the larger context of media literacy today.

Part One, Media Literacy: Past and Present, focuses on the growth of media literacy through a historical lens. The aim is to ground the book in a larger perspective over time, and beyond any specific theme, strand, or focus. Julian McDougall of Bournemouth University, U.K., opens the section with an exploration of how media education and critical inquiry have evolved over time. Tessa Jolls, Barb Walkosz, and Dee Morgethaler then present a series of interviews conducted with seminal media literacy scholars who offer their insight on their careers in media literacy and what they believe were and are the biggest challenges that face the movement today. This enlightening picture captures some of the most vibrant voices that have helped build the field over the last decades. Lastly, Neil Andersen, President of Ontario's Association for Media Literacy, offers his own look back at the evolution of the field in Australia, England, the United States, and Canada, where he grounds the evolution of media literacy in the early work of McLuhan. Andersen builds a critical look at media literacy today by tracing Canada's embracing of the movement and the strides they have made.

The concept of a participatory culture has been made relevant by the many new technologies emerging in the home and classroom today. However, the idea of participation in media has existed long before these technologies. How we think about learning and the interplay between technologies, literacies, and educational experiences take on new forms of understanding in a digital media age.

In Part Two, Digital Media and Learning, four chapters explore a host of perspectives on how learning is evolving in technological contexts, and what tools and platforms are facilitating this change. Paul Mihailidis, Director of the Salzburg Academy on Media and Global Change and Media Studies Professor at Emerson College, begins by exploring the phenomenon of curation, and arguing for its position as a core competency for digital and media literacy in participatory culture. Margaret Carmody Hagood of the College of Charleston uses the lens of participation to explore how educators can use collaborative technologies to engage students with disabilities. Erin Reilly of USC's Innovation Lab at the Annenberg School for Communication and Journalism explores how the concept of visualization can develop in youth more savvy and interactive relationships with data and information. Finally, Kent State Professor William Kist develops the "flat classroom" metaphor to ponder a broad concept of media literacy that incorporates multimedia texts and peer-to-peer tools in the education of all citizens. Kist sees the expanded classroom and discourse as mechanisms for more diverse voices and interactivity in classrooms around the world.

Part Three, Global Perspectives, explores the role of media literacy as it has developed in international scope and focus in recent decades. Facilitated largely by new digital technologies and social platforms, how students learn about the role of media in their daily lives must necessarily include global perspectives. Four scholars offer unique perspectives about different media education initiatives in progress around the world. Swedish Media Literacy Scholar Per Lundgren leads off the section by offering a "Nordic perspective" on media literacy education and specifically on policy concerns for media and information literacy as they impact local communities and geopolitical praxis. Australian media education scholars Michael Dezuanni and Annette Woods of Queensland University of Technology offer a thorough exploration of a new Australian Curriculum initiative to show where, how and to what extent media literacy education is implemented across primary school subjects. We hear from Lebanese scholar Jad P. Melki of the American University of Beirut about digital and media literacy efforts in the Middle East. Melki offers a case study of a movement underway in Beirut, Lebanon, to combat the notoriously low levels of media literacy education across primary, secondary, and higher education. Lastly, Alice Lee from Hong Kong Baptist University explores Web 2.0 enabled classrooms full of digital technologies. She highlights the need for media literacy education to help present these technologies as facilitators of critical, reflective, and engaging thinking skills.

Public Spaces is the fourth part of *Media Literacy Education in Action*, and explores the opportunities that media literacy provides for lifelong education and vibrant spaces for the public to engage with media in informal learning environments. Libraries, museums, parks, and community centers—often overlooked in conversations about media education—are positioned to embrace digital culture in unique and large scale ways. In this section we begin with Marcus Leaning from the University of Winchester, U.K., who argues for the integration of media and information literacy under one unified umbrella, overcoming the longstanding divisions that have largely kept public spaces on the periphery of media literacy discussions. From this theoretical work we move to explore the role of public libraries in empowering youth communities with a commercial free "third place" to explore, express, and communicate with media. Denise Agosto and Rachel Magee of Drexel University advocate for the informal learning that libraries can enable, and how they are best positioned to elicit interest-based media literacy for youth. Gayle Bogel of Fairfield University shifts the conversation to the school library, which she positions as the collaborative hub for students, teachers, and the larger community. Lastly, Brigham Young University Associate Professor Amy Petersen Jensen explore the concept of arts literacies—theatre, dance, music, and visual arts—as ways to engage K–12 learners with modes of critical inquiry and practice that harness their creative selves.

Whatever the specific design of media literacy learning programs, it can be argued that the goal of engaged citizenship is the umbrella for all media literacy activities. Whether its healthy lifestyles, political voice, or more production skills, these are all in the context of helping enable stronger, more critical and analytical voices. In Part Five, Civic Activism, we read about an array of media literacy explorations that involve the notion of the active citizen as their outcome. Katherine Fry, Professor at Brooklyn College, investigates notions of media literacy and power, through the lens of Freire's Pedagogy of the Oppressed. James Castonguay and Lori Bindig of Sacred Heart University use social movement theory to explore media literacy and community organizations as goal-oriented movements. Nick Pernisco of Santa Monica College follows this by look at the notion of combating social inequality with media literacy. He focuses specifically on erasing inequality, closing the digital divide, shrinking the participation gap, and fostering more active civic agency. Lastly, Eric Gordon of the Engagement Game Lab at Emerson College and Stephen Schirra of MIT explore civic activism in the context of designs for civic learning, which focuses on information and out of school learning spaces that are designed through digital technologies and that foster the engagement of youth with their local communities.

From civic activism, our book moves to Policy and Digital Citizenship. Creating media literacy policy has become an important aspect of the growth of learning in developing curriculums nationally and internationally. Along with policy has been the increase discussion on digital citizenship, Internet safety, cyberbullying, and cybersecurity, as they have become increasingly important topics both in and out of schools. In this section, four chapters explore how media literacy can be a voice in policy discussions on municipal and national levels. Sonia Livingstone and Yin-Han Wang from the London School of Economics and Political Science write about the struggles of the European Commission to find common ground in the definition, measurement and evaluation of media literacy across countries in the Eurozone. Frank Gallagher of Cable in the Classroom explores the concept of media literacy and digital citizenship as tools to combat cyber bullying, and issues of Internet security. As inappropriate content is made more and more available with less and less filters, how we teach young people about their information habits can go a long ways toward the culture of youth and protection online. Rhys Daunic of the Media Spot provides an in depth case study on New York City schools, and their embrace of new literacies is detailed with an eye towards developing more inclusive standards and policies that line up with the Common Core. Finally, Fairfield Professor and co-editor of this book Belinha De

Abreu provides a thorough account of U.S. educational policy and the Common Core to show how media literacy can push effective educational measures forward to ensure Internet safety for all youth in the curriculum of the K–12 schools.

Finally, Part Seven explores Future Connections, asking us to pause and consider the state of the field and ponder the question: Where is the field headed from here? To help provide direction, wisdom, experience and insight, we called on senior scholars of media literacy to point the way. David Considine, writing alongside his brother Michael, explore what is still missing from the media literacy process for students, and what challenges and changes are going to be necessary for the future. Gretchen Schwarz, Professor at Baylor University, suggests that we look at the university as a home for a "new rhetoric" of media literacy education. This argument positions media literacy students for more than a job or career, but for an inclusive and democratic lifestyle. To do so, university educators must incorporate many strands of media literacy into their courses, program and disciplines. Lastly, Art Silverblatt and his team at Webster University in St. Louis look globally again to see a maturing discipline that has made great inroads into education across all levels. The final chapter in this section details these trends and growth patterns to provide a look into the future of a field that is growing in scope, depth, and reach.

Our hope is that *Media Literacy Education in Action* can elicit new ideas, challenge existing ones, and help to form a unified network around media literacy educators around the world. Media Literacy is no longer an option. The question is not if we implement media literacy's competencies in society but when and how well we do so. We have learned through this process that this book could never be entirely "inclusive," but we hope it offers a grounding framework for those who are active in media literacy education around the world, and for those looking to help advance this ever more vital movement for our growing digital media culture.

ACKNOWLEDGMENTS

The authors would like to thank the many people who contributed their thoughts and ideas throughout the process of creating this book. We would most especially like to thank each of the authors who said "yes" quite readily when asked to contribute their thinking on the field. You have provided us with a diverse and wide range of ideas that we hope will grow the media literacy conversation. We hope you all appreciate the end result. We would also like to thank the team at Routledge, especially Naomi Silverman who accepted our proposal from the start and Andrew Weckenmann who helped to keep us organized and answered a multitude of questions throughout the process. Lastly, we would also like to thank Emily Fiskio who reviewed all of the material prior to submission.

INTRODUCTION

Belinha S. De Abreu and Paul Mihailidis

Why this book? Why now? Media literacy education has experienced significant changes over the last thirteen years. Traditionally, discussions of media focused primarily on conventional mediums such as television, film, radio, and so on, whereas today those mediums have merged into new social and mobile technologies that aggregate format, content, and message. As such, discussions of the meaning and understanding of literacy related to the outgrowth of this change have become documented and an ever-growing challenge for various scholarly communities. In order to better understand how media literacy has evolved, part of the challenge of this book was to reach out and acknowledge that media literacy is expanding and changing because of its extension in various new fields of study established in the last ten years, as well as disciplines whose traditions focused in other literacies are now seeing increasing connections to media literacy education.

Another obvious shift is that while media literacy is still traditionally defined as the ability to access, analyze, and create (Silverblatt, 2007), the production piece of this aspect was growing without necessarily having any discernment involved by the creator. The media have become both a learning instrument and an idea producer. However, they have also become a source of mixed messages that have both negative and positive influences on our youth (Flores-Koulish, 2005). This became more obvious when the Internet exploded in 2004 to incorporate social network platforms and shifted from what is known as Web 1.0 to Web 2.0. The ability for the user to interact with the computer changed the way people communicated, thus producing online exchanges which were collaborative, embedded, and participatory in nature. In essence, we were "alive." No longer was a stagnant piece of technology used for information perusal, but became a place where creation and circulation of information was happening regularly.

> The growth of networked communication, especially when coupled with the practices of the participatory culture, provides a range of new resources and facilitates new interventions for a variety of groups who have long struggled to have their voice heard. New platforms create openings for social, cultural, economic, legal, and political change and opportunities for diversity and democratization for which it is worth fighting. (Jenkins, Ford, & Green, 2013, xiv)

Despite this new wave of online dynamics, which for most people were exciting, it also created a tension in the general society as more Internet users became younger and younger. Their experiences were worrisome and controversial to school leaders and teachers, who began to turn technology off. Much like the way they once banned television or films, they attempted to do so with this medium. The issue became worse and worse as it became clearer that we had a generation of youths who were engaged by this medium and a generation of adults who feared it. Perhaps the biggest realization was that this issue was felt internationally.

Media literacy education has had a longer history in Europe, Canada, and Australia than in the United States (Silverblatt, 2007). The United States was in many ways late to the game. The growth of television in the United States between the 1940s and 1950s drove the concerns about media violence. Conversations began to take center stage with various interest groups from parents to child advocates about the need to curtail some of the imagery, messages, and representations being viewed through the television screen. In 1952, Congress held the first hearing on broadcast violence as a possible connector to real-world violence (Trotta, 2001). There was a real tug of war between the entertainment industry and children's advocates which continues until today; the difference being that now those concerns extend to online communities and video games. The concept of media literacy did not reach a consensus until 1992 when the Aspen Institute convened leaders from the United States and Canada to create a common language that would be inclusive of the various approaches to conveying media literacy/media literacy education (Tyner, 1998). Since that time, the extension of media literacy education in the classroom depended on the acknowledgement of schools, companies, the film industry, or even the federal government.

As television was the medium that seemed of most concern to parents and educators, much of the curriculum was based around this platform in the beginning. The Internet, however, proved to be the great equalizer worldwide. Concerns arose from educators and policymakers who were trying to work with this new access point into a virtual and online world that became referred to as the "Wild West," a new frontier needing taming (Yen, 2002). Questions about controlling this environment became contentious. Policymakers were considering implementing laws which would prevent certain materials from being posted or viewed by the general public. But the Internet was still being celebrated as being open and free, which meant that each time new laws were considered for this space, there was an outcry of censorship (*Wall Street Journal,* 2010). At the same time, there appeared to be a subtle belief that the Internet would not amount to much more than a platform that students and adults would use to gather information. When the Internet became interactive, an explosion took place that bridged connections with people globally, the number of ways in which people wanted to consume, share, and recreate became powerful. It caught many educators by surprise and it also created a division among educators—some wanted to include these new environments in the classroom, while others tried to keep these mediums at bay and not have them included within the school curriculum.

Students began engaging in behaviors that concerned parents and schools. The ability to share seamlessly through mobile devices was changing the nature and types of information students were putting on display to peers, with seemingly little thought or reflection. Incidents of cyberbullying increased and infiltrated schools and classrooms (King, 2010). Because of policies that were hindering the progress of teaching in learning as related to Internet usage, many schools ignored the incidents or shifted the burden to parents. That In the United States that has significantly changed of late because of new federal guidelines and state statues which demand teachers to be proactive in preventing these issues from developing. For example, California has "Seth's Law," which requires school policy changes and investigation processes be done if an incident of cyberbullying comes into play. Connecticut and Maine have passed laws to prevent cyberbullying in and out of school, and more states are heading in the same direction (Hinduja & Patchin, 2013).

Parents were also caught in the melee as they were forced to adapt to this new technological landscape that was advancing at an expansive and dizzying pace. Without a full understanding of the nuances of these networks and platforms, they began participating in the social networks and allowing their children to partake in those experiences as well. Parents were also keenly aware of the fact that they are playing a game of catch-up with their children. Their children would find places online that were engaging, but not necessarily open to the adult user. Parents and adults were for the most part on the outskirts looking at a technological sphere that was shaping the way their children behaved or connected with their peers. These networks were first designed for young people, making the relationship between adolescents and parents on social networks ambiguous. A level of unease was settling in and was creating a tug-of-war within the parent-child relationship on accessibility and freedom to use many of these new tools. Whereas the television provided parents with the ability to control their children's viewing, the Internet and its range of accessibility to transmit information were less controllable, and the issues created were complex, varied, and far-reaching.

In the same vein, political agencies began to see that television and radio—the predominant media channels for campaigns—were no longer reaching a new generation of voters. Political groups began to find places to vet their candidates on the World Wide Web, and in particular with social networks such as Facebook. The 2008 election in the United States, demonstrated the profound impact this tool had on changing the election when a sweeping number of young voters came out to vote for the president of the United States (Fraser & Dutta, 2008). More importantly, young people were able to leverage their social media platforms to express political opinions, share content, and extend the voice of their communities to new far reaching places. The use of digital media to engage with civic issues continued to grow with these new platforms, made evident by widespread conversations on a host of world topics and issues. It bridged discussion, and in fact took on wars and political agenda as seen in the MENA uprisings, or what has been called the "Arab Spring." Voice was given to the oppressed and was also an avenue for garnering support, assistance, and activism by the general public. Social media sites such as Twitter demonstrated that they were a force to be reckoned with when it came to organizing, protest, and dissent on a global level. People were turning to those who were sharing their stories online for the facts and experiencing truth using a method that was less controlled by governments and certainly not the mass media. As was stated in "'Convergence Culture' and Youth Activism in Egypt,"

> Social justice movements in Egypt have often been marginalized by mainstream communications systems, but are increasingly dependent on new media platforms to coordinate actions, mobilize and create networks, despite the fact that most of these movements have their origins in deprived communities. (Saleh, 2013, 202.)

In 2012, Invisible Children released their famous 27-minute campaign against Ugandan war criminal Joseph Kony. Social media users quickly propelled the video to become the fastest video to ever reach 100 million views on YouTube. This activity, which caused heated debate both on the content of the video but also the role of social media to affect political change, reflects the power of active and engaged citizens to leverage their voices through social media.

News agencies were increasingly struggling to adapt to a culture that increasingly utilized social networks for sharing news and information about events in real time. The traditional mechanisms for top down information gathering and dissemination were upended when citizens took reporting into their own hands. When Hurricane Katrina struck in 2004, when bombs went off in the London Underground in 2005, and when the Boston Marathon was stopped by senseless acts of terrorism, citizens were the first to share text, video, and photo that captured the scenes. News outlets still produced stories of depth and scope, but they relied much more on social technologies and groups of citizens to facilitate their stories and gather information. This new pressure on news business is now having a large influence on the ways in which students are taught about news, information, credibility, and reliability in the digital age.

Libraries and public spaces were also finding positives and negatives attributed to these new mediums. No longer were people coming into libraries to borrow DVDs and CDs, they were coming in to borrow time on computers that would help them connect to peers, families, and the world. Libraries were also seeing a change in the oldest medium—the book. New e-readers were changing the way in which their patrons were engaging with literature. There were a multitude of websites that provided users with information and opportunities for buying books. The idea of "sharing" online became a confused term for patrons. The legalities of how people were getting their information and putting into other documents became troublesome. Copyright issues were shifting and changing. Big companies online companies such as Google were stepping on the toes of authors. Librarians and educators were left to the task of teaching people the differences between "authorship vs. sharing." Yet, the flip side of these concerns were the increased number of patrons who wanted resources given to them and were willing to spend time in places where they were welcome to engage with new technologies.

As a result, more new literacies were introduced into the discipline. Digital literacy, information literacy, and visual literacy all began to splinter research and scholarship under the umbrella of media literacy. The argument for the perfect name continues, but in true form media literacy was still what most people understood and connected to how vitally important it was to teach and know how to critically think about the messages of whatever medium of choice is being used now or in the future (McDougall & Sanders, 2012; Buckingham, 2010).

Yet despite all of these changes, some things have still remained the same. Television viewing hasn't necessarily decreased because of these technologies. In fact, quite the opposite is true. Television viewing has diversified and expanded into various outlets, places, and situations. Indeed, television is now a dominant form of visual inquiry on the web. As was stated in "Educational Challenges in Times of Mass Self-communication," "Reception happens in places outside of the home, in bars, markets, shopping centres, restaurants, on public transport, in shop windows . . ." (Orozco & Navarro, 2012, 68). Further adding to this change was the mobile phone and tablet computers, which have become primary sources for engagement with mass media messaging from television, film, and radio. We now carry our entertainment with us wherever we are and to whatever place we are going. We are tethered to devices that keep us "connected" all the time, in real time, and to an information landscape more abundant than ever before. As reported by the Kaiser Family Foundation,

> The story of media in young people's lives today is primarily a story of technology facilitating increased consumption. The mobile and online media revolutions have arrived in the lives—and the pockets—of American youth. Try waking a teenager in the morning, and the odds are good that you'll find a cell phone tucked under their pillow—the last thing they touch before falling asleep and the first thing they reach for upon waking. Television

content they once consumed only by sitting in front of a TV set at an appointed hour is now available whenever and wherever they want, not only on TV sets in their bedrooms, but also on their laptops, cell phones and iPods. (Rideout, Foehr, & Roberts, 2010, 2)

The increased use of the mobile phone has also led to new forms of interactivity directed by each individual user. We are no longer looking at passive connectivity, but a unique form of participation which is selected by the interests and tastes of each person. This cultural change is worldwide and one that transcends community, cultural distinction, and language. The tool has helped to direct the media message. The media message is now influenced by the participant. The participant controls the medium. The medium controls the participant. The cycle seems to have increased, and it is not at a point of ceasing.

Media literacy education, then, holds the immense responsibility of preparing future citizens, parents, politicians, teachers, community leaders—society in general—to facilitate their daily lives in a digital media culture. In the opening of *Net Smart: How to Thrive Online,* Howard Rheingold (2011) writes, "The future of digital culture—yours, mine, and ours—depends on how well we learn to use the media that have infiltrated, amplified, distracted, enriched, and complicated our lives" (1). Media literacy is the field that will help us learn how to be critical, savvy, expressive, participatory, and engaged with media to help build a more vibrant, inclusive, and tolerant digital media culture. While media literacy takes many different shapes and forms, it is up to parents, teachers, scholars, and leaders to implement this movement that can help shape the future of teaching and learning about media's ever increasing role in the world. As Rheingold notes:

> The mindful use of digital media doesn't happen automatically. Thinking about what you are doing and why you are doing it instead of going through the motions is fundamental to the definition of mindful, whether you deciding to follow someone on Twitter, shutting the lid of your laptop in class, looking up from your Blackberry in a meeting, or consciously deciding which links *not* to click. (1)

The future poses a number of opportunities and challenges for the advancement of civic society around the world. Media literacy education should no longer be an option, but a priority, across private and public spaces, to help young people learn to lead digitally throughout their lives.

Further, as part of this common view of creating a harmonious and synergist relationship between the various literacies, UNESCO began creating and implementing curriculum that brought together the ideas of traditional literacies along with the consideration of new technologies. They termed their work "media and information literacy" and in doing so capitalized on the various delivery platforms of mass media (Grizzle, 2013).

MIL recognizes the functions of media and other information providers in our personal lives, knowledge societies and democratic societies. It promotes the individual's right to communication, express, seek, receive and impart information and ideas. It encourages the evaluation of information and media based on how they are produced, the messages being conveyed, and the intended audience. (Grizzle, 2013, 260)

In their conceptualizing of the teaching of media and information literacy, the primary goal is to empower children, youth, and citizens in all societies whether advanced or in a community that is struggling with the basics. Their work is just beginning, but its impact has already been felt by the many contributors of the documents they have created, as well as the teachers and students who have been educated using their materials worldwide.

Clearly, we are still working towards building and implementing media literacy education, and that is just fine. Some people might think this is a negative, but in fact it is a positive. The opportunity for opening doorways between disciplines, communities, and people exists. Theoretically, this field is beginning to take shape, which is represented by the many voices who have contributed to this book. What has become apparent is that no one group owns the term, and in fact all of the people who have contributed to this book as well as those we have met in our respective work environments have suggested that this is the exactly the right time for this book as we are in the midst of an exciting technological space. There is an opportunity to explore and create new conceptual understanding of how media literacy education can influence opinion, motivate people to participate in civic life, bolster critical thinking, open up creative avenues, and change one's perception of the world. As Marieli Rowe of the *National Telemedia Council* states, "This is a global instant and a totally invasive digital world in which all are equal, and at risk in power. We're all in the same boat. Media literacy's apex may very well be a road to new sensitivity for becoming a more civilized global society if we could develop common language through the rich variety of media" (Jolls, Walkosz & Morgenthaler, 2011.). We hope you find some of that language here.

References

Buckingham, D. (2010). The future of media literacy in the digital age: Same challenges for policy and practice. *Media Education Journal, 47*, 3–10.

Flores-Koulish, S. (2005). *Teacher education for critical consumption of mass media and popular culture.* New York: RoutledgeFalmer.

Fraser, M., & Dutta, S. (2008, November 19). Barack Obama and the Facebook election. *US News and World Report.* Retrieved from http://www.usnews.com/opinion/articles/2008/11/19/barack-obama-and-the-facebook-election.

Grizzle, A. (2013). Media and information literacy as a composite concept. In U. Carlsson & S.H. Culver (Eds.), In *Media and information literacy and intercultural dialogue*, MILID Yearbook.

Hinduja, S., & Patchin, J.W. (2013, April). A Brief review of state cyberbullying laws and policies. *Cyberbullying Research Center.* Retrieved from http://cyberbullying.us/Bullying_and_Cyberbullying_Laws.pdf.

Jenkins, H., Ford, S. and Green, J. (2013). *Spreadable media: Creating value and meaning in a networked culture.* New York: New York University Press, xiv.

Jolls, T., Walkosz, B, & Morgenthaler, D. (2011). *Voices of Media Literacy: International Pioneers Speak: Marieli Rowe.* Retrieved from http://www.medialit.org/sites/default/files/Voices_of_ML_Marieli_Rowe_1.pdf.

King, A.V. (2010). Constitutionality of cyberbullying laws: Keeping the online playground safe for both teens and free speech. *Vanderbilt Law Review, 63*(3), 845–884.

McDougall, J., and Sanders, R. (2012). Critical (media) literacy and the digital: Towards sharper thinking. *Journal of Media Literacy, 59*(2/3), 8–12.

Orozco, G., Navarro, E., & García, A. (2012). Educational challenges in times of mass self-communication: A dialogue among audience. *Comunicar, 38*, 67–74.

Rheingold, H. (2011). *Net smart: How to thrive online.* Boston: MIT Press.

Rideout, V.J., Foehr, U.G., & Roberts, D.F. (2010). Generation M2: Media in the lives of 8–18 year olds. *Kaiser Family Foundation.* Retrieved from http://kaiserfamilyfoundation.files.wordpress.com/2013/01/8010.pdf.

Saleh, I. (2013). "Convergence culture" and youth activism in Egypt. In U. Carlsson & S.H. Culver (Eds.), *Media and information literacy and intercultural dialogue*, MILID Yearbook.

Silverblatt, A. (2007). *Media literacy: Keys to interpreting media messages.* Westport, CT: Praeger.

Trotta, L. (2001). Children's advocacy groups. In J. Singer and D. Singer (Eds.), *Handbook of children and the media.* London: Sage.

Tyner, K. (1998). *Literacy in a digital world: Teaching and learning in the age of information.* Mahwah, NJ: Lawrence Erlbaum Associates.

Wall Street Journal. (2010, May 8). Julius Caesar of the Internet. Retrieved from http://online.wsj.com/article/SB10001424052748704370704575228152292941636.html?mod=rss_opinion_main.

Yen, A.C. (2002). Western frontier or feudal society? Metaphors and perceptions of cyberspace. *Berkeley Technology Law Journal.* Retrieved from http://www.law.berkeley.edu/journals/btlj/articles/vol17/Yen.stripped.pdf.

PART I

MEDIA LITERACY
PAST AND PRESENT

The first section of *Media Literacy in Action* focuses on the growth of media literacy through a historical lens. The aim is to ground the entire book in a larger perspective over time and beyond any specific theme, strand, or focus. In this section you will find holistic reviews of the growth of media literacy in specific parts of the world, across disciplines and grade levels, and in formal and informal education settings. Chapters develop narratives of media education practice in critical and historical contexts. Ideas focus on the evolution of media literacy movements in Australia, Canada, the United Kingdom, and the United States. Seminal media literacy educators are interviewed to offer their insight on their careers in media literacy and what they believe were and are the biggest challenges that face the movement today. A discussion of new literacies is also offered as a way to ground the notion of literacy in a theoretical context, and build towards a portrait of what literacies today require in a multimodal digital media culture.

1

MEDIA LITERACY

An Incomplete Project

Julian McDougall

The global project of media literacy for the twenty-first century is under review (Buckingham, 2010) and contextual formulations strive for an elusive consensus for this broad and fragmented community of practice.

This chapter will provide a genealogy of the various educational practices that have, in different countries and contexts, attempted to develop or enhance students' abilities to critique and create media towards more reflexively engaging with the mediation of life.

There are clear and present fault-lines and tensions between media literacy as a discrete area of or outside of the curriculum; between media literacy as a cross-curricular or extra-curricular practice and between media education as a formal subject and the broader field of literacy education. Notions of new, digital, and media literacies have served to undermine the project. This chapter concludes with suggestions for pedagogic strategies that might dispense with such unhelpful 'insulation' between categories.

Media literacy education, then, is an 'incomplete project,' generating 'its own aporias' (Habermas, 1993, 131) and can only be renewed by new forms of more reflexive and negotiated pedagogy that bear witness to the complexity of reading practices—ways of being literate—instead of focusing on the 'nouns' of media literacy—the dubious distinctions between forms of textual activity.

(Media) Literacy

In a response to an article I co-authored (McDougall and Sanders, 2012) for *Journal of Media Literacy* about the 'conditions of possibility' for critical media literacy, Cortes (2012) offered a hypothesis drawn from observing his cat:

> He can mess up our TV remote. And he can turn up my Bose radio, usually to the classical music channel. Yet, despite Tigger's media experience, I wouldn't classify him as media literate, certainly not possessed of critical media literacy ... Let's call it the Tigger Paradox, the gap separating experience and adeptness from critical analytical ability. (Cortes, 2012, 24)

Whilst educating people to be literate is broadly understood as part of citizen entitlement on utilitarian principles, there is a clear and important distinction in policy and rationale discourses surrounding media literacy. The reading and writing of words is rarely discussed as response to anything other than the obvious benefits of using language. Media literacy, however, is often justified as a response to something—the development of mass media, and more recently, digital and social media. Whilst there is great variance in how the axes of affordance and protection are drawn and how media literacy policy is mapped across them, this obvious difference is important to recognize. Before educators can successfully integrate media literacy into the 'day job,' there must be agreement that media in some way make a difference. In this sense the (incomplete) project of media literacy education is not the same as either literacy development in general or education's usual epistemological arrangements.

Media literacy as a response, then, has a genealogy and some distinct 'flavours.' Before making generalizations it is important to bear witness to the complexity of how media literacy is discursively framed in space and time, as Lin articulates in this description of Asian policy and practice:

> Sometimes, various discourses are adopted strategically. The citizenship discourse with a negative assumption from the protectionist discourses of media is an example of a hybrid discourse. As late-comers to media education, advocates in Asia are aware of the dangers of solely applying the protectionist discourse. They strategically adopt the negative effect as rationale for promoting media education while adding the flavour of the active 'civic engagement' rhetoric. The hybrid discourse carries contradictions in itself. (Lin, 2009, 40)

This is a revealing case in point. Whilst the inception of English Literature education was controversial, mobilizing arguments over its epistemological rigor, it is safe to say that educators wishing to teach children to read rarely have to behave strategically to combine ideas about both the power and danger of 'book learning.' At the risk of convenient simplification, there are four dominant discursive models at work in the international genealogy of media literacy, each of which is integrated in various ways into the formal institutionalized practice of media education. With these disclaimers offered, the following summary attempts to describe this 'history of the present.'

The **social model** has situated media literacy within a broader set of plural 'literacies.' Within this category we can locate elements of media literacy within 'new literacies' and 'multiliteracies.' There are some key areas of dissensus between and among these but by way of general mapping of the field we can say that these approaches share a belief that 'the competencies that are involved in making sense of the media are socially distributed, and that different social groups have different orientations towards the media, and will use them in different ways' (Buckingham, 2003, 39). In practice, this model seems to be marginalized in media literacy education.

Protectionist models, which are more or less explicit in this intention, sometimes share characteristics with attempts to determine competences and skills that can be benchmarked against ages and contexts. These are dependent on normative judgments and definitions of a media literate person, group, or whole society (Livingstone, Papaioannou, Perez, & Winjen, 2012, 5). Despite appearances to the contrary, this model—when combined with others—dominates the landscape of media literacy education.

The **citizenship model** operates within a broadly Habermasian model of public sphere communication and is partly discussed as a response to technology—media literacy as inclusion in the online consensus—and partly as affordance for a more participatory society—a 'new civics.' Whether or not digital and online media are understood as determining such social action (as opposed to offering active citizens an online space to share their existing offline engagement), the focus here is on active media use as civic action in response to and/or involvement in governance (Hasebrink, 2012). The most dominant form of the citizenship model is the 'employability' discourse, which is more politically neutral—indeed it entirely reproduces the neo-liberal hegemony—but nevertheless shares the assertion that media literacy competence is required for contemporary participation in the public sphere—of employment in the 'creative industries' (Hesmondalgh & Baker, 2011) in this case. A more specific 'flavour' of the citizenship discourse that could be applied in more or less protectionist or creative/participatory contexts is Erickson and Meletti's (2013) media literacy resources for young people sharing online remix and parody material. This intervention combines a potentially protectionist agenda (from unintended law-breaking) with the creativity and participation discourses (to encourage more 'safe' production), but also goes further to lobby for a change in U.K. regulation to allow more exemptions for such parodic work, in order for young people to be equally free to experiment and develop media (for creative employability, also) as their counterparts in the United States and much of Europe.

Creativity models are perhaps the most contested variant of the media literacy discourse and can only be fully 'unpacked' within much broader debates around the nature of creativity itself and its function in education. Gauntlett's (2011) research into the online exchange of everyday creative practice and the role of web 2.0 in facilitating this, has been the subject of an overly polarised academic fray over the need or not, for a *Media Studies 2.0* (see Berger and McDougall, 2011a, b). Readman (2011) describes the problem of implementation in the observation that 'if media educators are prepared to acknowledge that "creativity" is not a "thing" but rather a site of conflict where different definitions and interests compete, we are less likely to accept it as a useful assessment term or something that can be measured and rationalised.'

'**Subject Media**' is not a separate category, as it contains elements of the others, depending on how practiced, but it provides a powerful and distinct framing for media literacy education. 'Subject Media' describes the formal—and legitimated—curriculum teaching of Media Studies with attendant specifications and assessment regimes. The power of 'Subject Media' is exercised in its proximal relation to other disciplines—most notably English, and how in the daily work of teaching in institutions, media learning becomes a 'vertical discourse' as a conceptual framework is handed down and manifested in the provision of resources and text books.

At policy level, the 'broad brush' approach is most clearly manifested and combined with a failure to demonstrate scale. For example, European Union strategies from 2000 onwards have financed a plethora of media education projects, all related to a shared objective—teaching children and their parents, in the online age, to 'use the media effectively' but also 'having a critical approach to media as regards both quality and accuracy' and 'using media creatively' (EC, 2007:4) Likewise, in the United Kingdom, OFCOM, a regulatory body, was charged by Government with a media literacy strategy which also sought to bring these very different activities together in a '3c' model—communication, being critical, and creating. In these worthy developments, we can see the awkward 'lumping together' of protectionist, citizenship, and creative discourses, but little attention is paid to the social model of differently situated, plural *literacies*. At the same time, the failure of scale is a result of these projects and task force initiatives sitting outside of any formal curriculum—Media Studies or other. Hence the project of media literacy is framed as extra-curricular and by nature of the funding contexts, the sum of perennial pilot studies.

Matters of 'incompletion' are complicated further by the proliferation of media literacies. The shift to cross-media, transmedia, and spreadable media (Jenkins, Ford, & Green, 2013) make a difference to each discourse, but the degree to which new variants beyond media literacy—to *digital* literacy, *new media* literacy, *transmedia literacy*—are needed for an educational response, is no less an 'idea speech situation,' to the extent that some have argued for a dispensation with the idea of 'the media' altogether (Bennett, Kendall, & McDougall, 2011) or a resurrection as 'mediacy': 'the technical facility to use new machines, but also to understand and use the codes of conventions of each related medium' (Anderson, 2012 35–36).

So, on the one hand, it is difficult to resist Buckingham's blunt observation (2012) that all of the above is 'a bloody big mess.' But preferring the softer 'incomplete project,' in order to demonstrate how these discursive models overlap with lesser and greater degrees of intention, some contrasting examples will now be discussed. The educational 'content,' pedagogic practices and modes of assessment are not the focus here. Rather, the intention is to 'map' them against the models suggested above. Clearly these strategically selected examples cannot stand for the entire global practice of media literacy education. Rather, they offer a 'taster' for what will follow in this collection but with our attention at this point on the *differences* between them.

Reading and Making the Cave

In a review of Canadian/North American media literacy education, Pungente, Duncan, and Anderson (2005) offer this opening gambit from a school student as a rationale for a protectionist approach:

> The media can persuade anyone to do something or to think a certain way. It can promote drugs and violence, or it can preach good education and hard work. We learn from the media and we also get sucked into the media. It covers everything—campaigning, fashion, education, and most importantly, life. When I say life, I mean anything that can ever happen to you, from the clothes you wear to regular days at school to walking home from somewhere. (2005, 1)

This premise is reproduced in Pungente's more recent 'Inside Plato's Cave' initiative—an online course for media literacy educators, starting out from a statement of indisputable fact—that we can draw an obvious parallel between Plato's parable and contemporary media and that media literacy can liberate today's children from the plight of the prisoners in the *Republic*.

Zezulkova's (2013) research into media literacy education in urban and rural Czech elementary schools shows how the broader discursive formations can be locally situated:

> The protection against negative influences, mainly violence and manipulative promotion, is the main purpose of media education. Secondly, media education should enrich pupils' current lives, by teaching them not to depend on media while entertaining themselves, as well as their future job acquisition, by helping them to keep up with 'city children.' (Zezulkova, 2013, 20)

This example of the 'bad media' discourse combined with employability objectives is common. In this contradictory fusion of the protectionist and civic models, media proliferation and influence are at once to be resisted and at the same time the neoliberal economic drivers necessitate competence in using media. It is hard to think of another educational practice so fraught with confusion.

In a very different example that would be excluded from most discussions of 'media literacy,' Palkhiwali (2012) sought to give voice to 2- to 5-year-old children in a rural Jamaican village through their drawing, jotting and photographic experiential 'media.' This project explored the way children in this setting communicate lived experiences and perceptions of place through these 'old media.' Inclusion of this example—selected from an enormous range of similar ethnographic projects—is strategic here, as it serves to remind us how crude our boundaries are. Just as Berger and Woodfall (2012) argue that transmedia narratives make it no longer sustainable to separate books from 'media' in education, so too should we be highly skeptical of the 'insulation' (Bernstein, 1990) of media literacy from the kinds of situated literacies captured by Palkhiwali with paper and pencils.

Fraser's research (2012) explores the extent to which ideas from Jenkins and others about digital media creativity and participation have 'crossed over' to the formal institutional spaces of 'Subject Media'—here in the form of A-Level Media Studies in England, the 'massified' learning experience of 16- to 19-year-old students in school and college. Fraser draws on Jenkins's (2006) work to develop a model of key modes of online material that disrupt traditional producer/audience relations and as such offer new opportunities for Media Studies to disrupt student–media and studying media/making media relations. These are acting out, extended storytelling, animated remakes (including Lego and Machinima), fan art celebration, and remix/mash-up. This research is of key interest here because it explores the pedagogic response to these shifts or 'the epistemological frameworks teachers and students use to make sense of a changing media ecosystem' (Fraser, 2012, 74). The findings are sobering in that the 'messy reality' of the media classroom, inequalities in teacher approach, technological access, and student engagement mean that there is still scarce 'joined up' evidence of the creative use of technology in contemporary media classrooms on this 'mass' scale:

> A high proportion (of students) are uploading their video work to You-Tube or Vimeo, though few are generating much by way of comments or even views, suggesting that online communities of practice will not simply 'emerge' from an educational context. (Fraser, 2012, 76–77)

The Project: Pedagogy

A recent contextual formulation for media literacy education is offered by De Abreu (2012, 6–7), key elements of which that move away from the discourses operating above include a focus on pleasure, voice for students, empathy, and navigation. In particular, the suggestion that media literacy education 'engages the teacher and the learner simultaneously so that a give and take relationship can exist within the framework of the classroom' appears to develop the project beyond protection, competence, and mere participation.

The 'history of the present' for media literacy education offered above presents a simple observation—that the sustained debate around reframing literacy education in and for the digital media age has consistently given far more weight to the 'nouns' of skills and competence to the 'verbs' of learning and pedagogy. This is the fundamental reason why media literacy educators are stuck on the 'working out' of these design principles. An alternative educational approach to media literacy might be provided by a 'pedagogy of inexpert' curation (Bennett, Kendall, & McDougall, 2011; Andrews & McDougall, 2013 Potter, 2012).

This way of thinking about media literacy education reframes the project by accepting first that new digital media have not *in themselves* caused a temporal or paradigm shift. Instead, educators can now more clearly see the problem of reducing media literacy learning to producer/audience and teacher/student interactions and potentially develop the solution—a more reflexive engagement with media as fluid and flowing in the age of 'realised' participation.

Clearly, many of the examples and research findings discussed here are constrained by their rather conservative and restricting ways of understanding media and people as separate subject/object categories. The reason for not engaging more profoundly with a 'reboot' of (media) literacy education is the failure to move away from a model of 'the media' which was always alienating and exclusive, even in the 'analogue age.'

Potter's (2012) theory of curation as an active literacy practice, providing 'alignment between theories of media production, learner agency, voice and identity in a new formation around the concepts of curatorship, representation and exhibition' (2012, 11) offers a much more productive and liberating discursive formation for media literacy education than is manifested in much of the genealogy traced here. Most of the media literacy projects and outcomes focus on more or less deficient models of citizens in relation to media and literacy, but pay little regard for how the 'educational encounter' itself serves to reproduce or challenge media reading and making practices.

And so such a 'pedagogy of the inexpert' is required to redistribute power through a more collaborative literacy education for which students and teachers exchange and negotiate meaning making as the key component of media literacy. This shift would finally free media literacy education from its protectionist trappings and locate its praxis somewhere between Buckingham's rejection of all things '2.0' and the less measured versions of the creativity and citizen-participation discourses. It is vital if we are to complete the project.

References

Anderson, N. (2012). Reflections on the work of Julian McDougall and Richard Sanders. *Journal of Media Literacy, 59*(2/3), 33–41.

Andrews, B., & McDougall, J. (2013). Curation pedagogy: Further towards the inexpert. *Medijkske Studije, 3*(6), 152–165.

Bennett, P., Kendall, A., and McDougall, J. (2011). *After the media: Culture and identity in the 21st century.* London: Routledge.

Berger, R., & McDougall, J. (2011a). Apologies for cross-posting: A keynote exchange. *The Media Education Research Journal, 2*(1), 5–29.

Berger, R., & McDougall, J. (2011b). Media Studies 2.0: A Retrospective. *Media Education Research Journal, 2*(2), 5–11.

Berger, R., & Woodfall, A. (2012). The digital utterance: A cross-media approach to media education. In I. Ibrus & C.A. Scolari (Eds.), *Crossmedia innovations: Texts, markets, institutions, education* (p. 111–126). Oxford: Peter Lang.

Bernstein, B. (1990). *The structuring of pedagogic discourse*. London: Routledge.

Buckingham, D. (2003). *Media education: Literacy, learning and contemporary culture*. London: Polity.

Buckingham, D. (2010). The future of media literacy in the digital age: Same challenges for policy and practice. *Media Education Journal, 47*, 3–10.

Buckingham, D. (2012). *Hard Times: Media Education and the new Nineteenth Century Curriculum*. London: Keynote presentation to Media Education Association conference— available at https://www.youtube.com/watch?v=_fLEQm9CP1o.

Cortes, C. (2012). Tigger in Cyberspace: Reflections on McDougall and Sanders. *Journal of Media Literacy, 59*(2/3), 24–25.

De Abreu, B. (2012). Understanding media literacy in the context of today's digital technologies. *Journal of Media Literacy, 59*(2/3), 4–7.

Erickson, K., & Meletti, B. (2013). *Introduction to copyright law*. Bournemouth University: Centre for Intellectual Property Management and Research: http://www.cippm.org.uk/publications.html.

European Commission, 2007. *A European Approach to Media Literacy in the Digital Environment*. http://ec.europa.eu/culture/media/media-content/media-literacy/c_2007_833_en_1.pdf – accessed 8.10.13

Fraser, P. (2012). Media studies 2.0: A report on research to date. *Media Education Research Journal, 2*(2), 74–81.

Gauntlett, D. (2011) *Making is connecting: The social meaning of creativity, from DIY and knitting to YouTube and Web 2.0*. London: Polity.

Habermas, J. (1993) Modernity: an incomplete project. In T. Docherty (Ed.), *Postmodernism: A reader*. London: Wheatsheaf.

Hasebrink, U. (2012). The role of the audience within media governance: The neglected dimension of media literacy. *Medijkske Studije, 3*(6), 58–75.

Hesmondalgh, D., & Baker, S. (2011). *Creative labour: Media work in three cultural industries*. London: Routledge.

Jenkins, H. (2006). *Convergence culture: Where old and new media collide*. New York: New York University Press.

Jenkins, H., Ford, S., & Green, J. (2013). *Spreadable media: Creating value and meaning in a networked culture*. New York: New York University Press.

Lin, Z. (2009). Conceptualising media literacy: Discourses of media education. *Media Education Research Journal, 1*(1), 29–42.

Livingstone, S., Papaioannou, T., Perez, M., & Winjen, C. (2012). Critical insights in European media literacy research and policy. *Medijkske Studije, 3*(6), 2–13.

Palkhiwali, S. (2012). Belonging in my community: Exploring children's voices in Porus, Jamaica. Presented at *Crossroads in cultural studies*. Paris, 2–6 July, 2012.

Potter, J. (2012). *Digital media and learner identity: The new curatorship*. New York: Palgrave Macmillan.

Pungente, J., Duncan, B., & Anderson, N. (2005). The Canadian experience: Leading the way. In G. Schwarz & P. Brown (Eds.), *Media Literacy: Transforming curriculum and teaching*. Malden, MA: Blackwell.

Readman, M. (2011). Inspecting creativity: Making the abstract visible. *Media Education Research Journal, 2*(1), 57–72.

Zezulkova, M. (2013). Whole person media education. Presented at the Media Trends Conference *Crossroad Challenges: Children and the Media*. Geneva, Switzerland, 8–10 April 2013.

2

VOICES OF MEDIA LITERACY

Tessa Jolls, Barbara J. Walkosz,
and Dee Morgenthaler

Conditions today are ideal for teaching media literacy. The ease of media production is now taken for granted, and the Internet has focused renewed interest on issues of information credibility and responsible participation by consumers (Flanagin & Metzger, 2010). Outside of the classroom, children currently spend multiple hours of their day engaging with a range of media including computers, cell phones, video games, and television (Rideout, Foehr, & Roberts, 2010). Yet in a time that should be the halcyon of the field, media literacy remains difficult to implement in today's classroom. This dilemma prompts one to ask, "Why is media literacy so scarce? So invisible? And what might be done about it?"

To gain understanding, 20 media literacy pioneers, many of whom are still actively working and contributing to the field, were interviewed for the Voices of Media Literacy project, published by the Center for Media Literacy (2011). The stated goals of the project were to:

- capture the history of media literacy from a first-person point of view, with the pioneers speaking for themselves;
- shed light on past endeavors and also focus on what the pioneers envision going forward;
- uncover issues pertinent to the field, and points of departure from various perspectives;
- learn from the experiences of the leaders who have helped shaped the field to date.

From these expert discussions, a number of themes emerged that offer guidance on potential future directions of the field.

Teach *about* Media, not just *with* Media

A distinguishing characteristic of media education is that students learn to think critically *about* media, whether during media deconstruction or construction or participation activities, in order to discover how media systems operate in social, political and economic contexts.

As David Buckingham said,

> Today seven year-olds can edit films on iMovie or any other program. There is a danger of confusing media education with technology . . . this is a very dangerous moment for us. How do we insist on the critical dimensions of media literacy being important at a point when everybody seems to be rushing to get kids doing very functional things with technology, as though by wiring them up we are somehow going to solve the world's problems?

However, the lure of new media is appealing to students and their teachers, and in a sense, using the media to teach is a much simpler task than addressing the complex issues addressed by media literacy. Douglas Kellner shed more light on what media literacy is really about:

> New media is a much more exiting and encouraging field to American academia than media literacy . . . which is teaching people how to read [and write] the media. But it's not enough to read [and write] the media; you have to be able to critique it in terms of the politics of representation. What are the biases in terms of representation for women, people of color, gays and lesbians, different social groups?

Teaching about media inevitably brings up questions about teaching the business of media and how ownership, profit margins, and ideology influence the content—whether it be the content of a website, a television program, a game, or a tweet. Renee Cherow-O'Leary said, "In my view, media literacy [should] pay sophisticated attention to the business of media . . . we have to understand these tools, how they originate, the business of them." The business reasons behind media usage such as how personal data is collected and used, why advertising is targeted to certain audiences, how search results vary by individual, and how news coverage varies from different sources are key to empowering media consumers and producers in making their everyday decisions.

Identify Key Methodologies that Define the Field so that Media Literacy Education Is Replicable, Scalable, and Measurable

Any field must have a common vocabulary and a common way of defining the system that is the object of study. With that commonality, it is then possible to teach about the fundamentals in a replicable, scalable and measurable way. Otherwise, there is "no there there." Len Masterman contributed greatly to the media literacy field by defining key concepts that address how media operate as a system; these concepts have provided the backbone for media education worldwide. As Masterman himself said of his work,

> You've got to be able to say what stands inside and outside of the field. Any discipline worth its salt has to have a set of key questions and issues that it thinks are important. It has to have some key ideas and key concepts, and it has to have a particular and characteristic mode of inquiry.

Barry Duncan affirmed these ideas, and tackled the challenge of addressing new media through media education:

> The notion of "representation" is the central concept of media literacy. Because it is how we are represented and how we represent ourselves, or re-present ourselves. That notion is being propelled through the decades, through the '60's to today, and it is central that how well we talk about representation largely determines the nature of how good our media literacy is. So, representation, the core principles—what we in Canada call the Key Concepts—by having those key notions, which often are turned into questions—that has kept us on track . . . I want to see how [the concepts] can be situated in a pedagogy, I want to see [the concepts] having a major role in bringing the key ideas both of traditional media and new media—of bringing them together and making all of these things as meaningful in the curriculum and the so-called convergence and the culture of connectivity—all of the new directions—have to be reconciled with the traditional. And if we do a good job at that we will be successful.

But defining success can be a slippery slope. Is media literacy something that can be mastered or is it something that can only be improved upon? James Potter said,

> One of my biggest issues is sorting through the priority between teaching skills and competency. Competency is categorical; either you have that competency or you don't; you're the master or you're not. But with skills there's this huge continuum where you always get better; there's never really an ultimate end point. I think people look at us in media literacy and expect us to deliver competency . . . but what we're really dealing with here, is that we are on a continuum and we are trying to nudge people a little bit better and a little bit better. . . .

Incorporate Production, but Ensure that Students Are Doing *Critical* Production

The ease of using technology for production has created a wide range of opportunities for media education as well as adding to the means of societal participation. Buckingham emphasized,

It is exciting that children are capable of creating content but it needs to be accompanied by a kind of critical thinking about what you are doing and a certain level of reflection on the choices you are making, and undertaking the process consciously.

Kathleen Tyner pointed out the advantage and necessity of joining deconstruction with construction,

When we get into the realm of virtual worlds and gaming, most people do not yet have the aesthetic vocabulary to really discuss and thoroughly enjoy what they are seeing and to share that in the public realm. So I always thought that the best way to teach about media was to marry production with analysis.

But, the need for doing and thinking goes beyond the conceptual, according to Katherine Currier Moody: "If you are a child, you have to make and create and do something or experience it with your body first and brain second—make a motor commitment. I think you have to *do* the media."

Make Sure that Learning Is Student-centered and Process-oriented

The pioneers' emphasis is not to constrain students, but to give them a framework, a forum, and practice so they can thrive and expand their own horizons.

Buckingham explained,

Younger kids can do a lot of the stuff that we have been trying to teach 14 year olds. If you provide media education in a systematic way over time, and didn't just leave it until secondary school but put it in the primary school as well . . . what you would get at the end would be something that is quite challenging and complex.

The students who respond well to media education are not always the "best" students, as David Considine commented, "I came very early to believe that interested kids did not have behavior problems . . . a lot of the kids that I taught (were) using an Australian phrase, 'no hopers'—but my belief was just that school did not engage them."

Chris Worsnop also shed light on how to make education student-centered: "Treat young people in schools as thinking, reasoning, decision-making, creative, autonomous individuals and acknowledge that and encourage it, accept it in ways that don't demand that they toe the line like we had to."

Provide Pre-service and Professional Development for Teachers

Until teachers become media literate and understand their role as teachers of media literacy, they cannot be expected to teach the subject. Yet, teacher pre-service and professional development in media education are definitely the exception. Neil Andersen explained,

> In Ontario, we have media literacy mandated and we have very articulate learning goals but it still isn't happening in most classrooms. The faculties of education seem to have been stonewalling this at a time when media literacy is mandated for all of the teachers.

Where professional development takes hold, media education can take off. The evolution of media literacy in Australia is a case in point. According to Barrie McMahon:

> [Our professional development program was so successful] that one school couldn't handle it. We used . . . a caravan to go around the State and also the metropolitan area to teach teachers and also to give demonstrations . . . in Western Australia now, media education is part of the formal curriculum from kindergarten, preschool if you like, through to Year 12.

Provide High Quality Teaching Resources

Teachers not only need training themselves, but they also need teaching resources—frameworks, activities, lessons, curricula—that are easy to use and model how to teach about the media, while using the media itself. Duncan explained,

> We had the famous Canadian Ministry of Education Media Resource Guide—and that became—even in the U.S.—a kind of underground best-seller. . . . It came out in 1989. Everything was generated with reference to the Key Concepts. To a certain extent there were lesson plans but we didn't have a detailed set. People would adapt them to what we called "teach-able moments." The teachable moments are things like the War in Vietnam, 9/11, Katrina. All of those things are mediated by the media.

Cary Bazelgette described a comprehensive program that she helped produce while at the British Film Institute (BFI):

> We produced seven collections of short films for classroom study by primary children. More importantly, we set up a program of training provisions aimed at creating "lead practitioners," who were also supported by their local education authorities to train other teachers. In the end we trained such leaders in 61 of England's 147 local authorities and over the ten years since, the BFI has sold over 15,000 resources and probably reached well over a million children, as well as created sustainable media teaching. What's also interesting about this project is that it was done without any extra subsidy

from the taxpayer: it was all achieved on the basis of regular expenditure on our salaries and within the local authorities themselves, who collectively invested some 800,000 pounds in media education.

Such programs and resources are essential to replicating, scaling and evaluating media literacy programs; teachers need easy access, consistency, support, and results.

Teach Media Literacy as a Separate Subject, yet Recognize that Interdisciplinary Approaches Are Ideal

Unfortunately, the politics of education often interfere with the delivery of media literacy education. Inevitably, how departments are structured, how credit is given, and where media literacy curricula are included or excluded effect how media literacy is taught and learned. Andersen explained,

> There shouldn't be a separate media strand [for media literacy] in the English curriculum; it should be integrated with all other subjects. . . . [But] if we take the strand out, media literacy will be easier to ignore. The fact is that math, geography, history and science teachers . . . can and should be integrating media literacies into most of their lessons . . . they can do media literacy in five minutes in another lesson rather than having to make it a separate lesson or separate unit.

Tyner concurred, and offered a further challenge:

> There are concerns about current confusion of where media literacy belongs and how it should be taught—concerns that span all levels of education, from preschool through post-graduate work. Given that the current education system is divided into subject silos, it is difficult to encourage the study of media literacy, which spans all content areas.

Renee Hobbs said,

> Until we can have truly interdisciplinary programs that connect English education to education to literacy studies to sociology to media and communications, until we can actually study that all of a piece, then the scholarship of media literacy is going to continue to be at the margins.

Assess and Evaluate Results of Media Literacy Education

Until media literacy education efforts are replicable and measurable, they cannot be disseminated to a wide audience. This fact, plus the substantial cost of quality evaluations, has been a barrier to the spread of programs globally.

Bazelgette commented, "Until we gather better, more objective and more sustained evidence about media teaching and learning, we can't make judgments."

As Robert Kubey noted, evidence is also necessary for growing the field,

> To my mind, if a number of studies showed statistically significant improvement in students' critical thinking or reading and writing skills—using quantitative measures—you could sell media literacy like hotcakes. Or at least get education schools to sit up and take notice and begin to consider teaching media literacy.

Fortunately, efforts to implement media literacy are now being documented and recognized, according to Considine: "We are . . . seeing the first doctoral dissertations that have addressed media literacy in the U.S. . . . and articles in *Library Science* and in publications like *The Journal of Adolescent and Adult Literacy*."

Develop Partnerships

No field, no movement can be successful unless there are stakeholders who are willing to champion its adoption. While grassroots' support, often enacted by individual teachers, acts as the foundation to the movement, institutional support is also essential. Hobbs commented,

> I continue to be surprised at the diversity of stakeholder involvement . . . there are parents, business leaders, museum educators, computer programmers and civil rights activists and anti-poverty advocates and art teachers and school counselors . . . most importantly, media literacy is now finally a part of our public discourse, and we see that so clearly now in TV shows like *The Daily Show with Jon Stewart* and *The Colbert Report*.

The pioneers themselves affirmed how varied the sources of support can be. As Marilyn Cohen said,

> The opportunity to further media literacy education in our state (Washington) . . . came from the teen pregnancy group at our Department of Health . . . you can do some wonderful things with a media literacy-based approach and leave the kids to come up with their own conclusions, which has to be the bottom line in any case.

Not only a desire for physical health, but also an effort to encourage spiritual growth has been at the heart of some media literacy efforts. According to Elizabeth Thoman, "One of the greatest influences in '76–77 was the Protestant church . . . the Media Action Research Center adopted as its first project an education program known as Television Awareness Training."

Regardless of where partnerships originate, media literacy education can be strengthened through connections to communities who recognize the value of critical evaluation and discernment in both understanding and producing media messages.

Advocate for Media Literacy at the Policy Level

The experience of the media literacy pioneers shows that whether media literacy is supported at the policy level or not can have a profound effect. As Buckingham explained,

> The one difference between the U.S. and the U.K. is that in the U.S. system, it has been very hard to get media education into the mainstream curriculum. . . . Whereas in the U.K. we have had media education as a separate subject in school for about 40 years. It has stayed in the curriculum but let's be clear—it is not a compulsory subject. It's been an element of English . . . the government passed a communications act in 2003 which established a new, converged regulator for media to promote media literacy through OfCom (the Office of Communications). It is a combination of recognition at the top . . . this is what we have in the U.K. that we have not had in the past.

Getting support at the policy level is difficult, and there are many obstacles. Chief among them, according to Considine, is the education system itself.

> You are trying to put an innovation into an institution, which is actually an institution of inertia. The culture and climate of schools swallows innovation. Statistics tell us that by 2013 we will be spending 29 billion dollars a year on technology. . . . So even though the computer promises individual self-paced learning, we've turned it into "drill and kill." In other words, the system swallows the innovation and the innovation takes on the life of what's already been there.

Not only is the system inert, sometimes it is pervert, according to Worsnop:

> Traditionalism in education is not going to go away because there's too much profit for publishers and test makers for them to let go of it. And no government in its right mind wants to have a population of young people thinking for themselves. . . . There are awful and nasty, nasty powers in education that keep media literacy at bay.

The politics of education often determine where and how media education is delivered. According to Robin Quin, "Media studies is now a subject that counts for university entry (in Australia); it is externally examined; it does consist of both a production element and a written element: it's roughly weighted 50/50."

But regardless of how media education is perceived, its presence is a necessity in today's curriculum. The stakes are high, according to Jean-Pierre Golay. Having lived through the Nazi era and experienced its impact on his native Switzerland, Golay observed, "One wonders if such a discouraging portion of the population targeted by the Nazi propaganda would have fallen for such obvious traps if they had benefited from some media education." Considine raised the ultimate challenge by noting that "it's not just a 21st century skill, it's a survival skill," He said that "the whole notion, the American ideal of 'informed responsible citizenship' . . . you cannot be an informed responsible citizen if you are not simultaneously media literate."

The hope for developing these skills amongst students globally is tantalizing. As Marieli Rowe said, "Media literacy's apex may very well be a road to . . . becoming a more civilized global society, if we could develop common language (for critiquing) the rich variety of media."

References

Center for Media Literacy. (2011). Voices of media literacy: International pioneers speak. Retrieved from http://www.medialit.org/voices-media-literacy-international-pioneers-speak.

Flanagin, A.J., & Metzger, M.J. (2010). *Kids and credibility: An empirical examination of youth, digitamedia use, and information credibility.* Cambridge, MA: MIT Press.

Rideout, V.A., Foeher, U.G., & Roberts, D.F. (2010). *Generation M²: Media in the lives of 8-to-18 year olds.* Oakland, CA: Henry J. Kaiser Family Foundation.

3

MEDIA LITERACY EDUCATION IN ONTARIO

Neil Andersen

Ontario's media literacy education derives from U.K. and Australian models. U.K. models arose within an acute awareness of its class structure, which has translated into a media literacy education that is influenced by an awareness of power dynamics and socio-economic ideological differences. Australian models arose from a defensive response to American media content and its influences and contain a strong media production element. Ontario's media literacy education presents influences of both. Canadians purport to have little class structure (a naïve populist misconception) but are acutely aware of American media content. Canadians generally consume more American websites, TV, games, music and movies than they do their own. Yet, Canadians are also bemused that many of America's most successful and popular cultural figures of the last 100 years are Canadians-in-disguise: Mary Pickford, Mack Sennett, Lorne Greene, Lorne Michaels, James Cameron, Paul Haggis, Joni Mitchell, Neil Young, Leonard Cohen, Mike Myers, Jim Carrey, Matthew Perry, Michael J. Fox, Celine Dion, Bryan Adams, Diana Krall, The Barenaked Ladies, Nickelback, Brad Pitt (OK, not Brad Pitt—just checking to see if you are paying attention). Canadians often smile conspiratorially when these artists receive American accolades, as though to say to one another, 'LOL! Fooled them again!' What neither they nor Americans might notice is the covert influences these Canadians are exerting on American culture and, by extension, the world.

The cloaked success and influence of some Canadians' participation in American culture often gives Canadians an ironic view of Americans and American culture, one that nurtures their media literacy. Media literacy benefits from a measure of detachment that allows people to become reflective and analytical about what they are observing and experiencing. Living beside a nation 10 times more populated and the world's only superpower—both militarily and culturally—forces Canadians into a detached position that has made media literacy easier to exercise, understand and appreciate than if they were inside the U.S. culture.

Media Literacy's most famous scholar is a wonderful example of Canadian media literacy education's cosmopolitan awareness and attitude. Born in Edmonton, Marshall McLuhan was educated at the Universities of Manitoba and Cambridge in literature and philosophy. He began teaching in the United States and then spent most of his academic life in Toronto, founding the Toronto School of Communications and the Centre for Culture and Technology. He also, by virtue of Barry Duncan and the Association for Media Literacy, instigated and influenced Ontario's media literacy education.

McLuhan was an unapologetic mediaphobe and an English lit professor heavily influenced by James Joyce's writing and Harold Innis's systems analyses. He especially relished the ways that Joyce played with and hybridized language in *Finnegan's Wake*. It was his fascination with this novel that helped him appreciate that it was not its narrative content but its revolutionary form that made it such a compelling experience. McLuhan synthesized Joyce's linguistic playfulness and Innis's system analyses into McLuhanism and its most famous aphorism: The medium is the message (and the audience is the content). So the notions of remix or hybridization of communications and audiences making meaning have always been present in Ontario media literacy education, thanks to a genius literature professor and the teachers who adapted and applied his theories.

Barry Duncan, the founding president of the Association for Media Literacy (AML), studied under McLuhan and worked to make his ideas accessible to elementary and high school students. I studied under Barry Duncan as well as at the *McLuhan Program in Culture and Technology* and I continue that work. McLuhan's key concepts, extended by subsequent media literacy scholars, are present in the work of the AML. The AML is responsible not only for lobbying Ontario's Ministry of Education to include robust and articulate media literacy learning goals but also wrote those goals and several subsequent support documents.

While it is tempting to pursue a reductive version of media literacy because it is easier, Ontario media literacy educators endeavor to engage the full range of media literacy's complexities. By reductive, I mean an *effects theory* that often suggests that media effects are inherently evil or, if not evil, then an impairment to critical thinking. I also mean *technological determinism,* which suggests that technology's effects on society are inevitable, unchangeable and indefensible. McLuhan rejected the *effects theory* and *technological determinism* to a degree. He acknowledged media effects by admitting to being a mediaphobe, preferring words on paper to other media forms, and explaining that his theories were developed to sensitize people to the inherent effects of electronic media so that they might prepare for and mitigate them. He stated that media literacy was 'protection against media fallout.' (McCluhan, 1964). His use of a bomb-shelter metaphor may seem extreme now, but it originated when the Cuban Missile Crisis was current and the attacks on Hiroshima and Nagasaki were as recent as the World Trade Center attacks are to us.

Ontario's media literacy education arose from—and is still organizationally attached to—the high school English curriculum. Its language and literature genesis emphasized a narrative, language-based, theme-focused approach that originally prioritized story, language codes and conventions, and value statements. Because of the lit-crit model favored by English teachers, early media literacy education had a strong deconstructionist discourse that assumed that meaning was primarily in the text. Cultural studies is now a large part of the media literacy education curriculum, and was added to the text-centric 1970s curriculum in the 1980s as a result of increased awareness of audience research and cultural studies scholarship. Audience study has foregrounded the importance of the pleasures and multiple uses of texts. It has helped us understand that viewers are social beings with multiple subjectivities. Similarly, texts are now seen as polysemic—they use layered codes and conventions to convey many meanings and hence elicit many different readings. Social media have highlighted audiences' roles in meaning-making by visualizing processes and individual interpretations.

There is currently a mandatory Media Literacy component for the Grades 1–8 Language curriculum and a discrete Media Literacy box on the Ontario report card. There is also a mandatory Media Literacy component for the Grades 9–12 English curriculum, although its evaluations are blended with other language and literature evaluations on the report card. There is also an elective English Media Grade 11 course that is selected by 10% to 15% of students.

Frameworks are tools used by educators to formulize and support thinking and learning. In narrative study, frameworks use plot, character, setting, and conflict. In mathematics, frameworks include isolating the variable. In science education, frameworks involve testing hypotheses. As do other jurisdictions' curricula, Ontario media literacy education utilizes frameworks. These were first articulated as 'The Eight Key Concepts of Media Education' in Ontario's *Media Literacy Resource Guide* and have sustained as useful statements to apply to any media text or environment. The AML added a second framework—the *Media Literacy Triangle*—shortly after as an alternative. Teachers use either or both, depending on their own comfort with media literacy education and their students' learning activities.

Rather than presenting the original Eight Key Concepts, I am presenting a set revised by time, experience, and feedback.

1. Media texts construct reality.
2. Media texts construct versions of reality.
3. Audiences negotiate meaning.
4. Media texts have economic implications.
5. Media texts communicate values messages.
6. Media texts communicate political and social messages.
7. Form and content are closely related in each medium.
8. Each medium has a unique aesthetic form.

You will likely note similarities between these statements and those used in other jurisdictions, as they have become models. Teachers use these concepts by exploring with students how they apply to specific media texts. Rather than exhaustively considering all eight for one text, they concentrate on two or three that best inform students' understanding of one text then apply a different two or three at another time and for a different text. A way of making the concepts more accessible to students is to re-configure the concepts as questions. For example, Key Concept #2 might be re-phrased as *How might World of Warcraft help people understand that media texts construct versions of reality?*

Here is a version of the *Media Literacy Triangle,* again revised as a result of the bumps and bruises of history and use.

The triangle framework was a gift to Ontario Media Literacy educators from the *Scottish Film Council* via Eddie Dick, one of its educational consultants. While it implicates most of the ideas presented in the *Eight Key Concepts,* it organizes them into three categories: audience, production and text; it also presents them as a graphic organizer instead of a list—a significant difference. Students imagine a media text in the middle of the triangle and then explore it from each of the three points of view. Again, constructing questions from the arcane bulleted words helps to operationalize the analyses. For example, two questions informing the audience

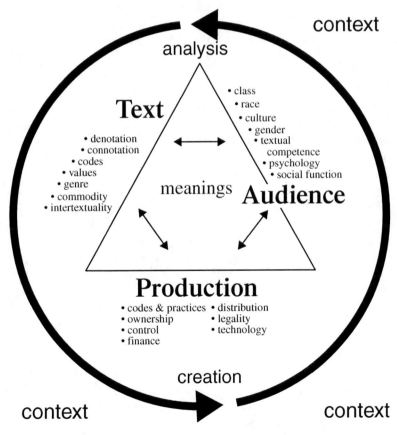

FIGURE 3.1 Media Literacy Triangle

side of the triangle might be, *How and why does Facebook appeal to its target audience?* and *What is pleasurable about this game?*

Ontario media literacy education rejects a good media/bad media dichotomy, postponing judgment until inquiry is complete, because the reductive leap to judgment often prevents people from seeing and benefiting from technology's usefulness or from understanding the larger context of its presence.

Some North American media literacy associations refer to 'big media,' specifically characterizing large media corporations as conspiratorial, malicious, self-serving, unethical, etc. While the charges against the United Kingdom's *News of the World* might support those notions, media corporations generally are not focused on the downfall of humankind, but rather on making profits for their shareholders. More dangerously, setting up a 'big media' construction suggests an 'us-versus-them' paradigm, where 'they' are big, and therefore denotatively dominant. While this worldview might afford some people self-satisfaction for being giant killers, most people know that they are neither giant killers nor aspiring to be. Most people prefer to operate within an ecological model, where media organizations and audiences interact in a variety of complex ways as they evolve. Social media websites are an example of such ecological actions, where some have been highly successful, then disappeared when audiences moved to a more useful one. More perilously, teachers who construct an 'us-versus-them' paradigm suggesting that adults/teachers know best and will protect children/students from evil creates a hegemony much like those they protest.

The same misstep is made by organizations that characterize media messages as evil. While a case can be made for such characterizations when an organization is promoting an ideology that violates human rights (homophobia, racism, ageism, sexism, etc.), it is (at this writing) legal to produce and market tobacco, fast food, and petroleum products extracted from shale and oil sands. Students need to be able to exercise critical media literacy skills autonomously in these cases.

The disservices that result from the 'big media' and 'evil media' discourses are that they encourage students to either fear or loathe media producers, each one a most unhealthy attitude. The 'big media' and 'evil media' discourses also set up the organizations that use them as caretaking students, fighting the battles on their behalf. Such feelings condescendingly discourage them from consuming media and thinking critically while simultaneously disempowering them from believing that they can change the situation proactively. Ontario media literacy education encourages students to engage with *all* media messages and to use critical media literacy skills to (a) select and use media forms and content that improve their lives and their society, (b) reject those that do not, and (c) actively resist the messages and organizations that they find unacceptable. Resistance might take the form of eschewing a particular product, website, or activity, but might also involve (a) lobbying government for changes to, or more effective enforcement of, legislation, (b) requesting that a corporation revise content or make a policy change, or (c) advocating a change in consumption behaviors among their peers.

Getting Started in Media Education (Pungente, 1985) identifies nine factors that appear crucial to the successful development of media education:

1. Media literacy, like other innovative programs, must be a grassroots movement and teachers need to take a major initiative in lobbying for this.
2. Educational authorities must give clear support to such programs by mandating the teaching of media education within the curriculum, establishing guidelines and resource books, and by ensuring curricula are developed and materials are available.
3. Faculties of Education must hire staff capable of training future teachers in this area. There should also be academic support from tertiary institutions in the writing of curricula and in sustained consultation.
4. In-service training at the school district level must be an integral part of program implementation.
5. School districts need consultants who have expertise in media literacy and who will establish communication networks.
6. Suitable textbooks and audiovisual materials that are relevant to the country/area must be available.
7. A support organization must be established for the purposes of workshops, conferences, dissemination of newsletters and the development of curriculum units. Such a professional organization must cut across school boards and districts to involve a cross section of people interested in media literacy.
8. There must be appropriate evaluation instruments.
9. Because media education involves such a diversity of skills and expertise, there must be collaboration between teachers, parents, researchers, and media professionals.

Based on Pungente's prerequisites for quality media literacy education, Ontario has fared well with the exception of numbers 3, 4, and 5, which occur in woefully rare instances. Ontario's Media Literacy curriculum statements are strong and articulate. Publishers have supported media literacy instruction. Ontario's Association for Media Literacy (http://www.aml.ca) has provided support provincially since 1978 and instigated the formation of media literacy education associations in many other Canadian provinces, now represented by the Canadian Association for Media Education Organizations (CAMEO). *Mediasmarts* (http://www.mediasmarts.ca) has provided support nationally since 1994.

Ontario's media literacy education subscribes to David Buckingham's (2000) recommendation, 'Preparation, not protection.' We cannot know the media experiences that our students have outside of and beyond school. We do know, however, that they will graduate into a world where their personal, vocational, and civic lives will be lived in and through mediated communications. Because media literacy is a crucial life skill, we prepare our students for a life of critical thinking that will help them maximize their communication skills for success in a democratic society and a multicultural world.

References

Buckingham, D. (2000). *After the Death of Childhood*. London: Polity Press.

Duncan, B., Andersen, N., Boles, D., Cole, S.G., Emid, A., Flynn, E. . . . Wheeler, W. (1989). *Media Literacy Resource Guide*. Ontario Ministry of Education and the Association for Media Literacy. Toronto: Queen's Printer for Ontario.

McLuhan, M. (1964). *Understanding Media*. New York: McGraw-Hill.

Pungente, J. (1985). *Getting Started in Media Education*. London: Centre for the Study of Communication and Culture.

PART II

DIGITAL MEDIA AND LEARNING

The concept of a participatory culture has been made relevant by the many new technologies emerging in the home and classroom today. However, the idea of participation in media has existed long before these technologies. In a digital media culture, how we think about learning and the interplay between technologies, literacies, and educational experiences take on new forms of understanding. In the Digital Media and Learning section, we explore a host of perspectives on how learning is evolving in technological contexts, and what tools and platforms are facilitating this change. The phenomenon of curation is explored as a pedagogical model for enhancing learning through remix, collaborative reproduction, and cultural production. Technology also has had a great impact on how educators can engage students with disabilities, as one chapter explores in this book. Using participatory culture to lead new pedagogical modeling for disability students is leading to new and innovative media literacy activities in the classroom. The concept of visualization as a digital media literacy is explored to discuss how visualization can increase how youth understand and comprehend information in a data rich and information rich society. To complete this section a discussion on the "flat classroom" ponders a broader concept of media literacy to incorporate more multimedia texts and peer-to-peer tools in the education of all citizens. This can expand classroom discourse and widen the opportunity to teach using diverse voices and vibrant dialog.

4

A CASE FOR CURATION AS A MEDIA LITERACY IMPERATIVE FOR PARTICIPATORY CULTURE

Paul Mihailidis

Introduction—Media Literacy and the Participatory Landscape

In his seminal white paper, *Confronting the Challenges of a Participatory Culture,* Henry Jenkins identified a core set of skills that "build on the foundation of traditional literacy, research skills, technical skills, and critical analysis skills taught in the classroom" (4). Collectively, these skills enable people to use new social platforms and spaces to facilitate critical inquiry and active collaboration online. Jenkins wrote (2009):

> Participatory culture is emerging as the culture absorbs and responds to the explosion of new media technologies that make it possible for average consumers to archive, annotate, appropriate, and recirculate media content in powerful new ways. A focus on expanding access to new technologies carries us only so far if we do not also foster the skills and cultural knowledge necessary to deploy those tools toward our own ends. (8)

The skills identified by Jenkins—play, performance, simulation, appropriation, multitasking, distributed cognition, collective intelligence, judgment, transmedia navigation, networking, and negotiation—have at their core the ability to engage multimodal inquiry, multimedia platforms, and information abundance through navigating collaborative spaces online.

In his 2008 book, *Mediacology,* Antonio Lopez writes about media literacy as a conduit for helping people find a "sense of place." Lopez grounds his exploration in critiques of media literacy education as a linear pedagogy that teaches youth to critically respond to media texts that they consume. Lopez rightfully sees this approach as both limiting and misguided. Instead, he offers an approach to media literacy that is grounded in what he calls a mediacology—a holistic approach to exploring media at the center of our sense of place, affinity to culture, and to the social ecosystems within which we function. Lopez writes (2008): "By focusing on media as a kind of "conduit" that transports information objects, we are failing to grasp how deeply our perception influences the manner by which we frame information, communication, and the world" (3).

Indeed, in today's ubiquitous media landscape, it is hard to envision future civic participants engaging with their local, national, and global communities without necessarily participating in the mediated spaces that will hold this dialogue. Statistics over the last few years can attest to this growth: A 2010 study found that "eight to eighteen year-olds in the US spend more time with media than in any other activity besides (maybe) sleeping—an average of more than 7½ hours a day, 7 days a week" (Kaiser). The Pew Center's annual State of the Media report (2012) reported information consumption habits in the United States migrating towards digital platforms across all age ranges.

As a result, citizens are increasingly asked not only to consume media content but to be *active participants* in the creation, sharing, and appropriation of media texts in their personal networks and beyond. This newfound participatory culture places more emphasis on the individual to possess the competencies necessary to effectively contribute to shared social and civic narratives that are created in social spaces.

Collectively, the skills Jenkins outlines in his paper embrace both the ecological approach to media literacy that Lopez explores above and a new reality for the competencies needed to critically and holistically engage with the new realities for media and a participatory culture today.

So what does this landscape mean for how we prepare future citizens for lives of inclusive and engaged citizenship? In the digital world, understanding how our actions engage and influence communities starts not from a linear response to media texts but rather from a point of seeing the value and purpose of our situated place and voice online. This extends beyond traditional models of evaluate, critique, and respond, and towards including those foundational skills in the act of curation online.

Role of Curation in Participatory Learning Culture

The word curate derives from the Latin root Curare, or "to cure." Historically, curation has denoted the gathering, organization, sorting, selecting for presentation, and preserving of material or objects. While this is mostly reserved for those who work with physical spaces and/or materials in public spaces—museums, parks, libraries, art galleries—curation now also incorporates the organization and cultivation of multiple forms of content in information spaces online. This has created a need to understand how youth choose to organize, sort, and present information within mediated spaces online.

Specifically, these new platforms for curation have shifted the way in which students share, appropriate, and organize content in peer-to-peer spaces. This has led to new collaborative capacities found in online networks that did not exist before the fast growth of such online spaces and tools. In their book *Connected*, Christakis and Fowler (2011) explore the new connective power of these new networks. They write:

> Our interactions, fostered and supported by new technologies, but existing even with them, create new social phenomenon that transcend individual experience by enriching and enlarging it, and this has significant implications for the collective good. Networks help make the whole of humanity much greater than the sum of its parts, and the invention of new ways to connect promises to increase our power to achieve what nature has foreordained. (286)

This new opportunity manifests itself in the ability for individuals to share, collaborate, and communicate with peers in new, dynamic, and participatory ways. From political opinions to movie and restaurant reviews, from travel tips to banking and shopping, people are now navigating and managing vast amounts of content. They are forming new connections with peers and acquaintances through their decisions of what networks to participate in, what to avoid, and what information to keep, what to discard, who to trust, what is credible, and how they can build meaningful daily information and communication habits in these spaces.

Media scholar Clay Shirky (2010) sees this new dynamic social environment as enabled by collaborative and curation-based technologies:

> The use of a social technology is much less determined by the tool itself; when we use a network, the most important asset we get is access to one another. We want to be connected to one another, a desire that the social surrogate of television deflects, but one that our use of social media actually engages. (14)

Of course, within this new user-driven landscape still exists some of the key issues around how people participate, how they respect others and how they positively contribute to information and dialog. Because these new mediated spaces are so vast, abundant, and diverse, the possibility for collecting mistakes, mistruths, and misinformation (Bartlett & Miller, 2011) are inevitable. Further, social networks like Facebook and Twitter and search engines like Google and Bing do play a significant role in how people locate, consume, and share information.

And this is exactly why and where media literacy education comes into the picture. If we are to prepare for a future society where mediated spaces facilitate a majority of public and personal civic dialogue, at the forefront of this must be teaching about the potential for empowered voices in social and digital platforms.

Because issues arise like best practices for sharing, remixing, and fair use (Lessig, 2008; Benkler, 2006; Hobbs, 2010a) curation should be at the forefront of how we think about and understand media education writ large.

In this context, media literacy education builds from foundations in critical analysis and evaluation of *messages* and towards building individual and social *agency* for behaviors within online spaces. I have identified three competencies— individual, participatory, and collaborative—(Mihailidis, 2013) that collectively position media literacy as the pedagogical movement oriented towards engaged citizenship in the digital age. Individual competency builds on foundations of media literacy and promotes the habits of engaged citizens proposed by Clark and Aufderheide (2009)—choice, conversation, curation, creation, and collaboration—as essential for participation in civic life through media. Collaborative competency implores embracing new media technologies to do more than simply keep in touch, share personal updates, or check in on friends. These tools are collaborative because we have enabled them to be so, and they can and should be seen in a larger context. Finally, participatory competency builds from the skills Jenkins (2009) identified—archive, annotate, appropriate, and recirculate—to build a more full understanding of networks, groups, audiences, and peer-to-peer sharing today.

These competencies will only develop in the context of media literacy education that premised on the development of smart and savvy navigation of information online. Curation can be the framework to help develop smart pedagogical approaches to thinking about participation, collaboration, and engagement online.

Developing Parameters for Curation as a Core Media Literacy Competency

Through education today, students enter the classroom with a certain level of familiarity with digital tools and platforms (Prensky, 2001; Ofcom, 2010; Rosen, 2010). While such familiarity does not necessarily translate into heightened levels of technological competence (Hargittai, 2005; Jones, Ramanau, Cross, & Healing, 2010; Kennedy, Dalgarno, Bennett, Judd, Gray, & Chang, 2008), it does provide a foundation of ready learners who have the basic foundational awareness of how to navigate online spaces.

Media literacy is premised on promoting critical thinking skills through the ability to access, evaluate, analyze, and produce information (Aufderheide, 1993; Ofcom, 2010; Potter, 2010; Silverblatt, 2001). Media literacy's overarching goal for teaching and learning outcomes are informed decision-making; individual empowerment; nuanced analysis of mediated messages; savvy consumption and production skills; and participation in local, national and global dialogue (Frechette, 2002; Gaines, 2010; Hobbs, 2010b, 2011; Tisdell, 2008). Media literacy scholar David Buckingham (2003) aggregates the myriad of approaches to media literacy in writing:

> [Media Literacy is] A critical literacy that involves analysis, evaluation, and critical reflection," that is possible only through the "acquisition of a metalanguage—that is, a means of describing the forms and structures of different modes of communication; and it involves a broader understanding of the social, economic and institutional contexts of communication, and how these affect people's experiences and practices" (Luke, 2000). Media literacy certainly includes the ability to use and interpret media; but it also involves a much broader analytical understanding. (38)

Like Lopez (2008) Buckingham does not separate media from the individual, instead seeing media messages and the critical inquiry of the individual as one and the same.

The emerging media literacy landscape, then, is one that is more fully integrated into the competencies needed for participation in an information age. Recent research I have conducted (Mihailidis 2013a, 2013b, forthcoming) shows that youth today primarily use aggregated and curated spaces for information consumption, sharing, and production. They no longer think of information in terms of specific outlets but instead in the context of their social information feeds. The implications for needing to prepare youth for agile and savvy navigation in this context is evident. In *Media Literacy and Semiotics* (2010), scholar Eliot Gaines elaborates on this need by acknowledging the sheer abundance of media in today's world:

> Every waking moment of contemporary life seems to be impacted by experiences that require the interpretation of signs taken to be messages from the environment, other people, or media. And while we are busy interpreting necessary information, the processes of communication and the media are in the background. Those processes have significant effects on the interpretation of meanings and the messages they convey. (5)

Recent investigations into youth and literacies in education have found that proper pedagogical methods that approach critical inquiry online, knowledge construction, reliability, and savvy web navigation can increase digital and media literacy (Kuiper & Volman, 2008; Sanchez et al., 2006; Taboada & Guthrie, 2006). Building on these, I want to offer six teaching approaches to curation for media literacy. I hope that these six points can help to start discussions and frame the approach to how curation fits into the media literacy landscape.[1]

1. **Where Top Down and Bottom Up Meet**—Social networks allow for the opportunity of fluid integration between information from media and news

organizations and from peer-to-peer civic voices. Traditionally media literacy has separated these voices in linear and top down fashion. Today, however, with the sharing of links, images, headlines, and thoughts, media literacy must account for this curation as a form of diverse, nuanced, and savvy information forum, where students can identify the point where top down information meets bottom up information.

2. **Integrating Mediums, Messages, and Platforms**—Along with the integration of organization and civic voices, teaching about curation can help students utilize convergence culture to better integrate formats for information online. Different delivery methods and platforms elicit different meanings and interpretations of information. Curation integrates these into spaces that don't distinguish mediums, messages, or platforms. Media literacy education can help to provide insight into the benefits and limitations of delivery systems and platforms.

3. **Sources, Voices, and Credibility Online**—At the center of media literacy will also be teaching and learning about vetting information for accuracy, balance, independence, and truth. Online, this takes a different and less linear reality. Do Facebook, Twitter, YouTube, and Tumblr provide credible sources? Can citizens alter reporting about an issue? How can we judge credibility online? Curation allows a deep exploration of the different voices that exist around an issue, and how those play into our own voices and modes of expression online.

4. **Frames, Bias, Agendas, and Perspective**—Beyond thinking about sources and credibility, media literacy can use curation to discuss how media frames, implicit bias, agendas, and perspectives are collectively developed through our social platforms. We no longer have one paper, or one channel that serves to "inform" us, but rather we live in a time of ubiquitous, constant, and vast information feeds, that never end. Who we have in our network and what algorithms we chose to listen to will have a significant influence on the way in which we receive, share, and re-appropriate information. Media literacy can utilize curation to help understand angles, perspectives and agendas build by networks online.

5. **Appreciating Diversity**—At no point before have people had such abundant, diverse, and vibrant information about any and all topics, ideas, and issues. Simply put, media literacy educators have this vast array of resources with which to teach about all the ways that this new media landscape can be used to be better informed, opinionated, understood, and engaged. This abundant information environment should not be seen as overwhelming, or put into linear "good or bad" compartments, but rather curation can help students learn to find, appreciate, and value the information that helps them become more tolerant, knowledgeable, and understanding.

6. **Civic Values and Civic Voices**—Lastly, what curation platforms have enabled above all is the build of civic voices. Citizens, of all ages, now have the opportunity to have a voice, to build dialogue, and contribute to discussions of all shapes and sizes. Using student-driven, creation-oriented learning, to

show this, is the first, middle, and last step towards activating these voices for engaged, inclusive, and active contributions in daily life.

Media literacy education is now more vital for participation and engagement in civic democracy than ever before. As youth and society both fast integrate media technologies and platforms to facilitate daily information and communication needs, it is up to media literacy educators to offer responses, pathways, and avenues to help cultivate inclusive, active, and engaged citizens across the mediasphere.

Note

1. Six teaching points adapted from P. Mihailidis & J. Cohen (2013), Exploring curation as a core digital and media literacy competency," *Journal of Interactive Media in Education* (forthcoming).

References

Aufderheide, P., & Firestone, C.M. (1993). *Media literacy: A report of the National Leadership Conference on Media Literacy.* Cambridge, UK: Polity Press.

Bartlett, J., and Miller, C. (2011). Truth, lies and the Internet: A report into young people's digital fluency. Demos. Retrieved from http://www.demos.co.uk/files/Truth_-_web.pdf.

Benkler, Y. (2006). *The wealth of networks: How social networks transform markets and freedom.* New Haven, CT: Yale University Press.

Buckingham, D. (2003). *Media education: Literacy, learning and contemporary culture.* Cambridge, UK: Polity Press.

Christakis, N., & Fowler, J. (2011). *Connected: How your friends' friends' friends affect everything you feel, think, and do.* Boston: Back Bay Books.

Clark, J., & Aufderheide, P. (2009). *Public media 2.0: Dynamic engaged publics.* Washington, DC: Center for Social Media.

Frechette, J.D. (2002). *Developing media literacy in cyberspace: Pedagogy and critical learning for the twenty-first-century classroom.* New York: Praeger.

Gaines, E. (2010). *Media literacy and semiotics.* New York: Palgrave.

Hargittai, E. (2005). Survey measures of web-oriented digital literacy. *Social Science Computer Review, 23,* 371–379.

Hobbs, R. (2010a). *Copyright clarity: How fair use supports digital learning.* New York: Corwin.

Hobbs, R. (2010b). Digital and media literacy: A plan of action, a White Paper on the digital and media literacy recommendations of the Knight Commission on the information needs of communities in a democracy. Washington DC: Aspen Institute.

Hobbs, R. (2011). *Digital and media literacy: Connecting culture and classroom.* Thousand Oaks, CA: Corwin.

Jenkins, H. (2006). *Convergence culture: Where old and new media collide.* New York: NYU Press.

Jenkins, H., Purushotma, R., Weigel, M., Clinton, K., & Robinson, A.J. (2009). *Confronting the challenges of participatory culture: Media education for the 21st Century* (a report for the MacArthur Foundation). Boston: MIT Press.

Jones, C., Ramanau, R., Cross, S., & Healing, G. (2010). Net generation or digital natives: Is there a distinct new generation entering university? *Computers & Education, 54*(3), 722–732.

Kaiser Family Foundation. (2010). *Generation M2: Media in the lives of 8–18 year-olds.* Henry J. Kaiser Family Foundation, Menlo Park, CA. Retrieved from http://www.kff.org/entmedia/mh012010pkg.cfm.

Kennedy, G., Dalgarno, B., Bennett, S., Judd, T., Gray, K., & Chang, R. (2008). Immigrants and natives: Investigating differences between staff and students' use of technology. In *Hello! Where are you in the landscape of educational technology? Proceedings ascilite Melbourne 2008.* Retrieved from http://www.ascilite.org.au/conferences/melbourne08/procs/kennedy.pdf.

Kuiper, E., & Volman, M. (2008). The Web as a source of information for students in K–12 education. In J. Coiro, M. Knobel, C. Lankshear, & D.J. Leu (Eds.), Handbook of research on new literacies (pp. 241–266). Mahwah, NJ: Lawrence Erlbaum Associates.

Lessig, L. (2008). *Remix: Making art and commerce thrive in the hybrid economy.* New York: Penguin.

Lopez, A. (2008). *Mediacology: A multicultural approach to media literacy in the 21st century.* New York: Peter Lang.

Mihailidis, P. (2013). Exploring global perspectives on identity, community and media literacy in a networked age. *Journal of Digital and Media Literacy.* Knight Foundation, *1*(1). Retrieved: http://jodml.wpengine.com/2013/01/21/perspectives-identity-media-literacy/.

Mihailidis, P., & Cohen, J. (2013). Exploring curation as a core digital and media literacy competency. *Journal of Interactive Media in Education,* forthcoming.

Mihailidis, P., Fincham, K., & Cohen, J. (2014). Towards a media literate model for civic identity on social networks: Exploring notions of community, participation, and identity of University Students on Facebook. *Atlantic Journal of Communication,* forthcoming.

Ofcom (2010). Children's media literacy audit 2010. London, UK. Retrieved from http://stakeholders.ofcom.org.uk/market-data-research/media-literacy-pubs/.

Pew Research Center's Project for Excellence in Journalism. (2012). *The state of the news media 2012: An annual report on American journalism.* Retrieved from http://stateofthemedia.org/.

Potter, W. J. (2010). *Media Literacy* (5th ed.). Thousand Oaks, CA: Sage.

Prensky, M. (2001). Digital natives, Digital immigrants. *On the Horizon, 9*(5), 1–6.

Rosen, L. (2010). *ReWired: Understanding the iGeneration and the way they learn.* New York: Palgrave Macmillan.

Sanchez, C.A., Wiley, J., & Goldman, S.R. (2006). Teaching students to evaluate source reliability during Internet research tasks. In S.A. Barab, K.E. Hay, & D.T. Hickey (Eds.), *Proceedings of the seventh international conference on the learning sciences* (pp. 662–666). Mahwah, NJ: Lawrence Erlbaum Associates.

Shirky, C. (2010). *Cognitive surplus: How technology makes consumers into collaborators.* New York: Penguin.

Silverblatt, A. (2001). *Media literacy: Keys to interpreting media messages* (2nd ed.). Westport, CT: Praeger.

Taboada, A., & Guthrie, J. (2006). Contributions of student questioning and prior knowledge to construction of knowledge from reading information text. *Journal of Literacy Research, 38*(1), 1–35.

Tisdell, E. (2008). Critical media literacy and transformative learning: Drawing on pop culture and entertainment media in teaching for media diversity in adult higher education. *Journal of Transformative Education, 6*(1), 48–67.

5

LESSONS LEARNED FROM AMANDA BAGGS

Implications for New Media Literacies Education

Margaret Carmody Hagood

In a world where those determine whether you have any rights, there are people being tortured, people dying because they are considered nonpersons because their kind of thought is so unusual as to not be considered thought at all. Only when the many shapes of personhood are recognized will justice and human rights be possible. (silentmiaow, 2007, http://www.youtube.com/watch?v=JnylM1hI2jc)

silentmiaow shared this perspective in an 8:36 *YouTube* video entitled "In my language." During the first four minutes she documented through sound and visual images her stim behaviors, repetitive motions often associated with people diagnosed with Autism Spectrum Disorders (ASD) and especially of those characterizes as LFA (Low Functioning Autism). She used assistive technology—that of type-to-talk computer software—to speak the captions she typed in the second half of the video. She summarized her video production in this way:

The first part is in my "native language," and then the second part provides a translation, or at least an explanation. This is not a look-at-the-autie gawking freakshow as much as it is a statement about what gets considered thought, intelligence, personhood, language, and communication, and what does not. (See comment section at http://www.youtube.com/watch?v=JnylM1hI2jc)

The video has received over a million hits since posted in 2007. It has resulted in over 5000 comments. silentmiaow also created a *YouTube* channel based upon her self-described work as an autism rights advocate who brings awareness to the literacies of individuals described as non-verbal/LFA. Her *YouTube* channel has received 1.8 million views.

silentmiaow is also known as Amanda Baggs. She maintains several outlets to share her thinking and to connect to others about autism rights activism. Besides *YouTube* video posting and commenting, she writes a blog at http://abaggs.blogspot.com. Her story was featured on *Anderson Cooper 360* and on CNN.com (Gajilan, 2007). In an article in *Wired Magazine,* (Wolman, 2008) she described the video, "In my language," as a political statement to call attention to stereotypes that underestimate the abilities of people with autism. She has also published her ideas about language and disability in *Disability Studies Quarterly,* an academic journal (Baggs, 2010).

In this chapter, I describe how individuals use discourse communities using new media literacies and participatory culture (as exemplified in the work of Amanda Baggs) and then explore issues that define and open up identities, in this case an identity such as autism. I argue that it is in this thoughtful and often difficult work that we identify implications for classroom instruction in media literacies education to improve students' critical thinking, ethical understandings, and various perspective taking within and across discourse communities that hold potential to ultimately transform learning about ourselves and others.

Brief Situation of Terminology

The following terms are central to this chapter:

> *New media literacies:* These are the literacies of the twenty-first century that connect foundational and traditional literacies of reading and writing of print-based texts with new literacies that include listening, speaking, viewing, and designing of both print and non-print based texts. New media literacies require abilities of both consuming print and nonprint texts (constructing meaning from texts created by others) and producing texts (creating one's own text and sharing it with others), be it in print or nonprint forms.
>
> *Participatory culture:* Jenkins (2006) coined the term *participatory culture* to describe the ways users engage in new media literacies, predominantly with online media. Characteristics of a participatory culture include the following:

- Openings for artistic expression and civic engagement
- Support for producing and sharing one's creations
- Informal mentorship between experienced and novices
- Members' contributions matter
- Social connections and care among members about each others' creations

Participatory cultures are created in online spaces where users form a shared discourse community around particular identities. It is within the discourse community that certain identities are recognized and valued as authentic while others are dismissed and critiqued as fraudulent.

Discourse theory, (identities/subjectivities), borderland discourse: Discourse theory is a way to imagine how identities and subjectivities come together. Gee (1990) explained a discourse as a way of being (in word, appearance, and action) within a particular context. For example, people use language, action, values, beliefs, tools, and objects to become a member of a particular discourse community. To be recognized as a member, a person must hold a particular identity valued among the other members. Simultaneously, people may well not identify with a particular identity within a discourse but still want to be a part of the discourse. To do so, people must actively position themselves using the language of power—their subjectivity—to shift and/or change the identities within a discourse (Hagood, 2002). Thus, people can change and impact acceptable identities and thus change and/or influence discourse, which can ultimately transform society (Gee, 1999). Knowing how identity and subjectivity work within a discourse community then allows people actively to participate in and to resist practices of that particular discourse and to observe how others engage in this work.

The Discourse of Autism Spectrum Disorder (ASD)

Autism Spectrum Disorder (ASD) is a neural developmental disorder that affects the brain's development and often impairs a person's social and communicative skills and interactions. The spectrum varies widely in character and severity but has a range of observable symptoms including measured intelligence, social interaction (understanding social cues, making eye contact, and demonstrating empathy), communication, repetitive movements (stim behaviors), sensory markers (responses to touch, smell, sound, taste, and feel), and motor coordination (http://www.cdc.gov/ncbddd/autism/signs.html). As of 2012, the Centers for Disease Control and Prevention estimated that 1 out of 88 children aged 8 has ASD. Boys are four times as likely as girls to be diagnosed with ASD.

Given its prevalence, many ASD discourse communities have formed, some as face-to-face, but the majority of ASD communities are online. And, given the inconclusive diagnosis of ASD, many different kinds of discourse communities support the various identities via the symptoms of the spectrum. Folks in ASD discourse communities have embraced new media literacies to facilitate their communication of ideas. And a participatory culture has formed within these discourse communities where folks share their stories and support each other's work.

Examining the controversial online presence of Amanda Baggs/silentmiaow reveals an interesting story about uses of new media literacies, participatory culture, ASD discourse communities, and associated identities and subjectivities of her advocacy work for people labeled with Autism Spectrum Disorder.

For many people, Amanda Baggs's online texts pushed them to think differently about themselves and others. On *YouTube* alone, silentmiaow has received

over 5000 comments on her "In my language" video. Many comments demonstrate an openness to understand the identity of autism differently:

> This is so touching, and a relavation [sic]. I have never been the type of
> person to make fun of or think people with disabilities as "bizarre", but I
> never thought about the things you've said in this video and it helps me
> understand things better, you are an amazing and courageous person for
> posting this. (posted by Uskyld)
>
> Bravo!! We "normal" people move too fast through life to realize the
> importance of many methods of communications, outside of verbal. We put
> too much emphasis on what's stated as opposed to what the meaning and
> purpose of what's communicated. There would be more peace on this earth
> if all listened and felt, instead of spoken and assumed. Thanks for your awe-
> some insight. The brain is powerful and hopefully people will realize that all
> human life is precious, regardless of differences. (posted by LavandaDolce)

And while some people thought the video thought-provoking, others felt that
silentmiaow's position of her own language was limited and further solidified
stereotypical withdrawn and uncommunicative identities associated with ASD:

> Interesting video. I do not see you as sub-human or anything of that nature,
> but I am uncertain that I see your language as a meaningful form of primary
> communication as it is non-standard even among those who are autistic.
> I mean, if I had spoke a language that only I knew, is it really a language?
> Also, is it really the burden of society to have to learn the individual lan-
> guage of each autistic person in order to communicate with them? (posted
> by marsman57)

Many posters in the online discourse community that silentmiaow/Amanda
created through her *YouTube* videos and blog have applauded her work in moving
beyond staid identities of those with autism. Some posters shared links to their
own created videos that they felt inspired to represent their own interpretations
of living with autism.

Within her online discourse community, examples of participatory culture
abounds. Amanda regularly comments on posts, answering people's queries, which
sometimes cover issues of autism while at other times deals with technological
support. Similarly, on her blog and in the academic journal article, she writes
about issues of language, communication, and identity, of living with a diagnosis
and identity label of autism, always advocating through print and nonprint texts
using her active subjective position to refute stereotypical labels that close off beliefs about those characterized with ASD.

Amanda embraces a participatory culture where the discourse community discussed issues of autism, activism, and general member support. She encourages
followers/readers to comment on her work and to share their own creations. She

supports others, and in the interactions online it is apparent that within these discourses members care about one another.

However, in other online discourse communities, members position Amanda Baggs's identity of autism as a hoax. For example, members of Wrongplanet.net have discussed it at length. This website is described as the online resource and community for those with autism and Asperger's and was developed by Alexander Plank, a young adult who was diagnosed with ASD when he was nine years old. This discourse community includes an online chat, a link to email Alex, video links and article resources for those affected by autism, and a thriving discussion forum with thousands of threads and posts. *Inconsistencies regarding Amanda Baggs' Past History???* (2011, July 8). Wrong Planet.Net. Retrieved February 14, 2013, from http://www.wrongplanet.net/postt167581.html. The following excerpts exemplify the various positions within the thread named "Inconsistences regarding Amanda Bagg's [sic] Past History???"

ShellyH wrote:

> Amanda Baggs is thought of as a hoax for several reasons. She talked growing up and didn't have [sic] speech delays.
>> Potty trained on time
>> Went to gifted college to study psychology
>> She didn't stim when other knew her at that time
>> She spoke and had friends . . . even an autistic girl she wrote about and admired

Amanda Baggs

When it all changed for her is after Amanda took LSD for months and smoked weed. After that she was found digging in the ground looking for mind control devices. The police found her and took her to an institution. She was diagnosed with paranoid schizophrenic. She was also diagnosed with multiple personality disorder. She wrote about this stuff online and she even had a different style of writing. Similar BUT now she writes alot like a lady named Droopy.

Wavefreak58 wrote:

> I guess I don't understand why this is important. The specifics about her history and RX don't change the efficacy of her advocacy work. So how does this minutia matter?

Amahanshi wrote:

> It does matter, because she's currently claiming to have autism (LFA), when the anecdotal evidence implies otherwise. I value honesty, and while I respect her eloquent writings regarding the request of not neglecting non-verbal/LFA individuals, that doesn't entitle her to call herself Autistic, unless she truly is it.

Wavefreak58 wrote:

> You're taking a very black and white stance here. The whole point of describing autism as a spectrum is that there are no clear divisions between high, medium and low function. In fact, there is a lot of disagreement on how to even define functioning levels. . . . The details of her history can tell us a great deal, but suggesting that it invalidates her point of view and diminishes her value to the autistic community does not bring anything useful into the conversation . . . How does her advocacy harm anyone?

Verdandi wrote:

> As far as I know, Amanda doesn't claim to be low-functioning, she simply describes how she functions. I am not sure what the point is to claim that her autistic symptoms started with drugs when she clearly describes them from childhood onward.

In this exchange, members use new media literacies in an online format and participatory culture to discuss issues of identity related to ASD. While ShellyH argues that Amanda cannot have autism because she doesn't fit the childhood label, Wavefreak58 refutes the critique, using the characteristic of being a spectrum to acknowledge that Amanda should not be labeled by others and should be able to present herself and her own identity. Futhermore, Wavefreak58 notes that Amanda's identity is closely associated with her advocacy work to open up the identity of those with ASD. And Verdandi clarifies the identity further, noting that Amanda "describes how she functions" but doesn't claim an identity of low functioning. Certainly, this discourse community also exhibits characteristics of participatory culture such as civic engagement, member contributions, and care for members' creations, all around the issues of Amanda's authenticity as a person with an accepted identity of autism.

The exchange about the authenticity of Amanda's identity as a person with autism and of her identity as an activist is discussed on many online discourse communities. This one exchange illustrates that within any discourse community members can accept identities that are given to them (as in the case of a label of autism), they can wholly refute those identities (as in the case of ShellyH's comment), or they can acknowledge a kind of borderland discourse crossing (Alsup, 2006), whereby "two discourses come in contact and there appears to be disparities between subjectivities that have potential for 'ideological integration of multiple senses of self' that can lead to some sort of identity growth, be it cognitive, emotion, and/or corporeal" (p. 36). Amanda seems to be doing the work of borderland crossing through her advocacy to open-up the label of autism and of the Cartesian mind/body split so that folks can examine closely their own thinking about the privileging of language and power over that of nonverbal interactions and its implications for identities. Using participatory culture and new media literacies, discussion and exploration can happen among many more people than if it were just face-to-face. Actually, in a response-post to someone on *YouTube*, she acknowledges that her identity shifts and changes too. In response to her video "In my language" she commented, "although I have my own way of relating to the world, I am often (not always) perfectly capable of doing what I said in the video and switching into other people's language if I have to."

Implications for Media Literacy Education in Schools

The purpose of the *Core Principles of Media Literacy Education in the United States* (2007) is to provide guidance to develop informed, reflective, and engaged citizens of a democratic society. This document presents media literacy as an expanded conceptualization of literacies. The development of media literacy must build on skills developed within all learners and must be integrated and interactive in the curriculum. To that end, media literacy education must instruct students in active inquiry and critical thinking about texts consumed and produced. This instruction must go beyond instructional technologies of the *how to use* tools. Instruction must address the nuances of the ways that new media literacies and participatory cultures get used to construct new identities and shift discourse communities. But new media literacies education must go beyond access to participatory culture.

As illustrated in this story about Amanda Baggs, representations are complicated; truths are evasive. Like Jenkins (2006) noted, media literacy educators must take an ecological approach that acknowledges the messiness of the interrelationships among different communication technologies. Further, we must provide opportunities to students to work within ethical frameworks from which to examine closely the identities and subjectivities that are shaped by and that shape discourse communities. So rather than ask the question, "Is Amanda or isn't she (you fill in the blank)?" it might be more useful in the study of media literacy education to have students examine how discourse communities, participatory culture, and literacies allow for deeper questions such as "How does Amanda Baggs's advocacy open up and close down identities, possibilities, and discourse communities for those interested in autism?"

References

Alsup, J. (2006). *Teacher identity discourses: Negotiating personal and professional spaces.* Mahwah, NJ: Lawrence Erlbaum.

Baggs, A. (2010). Cultural commentary: Up in the clouds and down in the valley: My richness and yours. *Disability Studies Quarterly, 30*(1). Retrieved from http://dsq-sds.org/article/view/1052/1238.

Centers for Disease Control and Prevention: Morbidity and mortality weekly report. (2012, March 30). Prevalence of Autism Spectrum Disorders. *Surveillance Summaries, 61*(3), 1–19.

Centers for Disease Control and Prevention. *Signs and symptoms of Autism Spectrum Disorders (ASDs).* Retrieved from http://www.cdc.gov/ncbddd/autism/signs.html.

Gajilan, C. (2007). Living with autism in a world made for others. Retrieved from http://www.cnn.com/2007/HEALTH/02/21/autism.amanda/index.html.

Gee, J.P. (1990). *Social linguistics and literacies: Ideology in discourses, critical perspectives on literacy and education.* London: Routledge.

Gee, J.P. (1999). *An introduction to discourse analysis: Theory and method.* New York: Routledge.

Hagood, M.C. (2002). Critical literacy for whom? *Reading Research and Instruction, 41,* 247–266.

Jenkins, H. (with Clinton, K., Purushotma, R., Robison, A.J., & Weigel, M.). (2006). *Confronting the challenges of participatory culture: Media education for the 21st century.* Chicago: MacArthur Foundation.

Matthews, E. (2006). *Merleau-Ponty: A guide for the perplexed.* New York: Continuum International Publishing Company.

National Association for Media Literacy Education. (2007). *Core principles of media literacy education in the United States.* Retrieved from http://namle.net/publications/core-principles/.

silentmiaow. (2007). *In my language.* Retrieved from http://www.youtube.com/watch?v=JnylM1hI2jc.

Wolman, D. (2008). The truth about autism: Scientists reconsider what they *think* they know." *Wired Magazine, 16*(3). Retrieved from http://www.wired.com/medtech/health/magazine/1603/ff_autism?currentPage=all.

6

VISUALIZATION AS A NEW MEDIA LITERACY

Erin Reilly

Defining Visualization

Every day, visualizations affect what we do. As data increasingly mediates our lives, visualization allows us all to be inquirers and interpreters so that we can represent data in meaningful ways. Today, we are able to combine multiple data sets resulting from our aggregation of knowledge from social media and multiple research resources, which allows us to philosophize about what we want and how we exist in the world to a wide audience.

Visualization is not a new phenomenon. Scientists have been collecting data to aggregate, analyze, and quantify information into visual presentations for some time. In the past, scientific visualizations were equated with numeric data rather than texts, images, and relational networks. Today, scientific research is not isolated in a lab. New forms of data aggregation and visualization allow scientists to collaborate across the world and across disciplines to hypothesize, solve complex problems, and offer new theories.

The use of images as visualizations in mass media is common today. Newspapers, such as *The New York Times,* employ an in-house interactive team to create custom visualizations for journalists to clarify large amounts of information. With the rise of free visualization tools (such as *Tableau Public, Many Eyes, Easel.ly*) and more accessible data sets open to the public, the process of making sense of our world and our place in it has become democratized.

Through social media platforms such as *Twitter* or *Facebook*, we now keep track of our actions and store personal data to better understand our thoughts, interests, and desires. Companies associated with every facet of life—economy, environment, education, health, transportation—collect data too. Combined, these companies have given rise to a world made up of pools of information gathered from multiple digital devices we use every day. Not only do companies collect data, they also share data with the public through visualizations.

Visualizations help us make sense of data, and of our society and our place in it. The traditional, top-down means of gathering data and analyzing content we now combine with grassroots aggregation of opinion and sentiment, or of nuanced actions that reflect what we like or don't like. Aggregated data gives us a broader, more complex view of the world provided to us from multiple sources rather than from singular experts.

> **Visualization**—*the ability to interpret and create data representations for the purpose of expressing ideas, finding patterns and persuading people to take action.*

Broadly defined, visualization means the act or process of interpreting in visual terms or of putting into visible form. But defining visualization as another new media literacy is more complicated. In 2006, *Confronting the Challenges of Participatory Culture: Media Education in the 21st Century* (Jenkins, Purushotma, Clinton, Weigel, & Robison, 2006) was released, where eleven new media literacies were identified as a set of social skills and cultural competencies to best equip young people to become full participants in the emergent media landscape and raise public understanding about what it means to be literate in a globally interconnected, multicultural world. From this white paper, a new research group, *Project New Media Literacies* emerged at MIT and currently is situated at USC's Annenberg Innovation Lab. This research group which I have led since 2007 as Research Director determined that the initial set of eleven new media literacies was not an exhaustive list and that as our society and cultural exchanges through media change, so too does the importance of new skills needed to be a full participant in our rich media landscape.

Adding to the original eleven new media literacies, **Visualization** as a new media literacy builds upon information visualization. As defined by Lev Manovich, visualization is "a mapping between discrete data and a visual representation" (Manovich, 2010). He includes in his discussion, the understanding of visualization as an important social skill to acquire in that it bridges the relationship between numeric and non-numeric data.

Visualization as a new media literacy is defined **as the ability to interpret and create data representations for the purpose of expressing ideas, finding patterns, and persuading people to take action.**

Type the word, "Why . . ." in Google's search box and up pops the most searched phrases, like "Why is the sky blue?" Traditional search, though, is not the only viable option for the web users of tomorrow. Netflix recommends movies you'll enjoy based on past films watched. *Wikipedia's* History page allows you to view the development of any entry back to its formation. *Twitter* shows you your friends and those to whom they are connected. Post images from your vacation and they will automatically geo-locate onto a map to share your journey with others. Want to make sense of the State of the Union speech? Load it into *Wordle* and the key themes will be revealed. Be motivated to make change in our world with artists like Chris Jordan who uses visualizations to issue strong statements about human consumption and waste? Jordan's visual images on Gyre, 2009 represent actual statistics relating to 2.4 million pieces of plastic, which are equal to an estimated number of pounds of plastic pollution that enter the world's oceans every hour.

Relationship to Other New Media Literacies

The Internet provides us with the ability to connect, on a global scale, our ideas, objects and actions. It provides the venue for fostering **collective intelligence**— the ability to pool knowledge and compare notes with others in order to achieve a common goal. The value of data is its ability to inform or to enable decision and action. Practicing visualization within social constructs enables us to communicate data effectively so that others can gain new insight into the data we shared.

With this ability to represent large amounts of data, we use visualization beyond numeric metrics, such as tables and charts, to make sense of our social constructs. The adage, "*A picture is worth a thousand words*," now includes the hundreds of pictures, hundreds of thousands of words, and multiple strands of layered stories we can create through visualization.

Computer scientists, designers, and artists like Jonathan Harris use visualizations to combine humanities with science. While new media offers ways to systematize information, it also offers a place for people to share and contribute their thoughts, ideas and feelings about themselves, others and society. In two works, Harris explores "Man in the Machine" (*I Want You to Want Me* [http://www.youtube.com/watch?v=GZUaXDm4qik]), an interactive installation about online dating; and "The Machine in Man" (*The Whale Hunt* [http://thewhalehunt.org/]), a "photographic heartbeat" of a traditional Alaskan Eskimo whale hunt consisting of over three thousand photographs that view the event from multiple perspectives and visual manipulations.

As visualization is more than a static image on a page—it is interactive—it provides new levels of data representation. It combines quantity and quality (numbers and text) so we can better understand, interpret and interact with art, science, and society. Visualization uses data as input and encourages users to manipulate the data, whether to explore a story or an argument, or to understand and interpret complex problems. Visualization fosters new questions; and often, by manipulating or combining data sets, new patterns emerge.

Confronting the Challenges of Participatory Culture white paper (Jenkins et al., 2006) also introduced the concept of **simulation**—the ability to interpret and construct dynamic models of real-world processes. As a complement to this idea, visualization provides powerful new ways of representing and manipulating information. It expands our cognitive capacity, allowing us to deal with larger bodies of information, to experiment with more complex configurations of data, to form hypotheses quickly and to test them against different variables in real time. Visualization can be effective in representing known knowledge or in testing emerging theories.

However, there are differences between simulation and visualization. Simulations create new data by modeling processes whereas visualizations translate data to evoke relationships. It is more likely that visualizations allow hypotheses to emerge from play rather than from scientific ruminations.

While data visualization has become more popular as a field of study, it is still an essentially rhetorical practice, able to influence people or engender action but only to the degree that it is leveraged in a larger social, cultural framework. Using visualization effectively also requires it to be complemented with the new media literacy, **judgment**—the ability to evaluate the reliability and credibility of different information sources. In other words, does the data shared in the visualization come from a trusted source? Is it collected in a reliable manner? Is its release timely and influential? Is it embedded in a good story? Bringing together the new media literacies of judgment and visualization encourages a balance of participation and experimentation and offers opportunities to bring the real world into the classroom.

Visualization as a New Form of Literacy

In today's media-rich world, we cannot think of language (such as print literacy) as the main means for representation and communication. New modes of meaning have emerged that need to be taken into consideration when thinking about literacy (Kress, 35). Though it is important to know how to read and write using traditional modes of communication, the new media literacies build upon these modes and offer new forms of reading and writing through social interaction with others. Visualization takes into account the importance of knowing how to read and write data *as images* and mediates our interaction with the visual information.

Learning how to read and write visual data will help make literacy accessible to everyone. **Like a lens on a camera, visualizations give us the ability to zoom out for the macro overview or zoom into the micro view and see the tiniest detail in the original context of the visualization shared.** However, we need to understand which structure works best with which type of data.

Visualization as a new form of reading and writing can also be identified as a new form of writing at the structural level. At the structural level, different types of visual methods are used to represent data, which requires the writer to clearly understand which mode of communication will best represent the inquiry.

Visualization methods provide a systematic graphic format to create, share and codify knowledge (Lengler & Eppler, 2007). For example, network visualization methods use macro representations of data. They give overviews of social constructs, the relationship between people, items or entities. Similar to bar charts found in Excel, network visualizations are readable by understanding spatial dimensions. The larger the spatial node, the more that node represents connections to a specific person. If nodes are clustered together, the connection of each node to the others becomes readily apparent.

Silobreaker is an automated search service for news and current affairs that aims to provide more relevant results to the user than traditional search-and-aggregation engines. Instead of listing articles matching a search query, *Silobreaker* displays people, companies, organizations, topics, places, and keywords associated with the search; it understands how they relate to each other in the news flow and puts them in context through visualizations.

The visualization of the network is optimized to keep strongly related items in close proximity to each other. In this way, the overall arrangement of nodes in the network clearly represents the connections between nodes (nodes that are far away are weakly related to each other). In this visualization, the size of a node is proportional to the number of edges emanating from it.

To interpret the data, however, we also need to *read* the presentation the visualization offers so that we can interpret the hierarchy and composition of the nodes as they are mapped onto the image. Where spatial arrangement has been the primary means of reading visualizations since the eighteenth century, color, saturation, and texture can also support how a fixed spatial layout (such as the geography of a country) is represented (Manovich, 2010).

A micro representation of data uses a different visualization method all together, like a phrase net diagram. *PhraseNet* can be used to look at literary styles over the century, to understand power relations between characters in a story, and to identify alliteration and assonance in poetry. *PhraseNet* explores the relationships between different words used in a specific text. It uses a simple form of pattern matching to provide multiple views of the concepts contained in a book, speech or poem. For example, through creating a word graph made from Jane Austen's *Pride and Prejudice,* the program has drawn a network of words; two words are connected if they appear together in a phrase of the form "X and Y."

We don't know what the characters said or what their actions were, just that they spoke with each other and which character had the most dialogue based on the size of the character's name and the thickness of the arrow in relation to the other characters. So the main characters are linked, and the positive attributes of the characters form a group. This strategy shows that Darcy, who is a main character, does not appear in the network. The visualization forces us to ask: Why is the main character of the novel not represented in the network? What does this absence tell us about his character? These questions emerge through identifying patterns within the visualization and offer readers a new way of entering the text.

Challenges to Consider

Data can be generated, stored, and used in ways that raise questions like these either well or poorly. Knorr (1981) questions whether visualization can convince anyone in any specific way about a text because many interpretations are possible. However, Latour (1983) argues that visualization supports making the invisible be visible. While it is true visualizations can convey a story in multiple ways, we must be mindful of the intent behind the data collected and shared visually.

To be media literate, visualizations should be transparent and allow a de-layering process, like peeling back the layers of an onion. An example of this process in action is being conducted at University of Southern California's Annenberg Innovation Lab led by Francois Bar. His research group is currently working to develop appropriate methods for better determining sentiment through *Twitter*. To determine sentiment in *Twitter*, researchers use tools to select keywords, hashtags (#), and users' handles (@____) to scrape and catalogue the tweets. The cataloguing of this data is often broken into positive, neutral, and negative, which can then be represented visually through spatial placement, color, and size and gives the readers a quick view of the pulse of the people. Though natural language processing, technology can quickly identify positive or negative language. When using these methods with the 2012 Presidential Campaign, Francois' research group quickly realized the limitations of visually representing sentiment analysis. The difficulty lies when false positives occur when people tweet language such as sarcasm. These are harder for a computer alone to determine, and the distributed cognition between the person and the tools becomes much more important.

Another problem in manipulating and representing data is determining which data to use. Each day, we add more data to our networked world. In a given month on *Facebook*, each user, on average, uploads 70 pieces of content. With half a billion members of *Facebook*, that's roughly 35 billion pieces of media shared. The key to overcoming this mass of data input is to determine what data to leave out.

If we added how much media is created and shared through *YouTube* and *Twitter*, you can begin to see the world of big data that we have entered. In a world of rapid change, representation is fluid and not static. When trying to represent any data that moves through our social communities, the schema would not be the same from year to year or, for that matter, from day to day. The more we add data, the easier it will become for numbers to be meaningless without context.

An important part of visualization as a skill is the ability to see and understand where potential points of relationships in the data can be analyzed. This begins with formulating specific questions to help narrow searches, find points of intersection to review and identify patterns in the data. Pattern recognition is an acquired skill and research has shown that encouraging interdisciplinary studies (such as combining art and math, or architecture and nature) and looking beyond the definitive to the ripples or echoes of decisions may help to foster this skill.

What Might Be Done in the Classroom

Educators should encourage students to participate in a community of practice that is interested in deepening their understanding of visualization. This offers a way for users to pool their knowledge together toward a deeper understanding of the representations and patterns different visualizations in discussion offer, and in turn, this provides a historical analysis of the data that will change over time since data continues to grow and therefore constantly changes the results we identify and can analyze.

A few platforms are *Tableau Public*, *Many Eyes*, and *MapTube*. Though each takes a different approach to visualizations, they all offer a suite of data visualization tools for you to create and share visualizations. Fernanda Viégas and Martin Wattenberg created IBM's *Many Eyes*, and to date it is probably the most robust visualization tool that incorporates many layers of social features into its platform. People can share comments, datasets, and data visualizations to support their discussion and arguments, including the ability to make comments on a specific view of the visualization based on the variables you are interacting with or the filters you have created to view the visualization. For novice visualization creators, this is an opportunity to offer a context for the design of the visualization and to receive feedback from others who have more experience.

Done correctly—using the right tools, data, and appropriate questions—visualization can promote transparency. By asking the right questions and telling a story, visualizations provide an outlet to understand the relationship between quantifiable numbers and quality of people's opinions and sentiments. Armed with more access to information, visualizations can encourage people to be active in civic life and turn data into action.

References

Jenkins, H., Purushotma, R., Clinton, K., Weigel, M., & Robison, A.J. (2006). *Confronting the challenges of participatory culture: Media education for the 21st century.* Cambridge, MA: MIT Press.

Jordan, Chris. (2007). *Running the numbers: Gyre* [painting]. Los Angeles, CA: Paul Kopeikin Gallery.

Knorr, K. (1981). *The manufacture of knowledge.* Oxford, UK: Pergamon.

Kress, G. (2003). *Literacy in the new media age.* New York: Routledge.

Latour, B. (1983). Comment redistribuer le grand partage? *Revue Internationale de Synthèse, 104*(110), 202–236.

Latour, B. (1985). Visualization and cognition: Drawing things together. *Culture Technique, 14*, 14–17.

Lengler, R., & Eppler, M.J. (2007). *Towards a periodic table of visualization: Methods for management.* Lugano: Switzerland Institute of Corporate Communication.

Manovich, Lev. (2001, Oct. 27). Info-aesthetics: Information and form. Retrieved July 2013 from http://www.manovich.net/IA/.

Manovich, Lev. (2010). What is visualization? Retrieved from http://manovich.net/2010/10/25/new-article-whatis-visualization/.

Tufte, E. R. (1983). *The visual display of quantitative information.* Cheshire, CT: Graphics Press.

Viégas, F. & Wattenberg, M. (2006). Communication-minded visualization: A call to action. *IBM Systems Journal, 45*(4), 801–812.

7

THE WORLD IS A VILLAGE

Conceptualizing Uses of New Media in "Flat Classrooms"

William Kist

Recently, I had the privilege of moderating a discussion on *Twitter* as part of the #EngChat discussion group. This group "meets" on *Twitter* at 7:00 p.m. Eastern each Monday to talk about topics of mutual interest related to teaching English. The coordinator of #EngChat is Meenoo Rami, an English teacher at the Science Leadership Academy in Philadelphia. According to Meenoo, more than 3500 users from all over the world have sent out more than 10,000 tweets using the #EngChat hashtag since August, 2010. (More information about the origin and current news about #EngChat is available at http://digitalis.nwp.org/resource/1802.)

Meenoo asked me to facilitate the discussion held on December 3, 2012. (Archives for all discussions can be found at the EngChat website: http://www.engchat.org/.) I suggested the topic of using social networking to foster global education, because I had recently written about this topic (Kist, 2013). Kicking off the discussion at 7:00 p.m. on December 3, I was soon left behind as the range and depth of the ideas tweeted by the group of participants were fast and furious. In fact, I soon lost count of the number of resources and projects available that were mentioned for helping to use social media for internationalizing one's classroom.

It is clear that never before have people had the opportunity to participate in discussions with peers and experts and friends all over the world so easily and so cheaply. And although taking part in online social networks sometimes comes in for criticism as creating a culture of people who are isolated from each other (Turkle, 2011), there is also increasing evidence that people who participate in online social networks may be more trusting, have more close relationships and be more politically active (Pew Research Center, 2011).

At one point in the discussion on #EngChat, I made the point that I had noticed, in talking to teachers, that, often the first step in getting kids globally aware is just getting them up to speed on how to work with digital media—because the way we collaborate with people via social networking is by reading and writing on screens. Because students are, often, not able to communicate face-to-face with international friends and colleagues, the way we empower our students to interface with international collaborators is via digital tools, whether it is via a wiki or a Google Doc or a video. Therefore, some teachers feel the first step in getting their students globally up to speed, is to teach them how to navigate within a wiki, how to work in *iMovie* or operate an iPad (before launching into classroom partnerships). I expressed my thoughts this way:

> Helping kids become digitally literate seems to be first step in getting into global collaborations such as Flat Cl. #engchat

A few minutes later, Meenoo tweeted this:

> Global connections are about more than use of tech or projects. They are about empathy, a key to all human progress. #engchat

This exchange has inspired the main focus of this chapter—indeed, in our increasingly hybridized lives, what comes first, the empathy (or whatever we are feeling) or the projects and technology that may inspire empathy (or whatever feeling we want to inspire) in our students? Of course, the educators I have interviewed over the past year are doing these kinds of projects not just for the sake of doing them. They're doing them to engender in their students any number of attributes. But, again, what comes first—the empathy or the digitalization of that empathy? In the increasingly hybridized world we live in, it may not be easy to tell.

Of course, I'm not the first to suggest that we are increasingly living in a hybridized world with all of its ensuing pedagogical implications (Alvermann, 2002; Gee, 2003). But, with the increasing explosion of online learning at all levels of education and with our greatly flattened world (Friedman, 2005) and the huge international rise of social networks such as *Facebook* and *Twitter*, the lines have never been less distinct between school-based learning and non-school-based learning, between so-called "fiction" and "nonfiction." In such blurry territories, our roles as ethics teachers may need to be more sharply defined than ever before (Luce-Kapler, Sumara, & Iftody, 2010).

When I have written about using social media and global education before, I have written about kinds of assignments and assessments used by teachers that I have interviewed. For this chapter, I have instead structured the descriptions according to the kinds of attitudes, aptitudes, and dispositions that these assignments are trying to help develop.

Expanding Point of View and Empathy

Many of the projects I observed over the past year ultimately involve helping students be able to take on the points of view of those from other cultures. Of course, such a goal has been part of global education from the very beginning. Several famous examples exist of assignments that have attempted to effect this broader stance in a pre-Internet era. For example, social studies teachers have shown students maps that were published in the southern hemisphere. In such maps, Australia and the Antarctic appear towards the top of the page. Maps made in the northern hemisphere show Australia and the Antarctic at the bottom of the page. Another famous pre-Internet activity is "If the Word Were a Village" (Meadows, 1990) in which a class of 25 approximates by percentage the number of Europeans, Asians, teachers, soldiers, and so on who make up the world. It is always surprising for students to see how few doctors the world has, for example. It has been an eye opening exercise for young people from North America who see the world in a very different way from the way most of the world sees it. The point of the exercise is for students to imagine how their experiences are actually not the experiences of most of the world. When North American students see how much of a minority they are, just in terms of population, it can be a truly "lightbulb" moment; for North American students who see the world only through the lens of U.S.-dominated media (Klein, 2009/1999), it's a new notion that their familiar home and life experiences aren't shared by most of the world.

With social media such as *Twitter*, and other more school-based social networks such as ePals (http://www.epals.com), it is no longer necessary to imagine the point of view of someone from a different country. *Google Earth* (http://www.earth.google.com) can pinpoint familiar daily locations of someone's life from across the world or look at historical sites read about in textbooks or in novels. Many classrooms with projection systems and Internet access can make faraway places and faraway experiences closer and less distant simply by going to this one website. Of course, it is about more than just presenting foreign places on a big screen. Many teachers are assigning students to read blogs written by those overseas. In schools in which *Twitter* is not blocked, students may also start to follow those in countries being studied. These could be experts in a field being studied or everyday people from the culture being focused on. All one has to do is search a specific country or culture by using the hashtag. Typing "#Spain," for example will lead to any number of tweeters from Spain. Finding out the daily practices and opinions of those from other countries makes very real the perspectives and points of view from other lands and backgrounds. To give a real idea of the complexity of many world situations, teachers may assign students to follow people who tweet from very different perspectives, say, on the Arab Spring or on gun control. Students are able to get a glimpse of the daily musings of those on the front lines of history and world cultures.

Collaborating

Many global education projects involve giving students practice collaborating on projects. One of the challenges that any teacher faces who wants to set up international collaboration is the differences in time zones. Students must understand the techniques of asynchronous communication and partnership. Teachers may arrange for special times when the students get to communicate in synchronous fashion, but most of the interactions between student partnerships occur at different points of the day. When one classroom is working on their part of the project, the other classroom may be vacant, with all students home in bed.

These international collaborations often take the form of vast research projects in which teams of students research various components of a topic. In such projects, the students approximate *Wikipedia* on a small scale, as teams of students divide up a large topic or concept and each team has the responsibility of creating the material that forms a page of the wiki.

Students who collaborate via the Flat Classroom Project (http://www.flatclassroomproject.org/) work on a multimedia project, such as a video that deals with a pre-set theme. A sub-project under the Flat Classroom umbrella is the Eracism project (http://www.eracismproject.org/), which requires students to collaborate on a debate. The goal of these projects is to foster the ability of students to work together. Of course, a twenty-first-century skills framework (Reich, Murnane, & Willett, 2012) has influenced many teachers who want to prepare their students for a global workplace. The thinking is that, students will probably have to collaborate on their jobs at some point, perhaps asynchronously. If students can learn to collaborate from a young age, across time zones, this will put them in good stead when they get their own jobs. Teachers may choose to begin such a collaborative project by having students read a common text that focuses on a certain topic. Students in all of the classrooms may post their comments in the form of a blog or within a discussion board of some kind. These discussions may form a kind of pre-writing activity, a springboard toward collaboratively writing an original text.

Sharing

Never have students had so many ways of sharing their work and their interests with a worldwide audience. In fact, the concept of "audience" has never been so broad. Indeed, students have the opportunity of reaching a worldwide audience. To be sure, there are many venues in which teachers may set up password protection so that only invited audience members may view student work, limiting the audience. Such sites as *ThreeRing* (http://www.threering.com), *Mahara* (http://www.Mahara.org), or *DropBox* (http://www.DropBox.com) to name just a few allow students to safely and securely show their work to pre-determined audience members. But there are other venues that are completely open to the world. Students may share their work via a blog or a wiki that is set up in such a way that anyone who stumbles upon the site is able to view the work. For some teachers, this openness is important. In fact, promoting a culture of sharing seems to be a prime goal for the etiquette and ethics that many teachers are attempting to teach via these kinds of social networking projects. Paul Allison's Youth Voices Twitter feed (@youthvoices) is a kind of compromise between being out on the web (via *Twitter*) and yet protected. Allison's students tweet the first few lines of an essay, and then there is a link to the remainder of the student essay (without last names attached) on the Youth Voices website (http://youthvoices.net/). Using *Twitter* in this manner, Allison's students may share their thoughts with, as of this writing, 1300 followers, while still staying safe online.

Another form of sharing allows students to simply comment on the various texts they are viewing or reading. Students may set up virtual book clubs (or text clubs) with members from across the world. A simple assignment to begin this process is to have students share what they're reading by setting up an account on *Goodreads* (http://www.goodreads.com). This website allows a reader to share the books he or she has been reading and rate and review the books. This kind of sharing may be extended to other kinds of texts, too. A favorite photograph may be shared on Flickr (http://www.flickr.com) or a film experience may be shared on the Internet Movie Database (http://imdb.com). Music may be shared on Ping (http://www.ping.com) or iTunes.

Some teachers express worry that their students are too "off task" when they share about pop culture texts or other hobbies or interests. But, in the end, I think most teachers who set up international collaborations or who promote sharing believe that it may be during this so-called "off task" time that some very meaningful conversations take place. Hearing what music students in other parts of the country enjoy, for example, may break down some substantial barriers between cultures, perhaps more than officially sanctioned classroom assignments do.

Acting

Ultimately, many classroom collaborations involve some kind of social justice project. One of the most famous early projects in this genre was the Free Rice project (http://www.freerice.com), sponsored by the World Food Programme. Structured in the form of a trivia project, students could earn ten grains of rice, to be distributed to the hungry, each time they get an answer correct. Projects that foster social justice activities are perhaps the most powerful in connecting students with others from across the world, because of their authenticity. There are many examples of these kinds of projects. Students can take part in the United Nations' Day of Social Justice each February 20 (http://www.un.org/en/events/socialjus ticeday/), for example. Or Amnesty International's Write for Rights campaign (http://takeaction.amnestyusa.org/). Many students around the world are taking part in online relief efforts related to natural disasters.

I am writing this on the weekend after the second most horrific school shooting in United States history, in which 20 schoolchildren and 6 educators were killed by a gunman. Because most people are not going to be able to drive to Newtown, Connecticut, to pay their respects to those who were lost, there have been many *Facebook* pages that have cropped up in response to this tragedy. On these pages, people may leave tributes to the teachers and children who died.

Social networking has allowed people to express their outrage and sympathy and whatever emotions they have felt—emotions that they may not have an outlet for in face-to-face situations. (It sometimes may even feel like we have crossed the ultimate divide in that victims' *Facebook* pages remain up long after death and may provide an illusion, albeit a one-sided one, that the lost one is still with us—at least on *Facebook*).

In recent days, a new social media movement has arisen for people to act on their feelings in response to this most recent abhorrent event. Ironically, it has been spearheaded by a person who is most famous for appearing via an "old" medium—television. In this case, NBC news journalist, Ann Curry has created an idea called "26 Acts" and/or "20 Acts." Her idea, promoted via her *Twitter* page and its own *Facebook* page (http://www.facebook.com/#!/26acts) encourages people to perform either 26 or 20 acts of kindness as a way of remembering the 20 children and 6 adults who were murdered. Teachers may choose to expose their students to such a pro-active use of social media as a positive role model for using social media.

There are so many examples of people all over the world who are using social networking to make arguments for acting and doing something about some cause, whether it be personal, political, or even spiritual. Just in the last few days, the foreign minister of Israel has resigned his post due to being indicted. He chose to defend himself on *Facebook* (Rudoren, 2012). Of course, as mentioned earlier, the famous "Arab Spring" of 2011 and 2012 has been credited to the ability of protesters to communicate via social media. And we have just witnessed the reelection, in the United States, of President Barack Obama, although as Lizza (2012) has pointed out this was in no small part due to the face-to-face persuasion executed by a huge volunteer army. Indeed, recent studies suggest that the lines between our online and offline literacy practices are more blurry and less distinct than we may have thought (Marsh, 2011).

Recent television commercials for various technology products seem to want to capitalize on this increasing blurriness. A recent series of commercials for the Google Nexus 7 (search Nexus 7: Curious and Nexus 7: Camping on *YouTube*) portrays children going back and forth from consulting a tablet to playacting in the backyard with their parents. In the "Curious" ad, a girl asks Google how many miles it is from the Earth to the Moon before she dons a play space helmet and runs outside to take a make believe voyage. While the cynic may see these ads as designed to placate those who worry that new technologies separate and divide us, it may also be seen that these ads portray a new hybrid reality, one in which the new media tools really are integrated (sometimes seamlessly, sometimes not) into our daily lives. These hybrid ways, then of designing our classroom spaces, probably will emphasize the "big picture" pedagogic goals, such as helping students extend their points of view, collaborate, share, and act—goals that probably wouldn't seem that strange and foreign to the typical one-room schoolteacher of the 1800s.

References

Alvermann, D.E. (2002). Preface. In D.E. Alvermann (Ed.), *Adolescents and literacies in a digital world* (pp. vii–xi). New York: Peter Lang.

Friedman, T.L. (2005). *The world is flat: A brief history of the twenty-first century.* New York: Picador.

Gee, J.P. (2003). *What video games have to teach us about learning and literacy.* New York: Palgrave Macmillan.

Kist, W. (2013). *The global school: Connecting classrooms and schools around the world.* Bloomington, IN: Solution Tree Press.

Klein, N. (2009/1999). *No logo: 10th anniversary edition.* New York: Picador.

Lizza, R. (2012). The final push. *The New Yorker.* Retrieved from http://www.newyorker.com/reporting/2012/10/29/121029fa_fact_lizza.

Luce-Kapler, R., Sumara, D., & Iftody, T. (2010). Teaching ethical know-how in new literacy spaces. *Journal of Adolescent & Adult Literacy, 53*(7), 536–541.

Marsh, J. (2011). Young children's literacy practices in a virtual world: Establishing an online interaction order. *Reading Research Quarterly, 46,* 101–118.

Meadows, D. (1990). If the world were a village. Retrieved from http://www.sustainer.org/dhm_archive/index.php?display_article=vn338villageed.

Pew Research Center (2011). Social networking and our lives. Retrieved from http://www.pewinternet.org/Reports/2011/Technology-and-social-networks.aspx.

Reich, J., Murnane, R., & Willett, J. (2012). The state of wiki usage in U.S. K–12 schools: Leveraging web 2.0 data warehouses to assess quality and equity in online learning environments. *Educational Researcher, 41,* 7–15.

Rudoren, J. (2012). Hard-line Israeli foreign minister resigns. *The New York Times.* Retrieved from http://www.nytimes.com/2012/12/15/world/middleeast/avigdor-lieberman-israeli-foreign-minister-resigns.html?_r=0.

Turkle, S. (2011). *Alone together: Why we expect more from technology and less from each other.* New York: Basic Books.

PART III
GLOBAL PERSPECTIVES

Media literacy has steadily grown in its international focus over the last few decades. As media technologies continue to expand in scope and reach, with little regard for physical or cultural borders, how we educate students about the role of media in their daily lives increasingly incorporates more global perspectives. In this section, we read about four distinct viewpoints of media literacy around the world that can collectively provide a global perspective from which we can see media literacy move across borders, cultures, and divides. We read about media literacy in the Nordic region and the policy concerns for media and information literacy as they relate to local communities and geopolitical praxis. A deep exploration of the new Australian Curriculum initiative is unpacked to show where, how, and to what extent media literacy education is implemented across primary school subjects. In Beirut, Lebanon, a movement is underway to combat the notorious low levels of media education noticed throughout the country. A detailed investigation of media literacy as revolutionizing education in a region with periodic civic strife and sectarian divisions provides a rich account of what media literacy education can do to help bond societies. Lastly, we move to Hong Kong, where a picture is painted of an educational culture that has heavily integrated Web 2.0 tools, and digital technologies into the K–12 classroom. This holds great opportunities for training intelligent media consumers and producers, but also critical, reflective, and positive thinking skills. This depends, of course, on the technology being harnessed in the right educational contexts.

8

TOWARDS A EUROPEAN NETWORK FOR MEDIA LITERACY

A Nordic Perspective on Challenges in a Global Society

Per Lundgren

"We are drowning in information but starved for knowledge."

—*John Naisbitt, Megatrends*

We Are a Global Society

But who is educating our youth? Who is imparting to them ethical and social values? Who is supplying them with role models to emulate? These are questions and concerns which have contributed to the growing body of work in the Nordic community.

When facing the challenges in the world of young people's communication, the fundamental questions now are: How can recent developments in international Media Literacy policies strengthen pedagogical praxis in a cultural context? And what strategies must be applied to speed up this development with inclusion of all?

The Alliance of Civilizations Media Literacy Education Clearinghouse[1] says that children and youth from industrialized societies spend at least double the time immersed in electronic media (television, Internet, video games, DVDs, radio, cell phones, etc.) than they do receiving formal education in schools. The website states that much of the media consumed by children and youth is aimed at selling them products or ideologies.

Recent technological developments demonstrate a widening gap between how children and young people as consumers and communicators use social and mobile media, including web TV and smart phones, in a much more effective and advanced way than their teachers and parents.

UNESCO's Media and Information Literacy Teacher training curriculum, the United Nations Alliance of Civilizations Media Literacy Education Clearinghouse, the Council of Europe, and the European Commission have through policymaking and action on media (and information) literacy, created important platforms for media literacy education developments internationally.

Will the adaption and piloting of UNESCO's media and information curriculum in teacher training institutions contribute to innovation and improvement in all levels of education as expected? How could research findings and European evaluation tools contribute to define and promote quality in media literacy education? These are some questions addressed in this chapter.

Nordic Collaborations

The current formal public Nordic collaboration[2] between Denmark, Finland, Iceland, Norway, Sweden, Greenland, the Faroe Islands, and Åland is recognized as one of the oldest existing official country collaborations between neighboring countries. With the first step taken in 1952, this collaboration between countries brings together 25 million citizens from the Nordic region with individual cultures and shared core values. Further, by sharing best practices, this adds Nordic value to the national goals.

The Nordic countries are in a uniquely strong position in terms of the broad use of information technology, the long tradition of public service television and existing film, press, and media education resources, and their long term regional collaboration.

Compared with other European countries the education systems in the Nordic region are highly decentralised, which partly explains the need for coordination within this specialised area.

The Nordic collaboration within media and information literacy is in 2013 organized through the Swedish chair with specific action through the Swedish Media Council[3] and the Nordic information center for media and communication research, Nordicom.[4] The Swedish Media Council is a government agency whose primary task is to promote the empowerment of minors as conscious media users and to protect them from harmful media influences. Thus, opportunities are created for the official Nordic Collaboration for both research and policy making which included Nordic and Swedish national coordination between individual stakeholders.

Nordic Perspectives on European Media Literacy

In Europe, within media literacy, film literacy is emphasized. As a dynamic tool for learning, social change and development, media literacy education has the potential to redefine active citizenship and democratic participation and advance the competence to cope autonomously and critically with the communication and media environment established within, and as a consequence of, the information society.

Europe will soon be 500 million people in 27 countries, with cumulative cultural identities, representing a variety of cultures and languages, and when facing the challenges of a globalized media saturated world, it can increase quality and development by sharing research findings, practice, good practice, and best practice in media literacy education. This involves the use of tools for evaluating progress, thus measuring the status of media literacy in the individual nations.

In 2001, within the European Commission Media Literacy initiative, I conducted a Nordic study for the European Commission's directorate for Education and Culture.[5] It was then concluded that most school curricula did not take into consideration the new paradigm of a globalized media saturated world. Indeed, to the extent that they addressed new technologies, schools primarily taught technical skills (i.e. how to use computers) but seldom critical thinking skills relevant to media content and digital learning. Surely, the curriculum states this inclusion, but given the complexity of this, as important as expanding Internet access is, so too is the development of educational initiatives that teach media consumers how to critically interpret the messages they receive.

The overall goal for the suggested activities to promote media literacy in the 2001 study remains the same today in 2013, though today within a digital competence context—to improve media literacy education in pre-schools, schools, and adult education for all students.

The target group is primarily the people who train teachers and student-teachers at all levels of education, as well as professional teachers, politicians, professionals, and administrators who have responsibility for the competent development of teachers at various levels of the educational establishment.

The selection of Sweden as host of the 2010 World Summit on Media for Children and Youth in Karlstad, made it possible to promote an international dialogue, with participants from 100 countries, between researchers, educators, media professionals, policy makers, youth organisations, and others who advocate for digital competence, media literacy education, and children's well-being,[6] further to be addressed at the next World Summit in September 2014 in Kuala Lumpur, Malaysia.

Pedagogical Approaches in Nordic Media Literacy Education

Important contributions to the Nordic pedagogical debate on media literacy education in the Nordic countries come from all countries. For example, Professor Birgitte Tufte, in Copenhagen Denmark, in her book *Media on the Blackboard* (my translation),[7] defines media pedagogy as teaching about and with media. This was also the perspective of Associate Professor Thomas Koppfeldt at the University College of Film, Radio, Television, and Theatre at Stockholm,[8] who has played a key role, especially in Sweden, in media education and pedagogical developments from the mid 1970s for more than 35 years. Sirkku Kotilainen, in Finland, articulated in her doctoral dissertation at the University of Tampere, Finland, the multidimensionality of media education and in her recent studies shows how media literacy education supports a public voice for youth.[9] Ola Erstad is a Professor at the Institute for Educational Research, University of Oslo, Norway.[10] He has been working both within the fields of media and educational research. He has published work on issues of technology and education, especially on media literacy and digital competence (*Nordic Journal of Digital Literacy*).[11]

Sirkku Kotilainen,professor at the University of Tampere, Finland, in the 15th Nordic Conference on Media in Iceland (held at Reykjavik in 2001), describes the elements for teachers' media competence,

> The later humanist and constructivist approaches have taken the media as a chance for better living and lifelong learning in a continually changing society. Media belongs to our reality, and they must be seen as a part of contemporary culture and western democracy. People ought to be taught new kinds of media literacy competencies which include wider understanding and self-reflection (see Varis 2001; Ljunggren 1996; Graviz 1996; Buckingham & Sefton-Green 1994; Masterman & Mariet 1994; Craggs 1992).

W. James Potter (2001, 7–12) has articulated the following fundamental ideas about media literacy:

1. Media literacy is a continuum, not a category. There are degrees in this continuum and we all occupy some position on the media literacy continuum. This is a lifelong learning perspective: media literacy as a potential skill, it is under modification through one's life. Media literacy is connected to one's age and other personal and social contexts.
2. Media literacy is multidimensional including cognitive, emotional, aesthetic and moral dimensions. The cognitive domain refers to mental processes and thinking. The emotional domain is the dimension of feeling. The aesthetic domain refers to the ability to enjoy, understand, and appreciate media content from an artistic point of view. The moral domain refers to the ability to infer the values underlying the messages. According to Potter, someone who is highly media literate realises that there is a synergy among the four.
3. The purpose of media literacy is to give us more control over interpretations because all media messages are interpretations.

The goals of media education in school are connected to this kind of formulation of media literacy (Tufte, 1995; Erstad, 1997; Buckingham & Sefton-Green, 1997;Varis, 1999). The specific goals (and skill demands) in media literacy depend on the context where media literacy is needed and used. To work as a teacher is one specific context, a professional one. Teachers in a comprehensive school need understanding to teach media literacy and to initiate active learning with children and teenagers. Teachers ought to learn both media literacy and media pedagogy, in other words learn to teach about media (Stigbrand, 1989; Stigbrand & Lilja-Svensson, 1997; Hart, 1998).

Media Pedagogy Should Be Based on Student-centered Learning.

In media pedagogy, issues are raised up from children's lives, and materials relevant to children, which means popular culture, enter the classroom (Buckingham & Sefton-Green, 1994). The working methods are experiential, cooperative, and problem-based, which can be used all together to initiate active learning among pupils Masterman and Mariet (1994) add parent-teacher collaboration and cooperation with media institutions as essential features of media pedagogy. The teachers' mission is to help children and teenagers to question, investigate, and question again, Professor Kotilainen argues.

Future Sights I: Change of Context for Media Literacy Education

Media literacy education represents a critical filter against the previously described technological and cultural changes through the swift trans-national development of information technology and the globalisation of media content. The requirements of a broader concept of literacy for the twenty-first century to encompass life-long learning must be set against the fact that the area of media literacy is drowning as it is being integrated in other subjects.

By placing media literacy education in a context where it plays a key role as the promoter of the development of the competence that is required in a knowledgeable society with a digital culture, these are the following activities required:

- to place media literacy education in a context as the central player in three areas of application: education, professional career, and citizenship;
- to place media literacy education in a context of life-long learning, where a broader concept of IT includes media competence in a digital culture, and where media creativity is a key competence for an individual to actively use technological opportunities;
- to relate media literacy education to technological development described in the national documents from the education departments;
- to clarify the significance of media literacy education and the role it plays in education, working life, and citizenship, and to strengthen the general public's interest in and use of media competence as a tool for development in all three areas;
- to be a strong link between researchers, schools, the community, and businesses regarding media competence;

- to cooperate with the media and IT sectors concerning media literacy education, partly to increase opportunities for young people to gain space in the media for their own thoughts, opinions, and stories;
- to support and participate in the work of producing an overview of know-how, development work, and research that can contribute to the development of media literacy education;
- to act as the body to which course proposals are referred for consideration and participate in development, production, and implementation of national curricula;
- to support and strengthen the professional development and status of media literacy educators;
- to act as a resource during the further development of regional structures for cooperation by spreading knowledge about activities throughout the country and initiating cooperation with the networks, associations, and organisations that work to develop and renew media literacy education inside and outside of the formal education system;
- to develop contacts and cooperation with international networks, organisations, and environments that work with didactic research and development of media and communication studies, such as Nordicom and the International Clearinghouse of Children, Youth and Media;
- to support cooperation between EU member states in this field, e.g. via European Schoolnet and a European Media Literacy Network;
- to promote the use of UNESCO Media and information literacy curriculum for teacher training[12] in universities;
- to support equality of opportunity in media literacy education regarding gender, socio-economic factors, and multicultural environments;
- to support the development of media literacy education for students who require special support and for students with special interests ;
- to facilitate transfers between different school forms between pre-school and university;
- to spread knowledge about media literacy education teaching materials and media didactics and support critical assessments of these materials in cooperation with producers of teacher materials;
- to act as the body to which proposals are referred for consideration regarding the development of teaching materials, web newspaper resources, and educational radio and television programs in cooperation with national film institutes, newspaper initiatives in schools, national education channels on radio and TV, etc.

Future Sights II: Towards a European Media Literacy Network

The experiences from the Nordic Collaboration in reviewing the past ten years, suggests that sharing best practices which include tools for teacher training and media literacy assessment as well as access to research findings can speed up progress. Further, a European media literacy network and a European Observatory for Media Literacy are about strengthening the European regions and bringing different stake holders together. Lastly, the creation of national networks and a European observatory supporting the transformation of information and practice into knowledge to be used in formal and non-formal education remains a challenge essential to speed up progress towards media literacy for all.[13]

Notes

1. http://www.aocmedialiteracy.org
2. http://www.norden.org
3. http://www.statensmedierad.se
4. http://www.gu.nordicom.se
5. http://ec.europa.eu/education/archive/elearning/doc/workshops/digital_literacy/position_papers/lundgren_par.pdf
6. http://www.karlstad2010.se
7. http://experts.cbs.dk/index_uk.asp?func=6.html&id=174
8. http://www.stdh.se/dramatiska-institutet
9. http://nordicom.statsbiblioteket.dk/ncom/da/publications/civic-media-education-supports-a-public-voice-for-youths(9ebb3a60–7aaf-11df-85ec-000ea68e967b).html
10. http://www.idunn.no/ts/dk/2010/01/art05
11. http://www.idunn.no/ts/dk
12. http://portal.unesco.org/ci/en/ev.php-URL_ID=15886&URL_DO=DO_TOPIC&URL_SECTION=201.html
13. http://ec.europa.eu/culture/media/media-literacy/index_en.htm

References

Buckingham, D., & Sefton-Green, J. (1994). Cultural studies goes to school: Reading and teaching popular media. London and Bristol, PA: Taylor & Francis.

Buckingham, D. & Sefton-Green, J. (1997). Multimedia education: Media literacy in the age of digital culture. In R. Julkaisussa Kubey (Ed.), *Media Literacy in the Information Age. Current Perspectives: Vol 6. Information and behavior.* New Brunswick: Transaction Publishers.

Craggs, C.E. (1992). *Media education in the primary school.* London: Routledge.

Erstad, O. (1997). *Mediebruk og medieundervisning: En evaluering av mediaundervisning i norsk skole: intensjoner, impelementering og laering. Universitetet I Oslo: Institutt for medier og kommunikasjon.* Doctoral Dissertation.

Erstad, O. (2010). Educating the digital generation. *Nordic Journal of Digital Literacy,* (January), 56–71.

Graviz, A. (1996). *Införande av mediekunskap i skolan: ett pedagogiskt problem? En fallstudie i Uruguay. Stockholm Universitetet.* Pedagogiska Institutet. Doctoral Dissertation.

Hart, A. (1998). *Teaching the media: International perspectives.* Mahwah, NJ: Lawrence Erlbaum.

Kotilainen, S., Arnolds-Granlund, S.-B. (2010). Media literacy education: Nordic perspectives. Nordicom, Göteborgs universitet.

Ljunggren, C. (1996). *Medborgarpubliken och det offentliga rummet: om utbildning, medier och demokrati.* Uppsala: Uppsala Studies in Education 68. Doctoral Dissertation.

Masterman, L., Mariet, F. (1994). *Media education in 1990s Europe: A teacher's guide.* Strasbourg, France: Council of Europe Press.

Potter, W.J. (2001). *Media Literacy.* Los Angeles, CA: Sage Publications.

Stigbrand, K. (1989). *Mediekunskap i skolan: En studie av massmedieundervisningen ABC.* Stockholm: Pedagogiska institutet I Stockholms Universitet. Doctoral Dissertation.

Stigbrand, K. & Lilja-Svensson, M. (1997). *Mediekunniga lärare? Om lärarhögskolorna och mediepedagogiken.* Stockholm:Våldskildringsrådet nr 18.

Tufte, B. (1995). *Skole og medier: Byggesaet til de levende billeders paedagogik.* Köbenhavn:Akademisk Forlag A/S. Doctoral Dissertation.

Tufte, B. (1998). *Tv på tavlen—om børn, skole og medier.* Akademisk forlag.

Varis,T. (1999). Media education:An urgent challenge for teachers and teacher education. In H. Niemi (Ed.), *Moving horizons in education: International transformations and challenges of democracy* (pp. 191–210). University of Helsinki, Department ofTeacher Education,

Varis, T. (2001). Towards a global learning society for higher humanity. A Keynote at the Sixth and Final Rochester Intercultural Conference, July 19, 2001. Rochester, NewYork.

9

MEDIA LITERACY THROUGH ARTS EDUCATION IN AUSTRALIA

Michael Dezuanni and Annette Woods

This chapter investigates the possibilities for creative and critical learning enabled through the inclusion of media arts in the curriculum. Media arts has been included as one of five Arts subjects for the new Australian Curriculum and will become mandatory learning for all Australian children from pre-school to Year Six, and elective for children in Years Seven to Twelve. Media education has historically been associated with English curriculum in Australia due to its development through the critical reading tradition. However, media literacy education in secondary schools has also occurred through the Arts since at least the 1960s and creative practice has almost always been included as an aspect of official media curricula. This chapter investigates the media learning of one primary school student, to consider the nature of creative learning and how this relates to the 'critical' aspects of media arts curriculum. We undertook this work as part of a large research project that has been investigating the relationship between digital media and traditional literacy outcomes in a primary school.

Media Arts in the Australian Curriculum

In Australia, media literacy education has typically been associated with educating students to think critically *about* the media. As early at 1956, students studying the Tasmanian English curriculum were introduced to critical analysis of film and television (Perkins, 1963). Subsequent curriculum documents introduced around the country have emphasised this 'critical reading' tradition, which continues through critical literacy approaches within English curriculum. Learning to be critical about media is also a key element of most current senior secondary media studies courses in Australian schools.

Creative practice has also been a significant aspect of media curriculum in Australia, with media production recognised as being integral to learning about the media. Most states have included media as one of five strands of the Arts since the 1990s. This was endorsed in 1994 when media was included as a strand of the Arts in the National Curriculum Statements (Curriculum Corporation, 1994). Most recently, the Arts have been chosen as the 'home' for media arts education in the new Australian Curriculum. This will be complemented by the Australian English Curriculum, which also includes statements about engaging students in critical responses to media.

Australia is currently drawing together eight state and territory systems through the implementation of a new national curriculum. Media education has been recognised as an entitlement for all Australian children through the inclusion of media arts as one of five strands in the Arts curriculum. The main justification provided for this is that young people are growing up in a digital, multimodal world and thus must learn to communicate creatively for social and cultural participation and for creative personal expression (ACARA, 2011). A media arts curriculum will be developed for all levels of school, from the first year of schooling to Year Twelve and will be mandatory learning for children for the first seven years of schooling.

The Arts focus and the compulsory nature of media arts curriculum for primary students necessitates some 'back to basics' thinking about the nature of media curriculum and the relationship between critical and creative practice. The Australian Curriculum divides learning in the Arts into 'Making' and 'Responding' strands, which seems to provide clear guidance about where to locate the creative and critical aspects of media learning. The relationship between making and responding is, however, complex because creative making and critical response are interrelated and complex processes. What it means to be 'creative' with digital media production tools and how young students can best learn to respond 'critically' as part of media production requires ongoing exploration. In this chapter, we present one Year Four student's media production work as an example of media learning to address these questions.

The Setting

The research discussed in this chapter was undertaken as part of a four-year project in a school with a student population of approximately 600. Of the total school population, 12% identify as Indigenous, and a further 14% are from backgrounds where languages other than English are spoken in the home. Many students live in families where poverty affects life experiences, and access to technologies in the home is limited for at least some of the students.

When we entered the school, a new leadership team and school staff were embarking on a reform process (Woods, Dooley, Luke, & Exley, 2012; Luke, Woods, & Dooley, 2011; Luke, Dooley, & Woods, 2011). Our research project has aimed to investigate the potential for digital learning to improve literacy performance in a low socio-economic and culturally diverse school (Dezuanni & Raphael, 2012). One component was the inclusion of media arts into the year four curriculum. A media arts teacher worked alongside the classroom teachers to develop and deliver an integrated media arts curriculum. The classes undertook media arts lessons for approximately two hours each week. The program focused on developing students' ability to generate and use digital materials through media production in the first half of the year. This involved knowledge and skills related to operating laptop computers and video cameras and the use of a variety of media production software. It included learning to create digital text, still and moving images, and audio files, eventually learning to combine these using web design templates and video editing software.

In the latter part of the year, students built on this knowledge and skill by engaging with more substantive projects. In Term Three they represented a scientific procedure through the production of a short procedural video; and in Term Four they created a micro-documentary about themselves for inclusion in a digital time capsule (Dezuanni & Woods, in press). These two tasks required the students to apply their media production knowledge and skills to communicate to an audience for a specific purpose. To achieve this, they had to be both creative and critical as explained in the following model.

The Building Blocks of Digital Media Literacy

The media arts program was organised according to a model theorised by one of the authors. The digital media literacy 'building blocks' consist of four categories: digital materials, media production, conceptual knowledge, and media analysis, all of which provide resources for being creative with communications technology and for thinking conceptually and critically about how media are produced and used (see Figure 9.1). This model formed the basis of professional development sessions with the teachers and was used to help conceptualise media arts learning throughout the year. While the model is not hierarchical, the focus was on digital materials and media production in Terms One and Two, and these were further developed through engagement with conceptual knowledge and media analysis in Terms Three and Four.

The model suggests that digital materials can be categorised into the three broad areas of images, audio, and text which have their own properties and are created and used according to convention. According to this way of thinking, students learn to handle and operate communication technologies to create these materials through media production and make aesthetic choices about how to arrange and organise them using software. Media production requires students to draw on and develop conceptual knowledge as they use and challenge available designs to create media products that are appropriate for specific purposes and audiences.

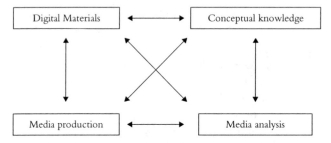

FIGURE 9.1 Four categories of digital media literacy building blocks.

Students undertake textual and contextual analysis to develop conceptual knowledge. For instance, they analyse how other productions have been created to understand how to identify available designs and they investigate social, cultural, and ethical issues to make informed choices about their own media production and use.

Danielle's Micro-documentary

Here, we illustrate the creative and critical work that is possible through the application of the digital media literacy building blocks model by discussing one production of a Year Four student. This example illustrates the potential for media arts to provide opportunities for young students to be both 'creative' and 'critical' in the primary school classroom.

The data comes from a Unit called 'Representing Self' in which students were required to produce a personal micro-documentary to be included in a digital time capsule prepared for students in twenty years time. The rationale was to have each student create a self-representation of things that were meaningful to them that would inform future students about their life at school, home and in the community. This was the culminating activity for the year, building on students' prior development of a range of media arts skills and knowledge. The unit was intended to provide students with an opportunity to engage in both creative practice with media technologies and a chance to develop a critical disposition towards—in this case—the representation of self as a concept. Table 9.1 provides an overview of the micro-documentary created by Danielle.

Creative Practice

'Creativity' is a complex concept within media arts. Media production often aims to reproduce existing designs in predictable ways and students are encouraged to replicate genre conventions so that their productions will be recognisable to others and this potentially curtails the creative choices they can make. Indeed, in the past some in media education have discouraged media production on the basis

TABLE 9.1 A Descriptive Summary of the Micro-documentary Produced by Danielle for the 'Representing Self' Media Arts Unit

Shot	Vision	Text/sound
1	Black-and-white title screen (starry background) generated in iMovie.	Written text: "Danielle's Time Capsule. Hope you like it!"
2	Camera "click" sound effect. Extreme close up of photographs on a key ring – with Danielle flipping through them	Recorded voice over: "These are my photos of when . . .
3	Close up of photographs on a key ring.	. . . I was little. That's when I got them."
4	Camera "click" sound effect. Medium shot of Danielle holding up photographs in front of the camera.	Recorded voice over: "These are my photos. It is important to me because I got them when I was little and my cousins are in them."
5	Wipe effect transition. Medium close up of teacher looking and smiling directly at camera.	"This is Lana. She is the most important person in the school because. . .
6	Medium shot of teacher clowning around.	. . . she is funny and nice." Sound effect: "Awww."
7	Medium close up of teacher holding a photo and looking directly at the camera, smiling.	Recorded voice over: "Miss Lana is always the best teacher."
8	Close up shot of Danielle holding an Angry Bird stuffed toy and looking directly at the camera.	Recorded voice over: "This is my Angry Bird. It is important because my aunty gave it to me."
9	Medium long shot of teacher working at the whiteboard.	Recorded voice over: "Miss Jenelle is my teacher. Miss Jenelle is teaching Issie some work." Sound effect: "Yaaayyy."
10	Long shot of teacher working at a desk with a student. Camera zooms out midway through the shot.	Recorded voice over: "Miss Jenelle is helping Stuart to do his work."
11	Tile transition to title screen – white writing on black with stars background.	Written text: Made by Danielle, Issie Thanks for watching :)
	Note – no music throughout.	

that it led students to reproduce commercial, ideologically problematic genres (Ferguson, 1981; Masterman, 1990). Additionally, students often use the templates available within the software. Danielle, for example, used digital materials available within iMovie, including title templates and sound effects. However, we contend that despite this Danielle made numerous creative choices while generating and combining digital materials for her production.

Danielle used a digital camera to gather a large number and range of individual shots to construct her video. She choreographed both her own use of the camera, in terms of the placement of the shot in relation to subjects and objects and others' use of the camera to capture her presentation of objects directly to the camera. She deliberately used different types of shots, for example, she cut between three different shots of her key ring photographs through continuity editing (an extreme close up, close up, and medium shot). Furthermore, she made the creative choice to control time and space by using a wipe transition between two sections. She also makes creative choices to address her audience through the use of 'audience' style sound effects 'Awwww' and 'Yaaaayyy' and competently timed the use of these effects. Likewise, the use of the 'camera click' sound effect helps to create an appropriate aesthetic for a digital story that consists of a series of photographic portraits. There is fluidity in Danielle's combination of digital materials to construct a self-representation that demonstrates awareness of aesthetic knowledge.

Developing a Critical Disposition

Our analysis of Danielle's production and the context in which it was produced suggests that it is more helpful to think in terms developing a critical disposition, rather than aiming to identify specific evidence of 'critical thinking.' Buckingham (Buckingham, 1998a, b, 2003) has written extensively about the difficulty of identifying evidence of critical thinking in student work and about the need to be cautious when making claims about the extent to which media education can empower or emancipate individuals. The unit described here aimed to help students become more critical about the process of representation through the process of selection. The thinking was that students become more pre-disposed to thinking about representation as they 'distanced' themselves from the representations they are creating.

The production of the micro-documentary provided Danielle with an opportunity to experiment with the concept of representation by sharing some of the things that matter in her life. She chose to focus on people who were important to her, which worked to construct a sense of her place and role in her family and community. For example, she explained that her Angry Bird stuffed toy was valuable and important to her because it was a gift from her aunty. She chose to include representations of Miss Lana, her favourite teacher and Miss Jenelle who plays an important part in her own and her classmates' learning. The choices Danielle made suggest that she understood that the process of representation is one of active construction of meaning that involves making choices and selections. The end result was that the documentary represented her as a complex individual for whom connection to family and significant adults, friends, and community is important.

Creativity and critical disposition are linked through Danielle's engagement with the concept of representation. Her creative choices help to make the process of representation more explicit. However, the extent to which these understandings were available to Danielle is unclear in the current data.

We do suggest that a process of structured discussion and dialogue about the representations selected would provide valuable opportunities for making these understandings and processes visible to the students involved. Combining creative experimentation in order to represent meanings, along with structured dialogue after the process has the potential to be a powerful media arts pedagogy in the primary years.

Concluding Thoughts—Creativity and Critical Thinking in Media Arts

Danielle's work illustrates that primary school students can develop their creative media arts practice and learn to think critically about the media through media production. Indeed, in an era in which media production tools have become increasingly available to younger people, it is hard to imagine why comprehensive media literacy education might occur without some form of creative practice. Furthermore, despite past claims that student production work might be inherently uncritical, our work in this school suggests that students can learn about representation as they create. We do not claim that all production work is 'critical', but believe that there are opportunities to explore all of the key concepts of media education: media languages, representations, audiences, and institutions within media arts production activities. We have found the digital media literacy building blocks model outlined in this paper useful for generating the creative and critical aspects of students' media learning. This model has the potential to assist teachers and students to participate in digital media culture in creative and critical ways.

Acknowledgment

This chapter reports data collected as part of an Australian Research Council funded research project. We thank the teachers, administrators, and students who are our research partners on this project and acknowledge the partnership of the School, the Queensland Teachers Union, and the Indigenous community of the school, along with the support of the Australian Research Council. Particularly we thank the year four teachers Miss Lana and Miss Janelle, and the students of this year four class. Special thanks also goes to Amanda Levido who is the media arts Researcher who supports the teachers at this school. Our colleagues on the project are: Allan Luke, Karen Dooley, Beryl Exley, Vinesh Chandra, John Davis, Amanda Levido, Kathy Mills and Katherine Doyle of Queensland University of

Technology, John McCollow and Lesley MacFarlane of the Queensland Teachers Union, and Adrienne McDarra.

References

ACARA. (2011). *The shape of the Australian curriculum: The arts*. Sydney: Australian Curriculum, Assessment, and Reporting Authority.

Buckingham, D. (1998a). Fantasies of empowerment? Radical pedagogy and popular culture. In D. Buckingham (Ed.), *Teaching popular culture: Beyond radical pedagogy* (pp. 1–17). London: UCL Press.

Buckingham, D. (1998b). Pedagogy, parody and political correctness. In D. Buckingham (Ed.), *Teaching popular culture: beyond radical pedagogy* (pp. 63–87). London: UCL Press.

Buckingham, D. (2003). *Media education: Literacy, learning and contemporary culture*. Cambridge: Polity Press.

Curriculum Corporation (1994). A statement on the arts for Australian schools. Melbourne: Curriculum Corporation.

Dezuanni, M., & Raphael, J. (2012). Media arts and learning in the digital world. In C. Sinclair, N. Jeanneret, & J. O'Toole (Eds.), *Education in the arts* (pp. 145–159). Melbourne: Oxford University Press.

Dezuanni, M. L., & Woods, A. F. (2013, forthcoming). 'These are my photos of when I was little': Locating media arts in the primary school curriculum. In P. Fraser & J. Wardle (Eds.), *Current perspectives in media education: A manifesto for media education*. London: Palgrave.

Ferguson, B. (1981). Practical work and pedagogy. *Screen Education, 38*(Spring), 41–55.

Luke, A., Dooley, K., & Woods, A. (2011). Comprehension and content: Planning literacy curriculum in low socioeconomic and culturally diverse schools. *Australian Education Research, 38*(2), 149–166.

Luke, A., Woods, A., & Dooley, K. (2011). Comprehension as social and intellectual practice: Rebuilding curriculum in low socioeconomic and cultural minority schools. *Theory into Practice, 50*(2), 157–164.

Masterman, L. (1990). *Teaching the media*. London, New York: Routledge.

Perkins, W. H. (1963). Screen education in Tasmania. *Screen Education* (July–August), 9–18, 30.

Woods, A., Dooley, K., Luke, A., & Exley, B. (2012). School leadership, literacy and social justice: The place of local school curriculum planning and reform. In I. Bogotch and C. Shields (Eds.), *International handbook on educational leadership and social (in)justice*. New York: Routledge.

10

SOWING THE SEEDS OF DIGITAL AND MEDIA LITERACY IN LEBANON AND THE ARAB WORLD

The Importance of a Locally Grown and Sustainable Curriculum

Jad P. Melki

Media literacy education has much to offer Lebanon and the Arab region, yet it remains in its infancy struggling to affirm its importance in academe. Decades of conflict, rampant corruption, authoritarian rule, and severe restrictions on freedom of expression and the press have turned much of Arab media education into factories that produce and sustain a "sensorial culture" and "prepare generation after generation of semi-educated journalists whose job is to promote the 'achievements' of the state" (Amin, 2002, 129). Nevertheless, the past decade has witnessed a revival in media education (Melki, 2011), thanks in part to a revolution in communication technologies and a wave of political and cultural uprising that swept the region and brought digital and media literacy to the forefront, especially in countries like Lebanon.

Lebanon has been a leader in promoting media literacy education both at the university and civil society levels, thanks to its relatively free media climate and high degree of academic freedom, in addition to the existence of many media programs and a diverse spectrum of curricula (Melki, 2009). It also has a talented media workforce and a vibrant civil society, with some 3,500 nongovernmental organizations (NGOs) spearheading a plethora of causes, some of which are related to media literacy (UNDP, 2009). Therefore, Lebanon offers a significant potential for developing a strong local media literacy brand and for advancing it throughout the region.

Simultaneously, Lebanese society stands to gain much from media literacy. At a societal level, Lebanon is made up of highly diverse, often clashing, religious and political cultures and identities. This distinguishing cultural characteristic is partly responsible for its curious freedom but also one of the main culprits behind Lebanon's confessional sectarian political system, its persistent discriminatory laws and practices (Hanafi & Tiltes, 2008; Farhood, 2009), the lack of social and cultural cohesion, rampant political and economic corruption (Khashan, 2011), and its constant state of political turmoil and instability (Shehadeh, 1998; Dawahare, 2000; Makdisi, Kiwan, & Marktanner, 2010).

Research extending back decades has shown how Lebanese media—traditional and new—reproduce social and political divisions and the entrenched confessional political system that has plagued the country for almost a century (Dajani, 1992; Nötzold, 2009; Melki, Dabbous, Nasser, & Mallat, 2012). Part of the problem is that almost all media institutions are tied to political groups (Al-Najjar, 2011; Melki et al., 2012), and Lebanese audiences tend to follow media that reflect their own ideologies and affiliations. Lebanon's news media echo the sectarian makeup of the country's population and closely reflect the agendas of their political sponsors (Dajani, 2006). Moreover, poor critical media literacy skills among Lebanese youth help perpetuate this problem (Melki, 2010).

But problems directly or indirectly related to low media literacy levels extend beyond the political sphere and may be linked to Lebanon's widespread consumerism and a growing materialist culture obsessed with physical appearance, titles and status, and additionally complicated with a conflicted identity that thrives for modernity—particularly in its Western form—yet clings onto contradictory traditional values. Add to that, widespread discrimination against women, who remain severely underrepresented in positions of power, especially in government and media industries and face an oppressive regime of discriminatory laws (Byerly, 2011), matched only by rampant sexually objectifying media stereotypes and a paradoxical culture of sexuality that conflates postmodern sexual body display with traditional expectations of sexuality (Mallat, 2011, 81). Moreover, Lebanese women—and increasingly men—face a "cosmetic surgery and beauty regime" and social pressures that normalize bodily modification and alteration (Doherty, 2008). The increase in demand for plastic surgery seems to never cease and the supply of steroids for overly muscular male figures is becoming increasingly obvious, especially in Beirut.

These and other issues make Lebanese society a fertile ground in need of the media literacy seed but also readily able, through its strong educational system, to spread its ideas and concepts throughout the Arab region.

State of Digital and Media Literacy Education in Lebanon

Media literacy in Lebanon has made some advances in the past five years, both on the academic and civil society fronts. One can attribute this progress to the efforts of several academics and civil society leaders, but an important contributing factor has also been the Arab uprisings and the role social media has played in these revolts.

The first full-fledged media literacy course to be offered at a Lebanese university was launched in Fall 2009, prompted by a curriculum developed at the

Salzburg Academy for Media and Global Change—a global collective that has been producing media literacy curricula since 2007. The course quickly attracted many students at the American University of Beirut (AUB), partly due to combing critical media literacy proficiencies with hands-on digital literacy skills. Later, it became designated a writing intensive course and began to incorporate more locally relevant modules and examples, such as religious sectarianism and political patronage of media institutions. Many students who attended the course also participated in the Salzburg Academy and helped add more local examples and case studies. As an extension to this course, and in an effort to promote media literacy education in Lebanon and the region, AUB hosted in 2011 an international conference titled *Digital and Media Literacy: New Directions*, with the support of the Open Society Foundations (OSF). The coincidental climaxing of the Arab uprising around the time of the conference strongly contributed to its success in promoting the need for media literacy in the region. Many attendees showed interest in teaching media literacy at their home institutions but complained of the challenges they faced, especially the scarcity of curricular material in Arabic and the lack of skills to teach the course. Subsequently, the conference outcomes report recommended the establishment of an annual academy that trains Arab media professors on teaching digital and media literacy and produces curricular material in Arabic. Supported again by OSF, the academy will debut in summer 2013. Moreover, at the request of a handful of Lebanese universities and schools, AUB faculty members have presented their media literacy curriculum in guest lectures around the country. Two universities adopted parts of the curriculum in their existing communication courses, and several confirmed interest in developing full media literacy courses after attending the summer academy. Several schools have also shown interest in incorporating media literacy in their teaching, but few concrete steps have been taken to implement this.

Other universities have also attempted to introduce courses related to media literacy. Lebanese American University (LAU) introduced in Spring 2010 a "Media, Culture, and Technology" course that included some basic media literacy modules (personal communication, February 15, 2013). However, the course was later renamed "Social Media" and became predominantly oriented towards professional online journalism and Web communication skills, including online content generation and dissemination. Other attempts include injecting media literacy modules within the traditional "media and society" courses. These, however, were a far call from the goals and aims of media literacy.

In addition, various media literacy modules have existed outside academe. Several civil society groups have been actively offering media and digital literacy training since 2008. Some target youth, underprivileged, and rural communities and minorities in Lebanon, such as Hibr Lubnani (Lebanese Ink), while others pursue small businesses, professionals, journalists, and activists, such as Social Media Exchange (SMEX). Most of the civil society groups tend to focus on teaching digital and social media skills, rather than emphasizing critical competencies. Many also tend to highlight the commercial and professional benefits, rather than communal and individual empowerment values, of these digital skills. SMEX, for instance, started in 2008 to offer workshops that train civil society activists on using digital tools in advocacy (SMEX, n.d.). Significant demand for these workshops led the non-profit organization to expand and add a for-profit arm: Social Media Exchange and Company (SMEX&CO) (personal communication, February 10, 2011). Hibr Lubnani, on the other hand, has been offering workshops that balance media literacy, digital literacy, writing, and audiovisual production skills. The media literacy component of their workshops covers training on analyzing media messages and asking the core media literacy questions but normally only occupies a small part of the program. Since 2009, it has trained over 650 people from various backgrounds (personal communication, February 14, 2013). Many of its workshops are conducted in remote rural areas and cater to underprivileged communities, although some still are centered in its Beirut headquarters and target youth aged 15 to 30. Hibr Lubnani's team has been planning for a while to launch a full-fledged digital and media literacy teaching and research center, but the lack of financial resources has delayed this project. Moreover, its staff note that the media literacy teaching has somewhat dwindled recently due to other exigencies and more interest in social media and production skills.

Other civil society groups have attempted to include media literacy learning within their media-related workshops. Maharat Foundation, a group that promotes free press and advocates reforming media laws in Lebanon, has offered workshops that include small components of media literacy. In 2008, a workshop on peace journalism included some message analysis and news comparison training, but such modules are not standard in their projects, as much of their capacity building initiatives focus on journalism training, media monitoring, and legal reform. The National Evangelical Union of Lebanon, too, sponsored a regional media literacy workshop for church leaders, but this was an isolated activity that focused on analyzing media messages "to reveal the values propagated vis-à-vis human rights in general and gender justice in particular" (WACC, n.d.). Finally, some individuals have also used the term media literacy to promote the reading of news among high school students, but they have been on a much smaller and infrequent scale.

Overall, the most systematic and growing efforts to generalize media literacy education in Lebanon—and the region—has been led by one university and is steadily but slowly expanding to other campuses. Civil society groups have also been a positive force in promoting media literacy training, although questions of sustainability and curricular direction raise many concerns about their future contribution. Although many schools have expressed interest in incorporating media literacy concepts and training in their curricula, they have not played a significant role so far in this domain. This makes them the natural next front for media literacy education in Lebanon.

Four Years of Media Literacy at the American University of Beirut

Four years of media literacy at AUB have provided strong evidence for its merit to Lebanese and Arab societies. A focus group with 10 undergraduates and qualitative interviews with two graduates who had taken media literacy at AUB between Fall 2009 and Fall 2012, revealed promising findings. The students came from various socio-economic and religious backgrounds. Seven were Lebanese, while the rest came each from Bahrain, Jordan, Sudan, Syria, and Turkey.

The course was an amalgam of conceptual teaching, critical thinking skills, and digital skills, as well as writing intensive skills. Student participants were easily able to recall both concepts and skills they learned, even those who took it four years prior. They highlighted core media literacy topics covered, such as media representation of gender, race, and minorities, news framing, ideal beauty in the media, objectification of women in advertising, media ownership and concentration of the industry, advertising and consumerism, media habits and its relationship to self-worth and self-esteem, and a slew of disorders, such as anorexia, muscle dysmorphia, obesity, hyperactivity, etc. They also remembered the specific digital skills and the applications they learned, many of which they continued to use after class. These included audio editing (audacity), blogging (Wordpress), video editing (Premiere Elements), photo editing (Photoshop Elements), and the many social media they had to research and present in class.

When students were asked about the main benefits of the course, three broad headlines emerged. Theses are delineated below.

Better Writing, Debating, and Blogging Equal Higher Confidence and More Participation

Students strongly believed that media literacy helped them become better writers and bloggers and that in turn empowered them to become more confident expressing their opinions publicly and virtually.

Because the media literacy course was designated a writing intensive course, students had to write several formal and informal essays and articles. The instructor closely edited the papers, and most students had to sit with a writing tutor to review their documents and make significant corrections before resubmitting, especially the first two papers. Many students had to go through two or even three phases of corrections, and many in the focus group admitted hating the process. However, they also noted how the critical writing style and the relevant media literacy topics they wrote about made the process more exciting. More importantly, participants mentioned learning a new form of writing that empowered them. "I became more confident about expressing my ideas. I learned that my opinion did matter, as long as I supported my arguments with evidence and citations. This made me more confident about myself and about what I write," noted one student. Another said she had spent most of her college life "citing other people's ideas, but this course taught me how to also express my own observations. I learned to confidently and effectively get my point through."

Better writing skills also meant more courageous, prolific, and engaging blogging. One participant said she had maintained a blog for years before she took the course, "but all my postings were private." The course required all students to create a new public blog and post all assignments in it. "After the class, I felt confident to make my own blog public and share my ideas without worrying about what others say." Other students who had maintained a blog before the course mentioned how the digital skills they learned, especially photo editing, podcasting, and vodcasting, made their blogging more engaging. Moreover, one participant noted that the course helped her sharpen the focus of her blog, and she now blogs about media literacy matters. Not all students had blogs before the course. In fact, eight did not, and only three of them continued to blog after the course. Still, those who did have blogs prior to the course said their blogging became more frequent and more engaging through their ability to use multimedia.

In addition to writing, students valued the skills they gained from debating. The media literacy course often entailed debating controversial issues, such as religion, race, gender, and sexual orientation. One student said the course made her realize the importance of voicing her opinions, even the most controversial. "I feel more confident doing so because I can get my points through more effectively." Another student who used to avoid debates because "they often ended in controversy" said the course changed her perception. "When I used to argue, I took matters too personally and was often offended. I avoided debates and frankly there were opinions I didn't want to hear about. The discussions taught me to debate more effectively by not taking matters personally. We can disagree and still discuss matters respectfully." A third student said the discussions rarely changed her opinion, but "I learned that incorporating and giving voice to ideas and opinions that went against my beliefs is worth it. It strengthens my own arguments."

According to Jenkins (2009), media literacy helps foster a strong participatory culture, and accordingly helps youth become empowered and engaged citizens able to confidently create diverse cultural expressions. Media literacy students at AUB echoed these learning outcomes. Stronger writing led to stronger arguments, which along with debate skills led to more confidence in engaging, exchanging, and challenging ideas openly and respectfully. And multimedia skills expanded the venues, reach, and forms of these exchanges, leading to more empowered, creative, and engaged citizens.

Nuanced Understanding of the Media Industry Equals Sophisticated Understanding of Media Influence and Processes

Participants in the focus group eagerly expressed their developed understanding of the media industry and how it influences individuals and communities.

Media literacy encourages students to ask critical questions about a message's author, intentions, purposes, persuasion methods, creative techniques, targeted audiences, and the lifestyles and values represented (Hobbs, 2011). These critical questions were extant in students' answers. One student explained, "Media literacy untangled the relationship between the advertising and media industries and between the viewer and producer." She said it helped her understand the interaction between these entities at the micro production level and how the outcome manifested itself at the macro societal level. "Before gaining this intricate understanding, I had a blanket view about the media—a conspiracy theory, and it made me angry that I could not understand it." Another student noted her understanding of information flow and the concentration of the media industry. "It made me realize that most of the information, entertainment, and technologies we use come from the U.S. Even the local advertising concepts often turn out to be imitations from U.S. media."

In addition, many noted their ability to view media messages in a different light—one that is critical and informed albeit tiresome. One student jokingly said "media literacy ruined the media experience for me and for my friends. I find myself critiquing every advertisement, every news piece, every song . . . My friends are always telling me, just stop analyzing and enjoy it, but I can't. There are so many things that I can now see in these media messages that I never saw before." Another student said she now possesses a "different criteria for analyzing messages, especially in music." Whereas she used to only analyze the aesthetic quality of a song, she now looks into "how the lyrics represent women and certain ethnicities and the role of business and profit in shaping that song."

Moreover, students noted their systematic approach to assessing information. "I have a way to evaluate the quality of online information. Before, I knew there was something wrong with some online information I read, but I couldn't always put my finger on it." Moreover, some students revealed how they've become "self-critical" and more aware of their media habits and how dependent they are on media technologies. The students all remember the "24 hours unplugged" assignment, where they had to give up all media and surrender their cellphones for 24 hours, then write about the experience. "That was a tough experience," one student noted. "But it made me aware of how much I depend on my cellphone and how addicted I am to Facebook."

In sum, media literacy at AUB has demonstrated success in honing student's critical skills and in garnering a sophisticated and informed view of the media.

Digital and Media Literacy Help Students Understand the Field and Make Intelligent Career Choices

Many students struggle with misconceptions about the media and communication field and industry. Most students, however, expressed how a critical understanding of the media industry helped broaden their scope of the field and consequently helped them make intelligent career choices. They also noted how the basic digital skills they learned helped them discover their passions and talents and simultaneously build their digital portfolio.

As mentioned earlier, media literacy at AUB strongly ties together hands-on digital skills and critical competencies. For example, a media literacy lecture about the power of images is tied to photo editing training. Students write a critical essay analyzing the images of a front cover news magazine article. Additionally, they use Photoshop to alter the front cover and create three alternative illustrations for the same story. They then comment about how the new images may influence the story. Other examples include tying analysis of propaganda in documentaries to basic video editing skills, linking assessment of Web content to creating and monitoring Wikipedia pages, and analyzing news construction to creating news podcasts.

All in all, this approach helped students become adept at using digital skills, reinforced their critical skills, and informed them about careers in the media industry. "I learned that the field of media and communication is more than just journalism and anchoring," commented one student. Another explained how confident she now is about pursuing graduate work in political communication. Yet another explained how the basic video editing skills she earned helped her realize that "editing is one of my strengths, and I hope to hone those skills and work in that domain." Several students mentioned that media literacy was their first ever communication course. "It intrigued me to consider a major in communication more seriously," one student said. A handful even decided to pursue graduate studies in the field based on this course.

Media literacy aims to help citizens become more critical and informed media consumers, but it also seeks to empower them to become media producers, and thereby full participants in contemporary culture (Hobbs, 2010). Media literacy at AUB, taught through both its critical analysis and digital composition aspects, has shown strong potential to build critical media consumers and producers. Moreover, because media literacy often caters to students from all majors, it indirectly helps them earn a better understanding of the various media professions, and thereby helps them make informed career choices. This could also mean attracting students to the field, a strong selling point to universities in Lebanon and the Arab world.

Challenges and Looking Ahead

Media literacy in Lebanon and the Arab world remains nascent but has the potential to grow. Several challenges, however, hinder its expansion.

The two most daunting are the lack of qualified instructors and the scarcity of curricular material in Arabic. These can be overcome by training a generation of university academics, school teachers, and civil society trainers and incentivizing them to introduce media literacy to their institutions. AUB's aforementioned summer academy is one step in that direction. The latter problem of lack of curricula is more daunting and needs a sustained long-term effort to generate research, case studies, translations, and multimedia examples. Documentaries and educational videos and case studies are also scarce. The few available tend to be in English or French. In addition, official records and reliable statistics about the industry, if available, are often difficult to access.

Another obstacle to media literacy education in Lebanon and the Arab world is the conservative reaction to some media literacy topics and teaching methods. When AUB instructors gave public lectures at other Lebanese universities, some students and academics voiced objections to certain topics raised. For example, while everyone welcomed the topic of Western media representation of Arabs, a handful objected to such topics as local media representations of religious minorities, women, and LGBT. Analyzing propaganda in Western media did not garner the same excitement as pointing out the same propaganda tactics in Arab media. Even lectures that were generally accepted generated a few objections about the teaching material used. In one public lecture, three students protested the showing of thin, scantily clad women in advertisements. The images illustrated the point of unachievable beauty and the sexual objectification of women. Although these images came from the numerous advertising billboards scattered around the country, the students nevertheless thought it was inappropriate to show them in a classroom setting.

Technological limitations and lack of resources could also hinder the advancement of media literacy in Lebanon, particularly in rural and impoverished areas. AUB's media literacy course requires a digital media lab and a seminar room. Many Lebanese universities and some private schools provide such facilities, but most public schools do not.

Nevertheless, the time is ripe for advancing media literacy education in Lebanon and the Arab world. The coincidental convergence of major technological, social, and political revolutions in the region offers an excellent opportunity for such an endeavor, especially if it was organically and locally grown—with the help of many international media literacy scholars.

References

Al-Najjar, A. (2011). Contesting patriotism and global journalism ethics in Arab journalism. *Journalism Studies, 12*(6), 747–756.

Amin, H. (2002). Freedom as a value in Arab media: Perceptions and attitudes among journalists. *Political Communication, 19*, 125–135.

Byerly, C. (2011). *The global report on the status of women in news media.* Washington, DC: International Women's Media Foundation.

Dajani, N. (1992). *Disoriented media in a fragmented society: The Lebanese experience.* Beirut, Lebanon: American University of Beirut.

Dajani, N. (2006). The re-feudalization of the public sphere: Lebanese television news coverage and the Lebanese Political Process. *Transnational Broadcasting Studies, 16.* Retrieved from http://www.tbsjournal.com/Dajani.html.

Dawahare, M. (2000). *Civil society and Lebanon: Toward a hermeneutic theory of the public sphere in comparative studies.* Parkland, FL: Brown Walker Press.

Doherty, S. (2008). Cosmetic surgery and the beauty regime in Lebanon. *Middle East Report, 39*(249), 28–31.

Farhood, D. (2009). *Family, culture, and decisions: A look into the experiences of university students in Lebanon.* Unpublished master's thesis, American University of Beirut, Lebanon.

Hanafi, S., & Tiltes, A. (2008). The employability of Palestinian professionals in Lebanon: Constraints and transgression. *Knowledge, Work and Society, 5*(1), 1–15.

Hobbs, R. (2010). *Digital and media literacy: A plan of action.* Washington, DC: Aspen Institute and Knight Foundation.

Hobbs, R. (2011). *Digital and media literacy: Connecting culture and classroom.* Thousand Oaks, CA: SAGE.

Jenkins, H. (2009). *Confronting the challenges of participatory culture: Media education for the 21st century.* Cambridge, MA: MIT Press.

Khashan, H. (2011). Middle Eastern upheavals: the view from Syria and Lebanon. *Middle East Quarterly, 18*(3), 25–30.

Makdisi, S., Kiwan, F., & Marktanner, M. (2010). Lebanon: The constrained democracy and its national impact. In I. Elbadawi & S. Makdisi (Eds.), *Democracy in the Arab world: Explaining the deficit* (pp. 115–141). New York: Routledge.

Mallat, S. (2011). More than just another pretty face? Understanding motivations for plastic surgery among Lebanese female youth. Unpublished master's thesis, American University of Beirut, Lebanon.

Melki, J. (2009). Journalism and media studies in Lebanon. *Journalism Studies, 10*(5), 672–690.

Melki, J. (2010). Media Habits of MENA Youth: A three–country survey. *American University of Beirut Issam Fares Institute Youth in the Arab World Working Paper Series, 2*(1), 3–50. Retrieved from http://www.aub.edu.lb/ifi.

Melki, J. (2011). The Plight of Media Education and Research in Arab Higher Education. In Chi-Kim Cheung (Ed.), *Research in media education* (pp. 83–108). New York: Nova Science Publishers.

Melki, J., Dabbous, Y., Nasser, K., & Mallat, S. (2012). *Mapping digital media in Lebanon.* Open Society Foundations. Retrieved from http://www.soros.org/initiatives/media/focus/mapping-digital-media.

Nötzold, K. (2009). Defining the nation? Lebanese television and political elites (1990–2005). Berlin, Germany: Frank and Timme.

Shehadeh, L. (1998). The legal status of married women in Lebanon. *International Journal of Middle Eastern Studies, 30*(4), 501–519.

SMEX (n.d.). *Meet SMEX.* Retrieved from http://www.smex.org/.

UNDP (2009). Assessment of capacity building needs of NGOs in Lebanon. *Publications.* Retrieved from http://www.undp.org.lb/communication/publications/index.cfm

WACC (n.d.). Lebanon/Egypt: Regional media literacy workshop for church leaders. Retrieved from http://waccglobal.org/en/programmes/2956-lebanonegypt-regional-media-literacy-workshop-for-church-leaders.html.

11

HONG KONG MEDIA EDUCATION IN THE WEB 2.0 ERA

Engaging with the Net Generation

Alice Y. L. Lee

Young people in Hong Kong have grown up digital. The members of the Net Generation are living in a participatory media environment and they are increasingly enclosed by various digital devices. How to reform media education for the Net Generation has become a great challenge for media educators in the city. Local educators have realized that it is not good enough to only update the content of the media education curriculum. The format and pedagogy of media education have to be changed too, and that demands a full understanding of the Net Generation and a shift of media education paradigm in the Web 2.0 era.

The Net Generation in Hong Kong

The local young people of the Net Generation are growing up in a media saturated and technologically advanced society. In the mid-2000s Hong Kong, like other developed cities, marched into the Web 2.0 era. "We media," its content not produced by media professionals but by ordinary people, has flourished in the city. It includes *Facebook, YouTube, Twitter, Weibo, Wikipedia*, blogs, and citizen journalism sites. By February 2013, the household broadband penetration rate reached 85.7%, while the mobile subscriber penetration rate was 229.3% (OFCA, 2013). In terms of the Internet connection speed, Hong Kong ranks third in the world, after only Korea and Japan (House News, 2012).

Hong Kong youngsters are heavy media users, and they are technologically savvy. They own the most gadgets when compared with other young people in Asia. They have on average 4.1 devices—two more than the regional average (Synovate, 2010). For example, the Hong Kong youth top other Asian youth surveyed in owning the most mobile phones and desktop computers. It is estimated that over 90% of them have a mobile phone and 31% of them even have smartphones (Szymanski, 2011).

According to a survey on post-1990s college students, they use a wide variety of media in a multi-tasking manner and spend 13 hours a day engaging in media activities. On average they spend at least four hours a day on the Internet (So, 2011). For primary school students, all of them also go online every day and the heavy users spend more than one hour on Internet activities (Lee, 2011). Youth in Hong Kong are the top group in Asia in forum discussions and blog visits. They are also heavily engaged with social networking, particularly with *Facebook*. Recently, young people are replacing their PCs with tablets. A TNS (2011) survey puts Hong Kong at the forefront of expected global tablet sales explosion.

Apart from living online and using the new media devices, the Hong Kong Net Geners share some common characteristics of their counterparts in the West, such as being keen on participation and sharing, belief in freedom of choice, love for exploration, enjoying experiential learning, and preference for playing and looking for fun (Tapscott, 2009). Spoon-fed education is what they hate most. They are good at active information search and interested in collaborative learning.

What is worth noticing is that they no longer just learn from the school. With their ICT skills, they seek knowledge and skills from non-school platforms such as the Internet. More important, the Net Geners not only are media consumers but have also become prosumers. They are exercising their newly acquired communication power for producing user-generated content and participate in social movements. In Hong Kong, Scholarism, which is an association set up by a group of secondary school students, used the social media to recruit members and launched an "Anti-National Education" social movement together with the parent groups. The movement finally forced the government to put aside the ideological loaded and controversial school curriculum (Lee, 2012). However, online malpractices such as cyberbullying, rumor spreading, and demonstration of violence are also very common. Guiding young people to constructively use their communication power is regarded as one of the essential tasks of media education in the Web 2.0 age.

The technological and generational change in Hong Kong creates an urgent call for local media educators to have a fresh look at their media education practices. Many of them have started exploring new ways to launch the territory's media education programs in both classroom and non-classroom settings. The following two cases demonstrate that local school students are now using iPads and Web platform to learn media literacy. They are also engaged with social media and social sharing sites outside the school to explore and discuss media issues.

Learning Media Literacy through iPads and Web Platform

Since 2009, two primary schools in Hong Kong have tried to integrate media literacy training with information technology education. The Shak Chung Shan

Memorial Catholic Primary School and Good Counsel Catholic Primary School in Hong Kong conducted a media education project entitled *21st Century Skills Learning: Creative Information Technology Education Project* (Tsang, 2009). The Project was supported by the Quality Education Fund of the Education Bureau, HKSAR Government and was supposed to last for two years. Yet, the two schools continue to offer this media education program after the Project ended in 2011.

The Project combines General Studies with Computer Studies and forms a new integrated curriculum. Teachers from the two schools set up a media literacy website, developed media literacy e-books, collected online and offline teaching materials, and formed cyber forums. In the classroom, while students are attending class lectures, they use desktop computers and iPads to access the Web platform and interact with peer classmates. After class, they go online to do their assignments and discuss with their fellow classmates. By the end of the term, the students are also required to work together in groups to produce a piece of media product which addresses a particular issue.

This Project has three objectives: (a) to cultivate media literate Millennials—In the General Studies class, students are guided to analyze and communicate with the media, while in Computer Studies they learn media production skills, creative expression and ethical use of the media; (2) to train competent knowledge workers—the media literacy curriculum is also designed to enhance students' 4C skills (Critical thinking, Creative, Communication, and Collaboration skills); and (3) to guide the students to learn through information and communication technologies.

In this Project the Web platform is able to create an open-ended learning environment which promotes inquiry-based learning and problem-based learning. Students can use this online platform for class discussions and online debates. Course assignments are uploaded to the Web for sharing. Meanwhile, the iPad and the Internet have created a user-friendly and stimulating learning setting. Teachers also adopt a student-centered pedagogy and facilitate collaborative learning in the media literacy class.

Findings of the evaluation survey indicate that the participating primary school students are experienced information technology users. They picked up the use of iPad quickly. The new pedagogic approach and the open-ended learning environment match the style and needs of these Net Geners. About two-thirds of them considered the media education curriculum as novel, interesting, and fun. About 60% of students praised it as practical. The Web platform and the iPads have offered an interactive, lively, and stimulating learning environment for these students who were excited about the new format of the curriculum. In the focus group section, the young students said they were so happy to have the opportunity to "play" with the desktop computers and the iPads in classroom. To them, these gadgets are "tools," "teachers," and "toys" (Lee, 2011).

Moreover, the students expressed that they enjoyed free discussion in class very much. They debated media issues in groups and then compared their views with other groups' opinions via iPads and the Web. Through interaction and team effort, problems were solved and conclusions were reached. Guided by their teachers, they also learned how to analyze media issues from multiple perspectives. In addition, using iPads to access *YouTube* and other social sharing sites for videos were also attractive to them. The Net Geners loved watching moving images and then examining the underlying values of the video stories. Participation, sharing and interactivity seem to be the key elements that make this curriculum appealing to the Millennials.

In the end of each course, evaluation results show that students' media literacy was generally enhanced. They were more aware of the media influence on their everyday lives. They understood how news is produced, knew the characteristics of each medium, acknowledged that every newspaper has its own editorial stand, and knew how to distinguish fact from opinion. To them, online information is not necessarily reliable while media coverage is media construct rather than objective reality. Findings also indicate that they know the importance of using the media in an ethical way and understand that they should act as responsible media producers. The survey finds that students have greater confidence in their 4C skills after taking the course.

The MARS MEDIA Community Project

Local media educators are aware that in the Web 2.0 era, many students actually learn from other channels outside the school. The Net Geners enjoy surfing on the Web and they are heavily involved with the social media. A group of professors at the Chinese University of Hong Kong then designed an innovative media education program called MARS MEDIA, targeting secondary school students. The program was supported by the university's Knowledge Transfer Project Fund. First of all, an online media literacy site was established and a series of media literacy educational videos produced by the college students were delivered through the site. At the same time, these original local materials were also uploaded to the social networking media including *Facebook*, *YouTube*, and *Vimeo*. Through the promotion and sharing on *Facebook*, young students in the territory were encouraged to access these media literacy materials and interact with them.

In addition, a media literacy summer school plus summer camp program was launched for secondary school students in 2012. The aim of the summer school and the camp was to foster young people's creativity and cultivate their media criticism skills. In the summer school, there were media literacy workshops on news analysis, MV production, movie making, advertising, and image building (Chu, 2012). Apart from lectures offered by local media professionals, hands-on training for media production was also provided. Young participating students had an opportunity to experience the media production process and their final products were uploaded to the Web for public sharing.

A MARS MEDIA Fan Club was also set up on *Facebook* to create a media literacy community for these summer camp participants. Before the Chinese Lunar

New Year, these young students and their friends were invited to participate in a talent show which was then produced as a video program for online public viewing. The objective of the activity was to demonstrate to the young participants how an amateur show can be packaged as a professional piece.

Media Education Paradigm Shift

Media education in the Web 2.0 has to respond to the technological environment and accommodate the needs of the Net Generation. In Hong Kong, media educators have developed new ways to engage Net Geners in media education programs in the participatory media environment. The cases presented above show that some of the educators use new gadgets such as iPads to involve students in learning while the others adopt Web 2.0 services such as social media and interactive web platform to package the curriculum. The new delivery format of our two cases shares the following components:

1. Invites participation;
2. Encourages sharing;
3. Enhances interactivity;
4. Promotes collaborative learning;
5. Facilitates active exploration and discovery;
6. Stimulates creative media production; and
7. Creates fun.

All these components are in line with the characteristics of the Net Generation. In fact, the media education program in Hong Kong has already undergone a paradigm shift. Its assumption, task, goal, pedagogy, curriculum delivery format, and thinking skills cultivation have been changed (see Table 11.1). The aim of media education 2.0 is to train not only intelligent media consumers but also responsible prosumers. In terms of pedagogy, the focus is moving from "teaching" to "learning." The ultimate goal of media education program is to guide students to achieve critical reflexivity. It means that apart from mastering critical media analytical skill, youngsters need to be reflective on their motives of consuming and producing media content. They are invited to use their communication power in a positive and constructive way.

Looking into the Future

While we have just entered the Web 2.0 era, Web 3.0 is already around the corner. Hong Kong is expected to move into another new age in 2016 (Tsoi, 2011). The next society will be a world of semantic Web, artificial intelligence, Big Data, and mobile communication. In Hong Kong, a cloud learning program has just been introduced and mobile learning is being developed. Media education will

TABLE 11.1 Old Paradigm vs. New Paradigm

	Media Education 1.0	*Media Education 2.0*
Assumption	–Audiences only receive media messages –Media audience know very little about the media and they need to be educated	–Audiences are media users (as media consumers and producers) –Media users have a lot of media experience
Task	–Trains critical media consumers	–Cultivates reflective prosumers (critical media consumers and socially responsible producers)
Goal	–Critical autonomy	–Critical reflexivity
Pedagogy	–Analytical skills and production techniques teaching	–Participatory learning (knowledge exploration and discovery) –Collaborative learning
Curriculum Delivery Format	–Media analysis lecture –Media production workshop	–Using new media gadgets and online platforms –Through Web 2.0 services (Interactive websites, blogs, social media, social sharing sites, wikis, etc.)
Thinking Skill Cultivation	–Critical thinking skill	–Critical thinking skill –Reflective thinking skill –Positive thinking skill –Creative thinking skill

continue to respond to the technological changes. There is already a call for extending media literacy training to media and information literacy (MIL) education. How to cultivate our Net Geners as competent knowledge workers for the future knowledge society will certainly be the next challenge for local media educators.

References

Chu, D. (2012). *Introduction to MARS MEDIA summer school camp.* Hong Kong: School of Journalism and Communication.

House News (2012, November 2). Hong Kong connection speed ranks third after Korea and Japan. Retrieved from http://thehousenews.com.

Lee, A.Y.L. (2011). The 21st century skills learning: Creative information technology education project—Action research report. Report submitted to the Quality Education Fund of the Education Bureau, HKSAR Government.

Lee, F. (2012, October 22). Behind the scene of the national education saga. *Ming Pao Daily*, p. A24.

OFCA (2013). Media focus: Key communication statistics. Retrieved from http://www.ofca.gov.hk/en/media_focus/data_statistics/key_stat/index.html.

So, C.Y.K. (2011). Revelations of media "24-hour famine." *ICAC Moral Education Periodical (Expanding Thinking), 64*, 18–20.

Synovate (2010, August 2). Hong Kong youngsters own the most gadgets across Asia. Fact sheet from the Synovate Ltd. Hong Kong: Synovate Ltd.

Szymanski, P.J.J. (2011). *Truths and myths about mobile youth in Asia.* Hong Kong: TNU Hong Kong.

Tapscott D. (2009). *Grown up digital: How the Net Generation is changing your world.* New York: McGraw-Hill.

TNS (2011). TNS survey puts Hong Kong at forefront of expected global tablet sales explosion. Retrieved from http://www.tnsglobal.com/press-release/tns-survey-puts-hong-kong-forefront-expected-global-tablet-sales-explosion.

Tsang, S.S. (2009). *21st century skills learning: Creative information education project.* Hong Kong: Shak Chung Shan Memorial Catholic Primary School.

Tsoi, A. (2011). When the post 80s generation meets Web 3.0. A speech presented at the Distinguished Speakers Seminar held on April 2, 2011, at the School of Communication, Hong Kong Baptist University, Hong Kong.

PART IV
PUBLIC SPACES

Much has been made of how public spaces will continue to have relevance to lifelong education in the face of exponential growth of personalized media technologies with growing presence in the home. Media literacy education sees great opportunities to re-envision these spaces as vibrant education centers with opportunity to harness new technologies for more immersive experiences. Libraries and museums sit as the primary "public" spaces where people are influenced by media, use media environments, or even interact with them. The Public Spaces section provides a look at an area that is often overlooked in the discussion of media literacy education. Here we read arguments for the integration of media and information literacy as one cohesive movement, overcoming long standing divisions in the use of the term and its application. We explore the role of public libraries in empowering youth communities with a commercial free "third place" to explore, express, and communicate with media. Likewise, the school library offers students the opportunity to interact with media in all forms, in an inquiry based way. Here the school library is seen as the collaborative hub and link to the larger community, where students and others can learn to utilize media for critical thinking. Lastly we explore the concept of arts literacies—theatre, dance, music, and visual arts—as ways to engage K–12 learners with modes of critical inquiry and practice that harness their creative selves. Public spaces, in this section, are engaged with as vibrant media literacy hubs for engaging youth.

12

TOWARDS THE INTEGRATION OF MEDIA AND INFORMATION LITERACY

A Rationale for a Twenty-first-century Approach

Marcus Leaning

Media and information literacy are two related but distinct fields of intellectual enquiry and educational practice. Both fields are widely recognised as important aspects of general education and in a number of instances have been identified as integral to furthering the wider political projects of democratic citizenship and the enhancement of civil society (Correia, 2002; Hobbs, 1998; Martinsson, 2009). While the two fields have historically had different emphases, in recent years there have been several calls for the two fields to be integrated (Cheung, Wilson, Grizzle, Tuazon, & Akyempong, 2011; Leaning, 2009; Moeller, Joseph, Lau, & Carbo, 2011). A key issue with this is that historically the fields are quite separate and that they occur in different locations: media education in educational institutions and information education primarily in libraries.

This chapter addresses the logic of integrating the fields and consists of two main sections: section one will consist of brief accounts of media and information literacy. The aim here is not to 'unpack' and describe the fields; this task has been performed many times before (for media literacy see Penman and Turnbull [2007]; for information literacy see Bruce [2000]). Rather the intention is to highlight that both fields have discrete histories and changing emphases. In section two the case for integration will be proposed. Here, attention will focus on three key points: that both fields share a progressive intent; that integration best meets the needs of audience members and users of information in the contemporary and future media and information landscape; that there is a pedagogic logic in combining the two. Finally, in the conclusion it is argued that an integrated approach to media and information literacy requires greater cooperation between formal educational institutions and institutions of information access such as public libraries.

The Context of Media and Information Literacies

Literacy in a particular field may be understood as the result of a successful course of education—through a programme of instruction we achieve a state of literacy or competence in a specific field of practice or attain understanding of a body of knowledge. The achievement of literacy in media and information has traditionally been carried out in different settings, been conducted in different ways, and been rationalised with different arguments. Media literacy has a relatively long history, and its evolution to its current form has not been in a straightforward and linear manner. Many commentators identify three key stages in this evolution: A first stage commenced in the early to mid-twentieth century responding to a concern that new technologies such as radio, cinema and television would result in a range of problems in 'mass society.' In the United Kingdom and other Western European countries the chief concern was that an 'alien' (read American) form of popular culture presented an easier and less intellectually demanding alternative to the native 'high culture' of classical European education. As such, the role of media education was to teach the audience to judge and be able to discern good from bad (Masterman & Mariet, 1994). In this way the intention of media education was to protect or inoculate the audience against bad media content (Buckingham, 2003).

Interestingly this approach was popular both on the paternalistic Right—drawing upon the literary theories of Leavis and traditions of Elliot and Pound and actualised in government report such as the British Board of Education's *Spens Report* (1938)—but also with the Marxist work of the Frankfurt School. Moreover, it still has strong cultural resonance in certain contemporary media education programmes aimed at children and other groups perceived as vulnerable.

A second approach began to emerge during the 1960s. This drew upon developments in cultural and literary theory, philosophy, and the gradual counter-cultural shift that took place in many Western democracies. While still having a concern with defending certain audience groups against what was perceived to be rapacious cultural influences, this approach was facilitated though educational activities that would 'empower' the audience. The perspective developed involved teaching audiences how to de-code inherently ideological media content so as to 'reveal' its underlying premises and structures (Penman & Turnbull, 2007). Over time it came to be known as the 'demystification approach' with students gaining what Kellner (2000) terms 'critical literacy.' The approach was avowedly politically progressive and found favour with many on the left as well as with other progressive and critical educational projects emerging during the 1960s, 1970s, and 1980s.

By the 1990s, a third approach had emerged and soon became dominant. This 'participatory approach' drew upon developments in how audiences are conceptualised (Buckingham, 1998), advances in pedagogy from constructivist and constructionist perspectives (Leaning, 2013), and the impact of the ubiquity of computers and creative media technology (such as domestic video cameras and mobile phones with cameras) in a range of settings. The participatory approach comprises a range of practices but is typified by students directly engaging in media text creation and other critical and creative processes (Buckingham, 2003; Livingstone, Van Couvering, & Thumim, 2005).

While the approaches noted above are presented in sequential order it is important to recognise that contemporary media education is a heterogeneous field and all three models of education are currently used to rationalise programmes. The 'location' of media education within educational systems is equally heterogeneous. Learning (2009b) draws attention to five separate models. These are the absence of any formal media education—any activity being initiated by individual teachers, grass-roots teacher-based organisations providing guidance and assistance to teachers, pressure groups external to the education system organising the development of materials and external activities, the formal incorporation of media education into the school curriculum, and government agencies developing materials in an advisory capacity without direct impact upon the structure of the curriculum.

The history of information literacy is a much less explicitly political affair with broad agreement as to the need for information skills training but disagreement over the exact nature of this. Information literacy is a decedent of the earlier practices of library and bibliographic literacy (Bruce, 2000) and deeply linked to the more technology specific practices such as computer, technology and Information, and Communications Technology (ICT) literacy (Belshaw, 2011). The term was first coined in a report by Paul Zurkowski (1974) for the U.S. National Commission on Libraries and Information Science. In this text, Zurkowski proposes that information literacy was such a valuable skill that it should be universal (at least within the United States) within the decade. The exact constitution of information literacy has proven to be a contested area with numerous manifestos, approaches and reports offering a range of refinements and definitions (Bruce, 2000). The majority of scholarship on the topic has sought to determine what should be the skills imparted by the activity and how best to deliver information literacy rather than with a sustained debate on the explicit rationality of the activity beyond a general agreement that it should occur. In this regard it is often constructed and contextualised as a solution to a range of problems such as unequal access to (and lack of knowledge of) information technology resources (Selwyn, 2004).

Information education is an activity that primarily occurs in school, higher education and public libraries (Lau, 2006). However it has been integrated into educational courses (see Pope & Walton [2009] for example) and is additionally offered as standalone courses in many countries (Virkus, 2003).

A Rationale for the Integration of Media and Information Literacy

Where information literacy offers a strong grounding in the skills of understanding information need, location, retrieval, evaluation, and even production; media literacy retains its strongly critical orientation towards meaning and the processes of semiosis. It is contended that these different aims be integrated into a common educational practice. We may consider this integration of media and information literacy programmes as an appropriate development for three key reasons. First, the participatory approach to media education (noted above) and information literacy are significantly aligned in their progressive intents. Indeed, as Moeller et al. (2011) note both areas concur on an explicit democratically orientated approach to empowering people. Moreover, Moeller et al. (2011) contend that the fields should be integrated to ensure that Article 19 of the Universal Declaration of Human Rights (Right to Freedom of Expression) is enjoyed to its fullest. Media and information literacy should be integrated as they both intend the same progressive outcome.

Second, for many the experience of being a user of information resources and a consumer of media is so similar that the two cannot be separated. Accordingly, having two separate forms of education seems inappropriate. Jenkins (2006) notes that the convergence of various information retrieval and media consumption systems into single platforms demonstrates what has been happening 'culturally' for a number of years; media and information culture does not exist in discreet 'silos,' but audience members draw from across the media and information spectrum to create new and vibrant cultural forms. This approach has been a mainstay for corporate media who have used multi-channel and multi-modal methods to reach audiences with increasing sophistication (Rangaswamy & Van Bruggen, 2005). Clearly the emphases of media and information education are needed to engage with such an environment. The free flowing nature of media content, brands, and symbols disseminated through numerous channels and platforms means the division between an 'active' information user and a 'passive' audience member collapses. Consumers of media need both the information handling and manipulation skills of information literacy and the critical, interrogative approaches of media literacy to meet the progressive intents noted above.

Third, regarding the two practices as separate is pedagogically 'wasteful' as it uses more resources and timetable space to offer two separate activities as it does one. Moreover integrating the activities means that the opportunities to reach people can be combined as the activities can 'piggy back' off each other to reach new learning spaces and occasions.

In conclusion, the integration of media and information literacy should be considered imperative for both disciplines. The information and media landscape of the twenty-first century presents new challenges and opportunities. Media and information literacy education must adapt themselves to this changing environment and should consider integration as a key way forward. Moreover, facilitating this integration requires not just a recombination and modification of the actual educational activities but also a reconsideration of the institutional 'location' of this education. A combined media and information literacy should not be the preserve of either educational institutions or that of libraries and institutions of information access, public or otherwise. Instead it is argued that greater cooperation, deeper integration, and an enhanced sense of shared interest between the two types of institution be fostered in order to facilitate the combination of the practices of media and information literacy.

References

Belshaw, D. (2011). *What is digital literacy? A pragmatic investigation.* Durham, UK: Durham University.

Board of Education (1938). *Report of the Consultative Committee on Secondary Education with special reference to grammar schools and technical high schools.* London: HM Stationery Office.

Bruce, C. (2000). Information literacy research: Dimensions of the emerging collective consciousness. *Australian Academic & Research Libraries, 31*(2), 91–109.

Buckingham, D. (1998). Media education in the UK: moving beyond protectionism. *Journal of Communication, 48*(1), 33–43.

Buckingham, D. (2003). *Media education: Literacy, learning, and contemporary culture.* Cambridge: Polity Press.

Cheung, C., Wilson, C., Grizzle, A., Tuazon, R., & Akyempong, K. (2011). *Media And Information Literacy Curriculum For Teachers.* Paris: UNESCO.

Correia, A.M.R. (Ed.). (2002). *Information literacy for an active and effective citizenship.* Prague: UNESCO, U.S. National Commission on Libraries and Information Science, National Forum on Information Literacy.

Hobbs, R. (1998). Building citizenship skills through media literacy education. In M. Salvador & P. Sias (Eds.), *The public voice in a democracy at risk* (pp. 57–76). Westport, CT: Praeger.

Jenkins, H. (2006). *Convergence culture: Where old and new media collide.* New York: NYU Press.

Kellner, D. (2000). Multiple literacies and critical pedagogies. In P. Trifonas *Revolutionary pedagogies—Cultural politics, instituting education, and the discourse of theory* (pp. 196–221). New York: Routledge.

Lau, J. (2006). *Guidelines on information literacy for lifelong learning.* The Hague: International Federation of Library Associations and Information Institutions.

Leaning, M. (2009). *Issues in information and media literacy: Criticism, history and policy.* Santa Rosa, CA: Informing Science Institute.

Leaning, M. (2013). Framing collaboration in media education. In M. Leaning (Ed.), *Exploring collaborative learning in higher education media education programmes.* York, UK: Higher Education Academy.

Livingstone, S., Van Couvering, E., & Thumim, N. (2005). *Adult media literacy: A review of the research literature.* London: London School of Economics and Politcal Science.

Martinsson, J. (2009). *The role of media literacy in the governance reform agenda.* Washington, DC: International Bank for Reconstruction and Development/World Bank.

Masterman, L., & Mariet, F. (1994). *Media education in 1990s' Europe: A teacher's guide.* Strasbourg: Council of Europe Press.

Moeller, S., Joseph, A., Lau, J., & Carbo, T. (2011). *Towards media and information literacy indicators—Background document of the expert meeting.* Paris: UNESCO.

Penman, R., & Turnbull, S. (2007). *Media literacy: Concepts, research and regulatory issues.* Melbourne: Australian Communications and Media Authority.

Pope, A., & Walton, G. (2009). Information and media literacies: sharpening our vision in the twenty first century. In M. Leaning (Ed.), *Issues in information and media literacy: education, practice and pedagogy* (pp. 1–29). Santa Rosa, CA: Informing Science Press.

Rangaswamy, A., & Van Bruggen, G.H. (2005). Opportunities and challenges in multichannel marketing: An introduction to the special issue. *Journal of Interactive Marketing, 19*(2), 5–11.

Selwyn, N. (2004). Reconsidering political and popular understandings of the digital divide. *New Media & Society, 6*(3), 341–362.

Virkus, S. (2003). Information literacy in Europe: a literature review. *Information research, 8*(4). Retrieved from http://informationr.net/ir/8-4/paper159.html.

Zurkowski, P.G. (1974). *The Information Service Environment Relationships and Priorities. Related Paper No. 5.* Washington, DC: National Commission on Libraries and Information Science.

13

A PROMISING FUTURE

U.S. Public Libraries as Informal Media Literacy Educators

Denise E. Agosto and Rachel M. Magee

Introduction: Media Literacy and Public Libraries—A Perfect Pairing

Since their initial founding in the mid-nineteenth century as institutions of informal learning, a major focus of U.S. public libraries has been on providing the public with opportunities for literacy improvement via books and other information media. Today's public libraries provide their communities with access to a wider range of media than ever before, from books, to movies, to music, to video games, to free Internet access, and they blend these various media into their public programs and services. As one of the few remaining commercial-free "third places" (neither work nor home) (Oldenburg, 1989) in contemporary society, public libraries continue to focus much of their programs and services on literacy efforts with the intent of creating a more informed citizenry. As such, U.S. public libraries are ideally suited to providing media literacy opportunities as informal media education outside of the school environment.

What Is Media Literacy within the Context of Public Library Services?

"Young people's lives are increasingly mediated by information and communication technologies at home, at school and in the community" (Livingstone & Helsper, 2010), and while these mediations have increased, discussions of literacy and types of literacy have also grown in popular discourse as well as in education, government, and policy conversations. Media literacy has traditionally been defined by governments and educators as the ability to access, analyze, evaluate, and produce content in a variety of forms (Aufderheide, 1993; Ding, 2011). Livingstone argues that "we must consider the possibility of literacies in the plural, defined through their relations with different media rather than defined independently of them" (2004, 8), also highlighting the importance of "learning from users themselves," to understand the way literacies are changing (10).

One potential example of changing literacies is the importance of the ability to share media. While this may be considered a part of creating or producing communications, content creation and sharing have different levels of engagement and may not be treated in the same way by young adults (Hargittai & Walejko, 2008). Though not explicitly addressed in the above definition, the element of sharing is a significant element in social networking site (SNS) use as well as other online participatory media (Forte & Bruckman, 2009). Libraries provide support for learning more about accessing, analyzing, evaluating, creating, and sharing content with their collections, but some are also actively engaging by helping communities develop these skills via programming, equipment, and staff. This continues a long tradition that started at the beginning of U.S. public libraries.

Media Literacy in U.S. Public Libraries

Since the founding of the U.S. public library movement not long after the civil war, a driving force behind the provision of U.S. public library services has been the promotion of a more literate, informed citizenry. The main vehicle for reaching this goal was originally the provision of paper books, and the general public continues to think of books first and foremost when they think of public libraries (De Rosa et al., 2010). However, in light of the digital information explosion today's informed citizens must be able to access, analyze, evaluate, create, and share information in an ever-expanding range of formats, especially new digital formats. This means that for today's public libraries, "The key challenge is to make sure that digital citizens are well-informed citizens in both information understanding and in their ability to evaluate and analyze what they are seeing" (Swiggum, 2008, 16). Contemporary library services consequently focus heavily on the provision of digital information resources for their communities of users.

This large and ever-growing emphasis on non-print materials is not a new path for U.S. public libraries. Although best-known for collecting, organizing, and circulating paper books, U.S. public libraries have also collected, organized, and even circulated a wide-range of non-book materials since the beginning of the twentieth century, from film and audio materials to more recent digital resources (Widzinski, 2001).

Initially these services were limited to non-book materials collection and organization (Widzinski, 2001). However, "the changing media environment—in which the media user is more and more a producer as well as a consumer—asks for new media policy to ensure an open public sphere in which everyone can participate" (Nijboer & Hammelburg, 2010, 39). Today the public library's focus is shifting to include active services and programs intended to help library users—especially youth—become more educated, discerning media consumers and creators.

As a result, U.S. public libraries are uniquely positioned to take a leading role in promoting public media literacy education. The vast majority of U.S. public libraries offer free Internet access and computer access. Many public libraries also offer free courses in basic computing skills. Far fewer libraries reach the point of acting as true media literacy educators, teaching users how to create digital resources and how to analyze and interpret the messages embedded in modern information media. As Hall explained, public libraries as a whole need to move more fully into media literacy education:

> The new literacy studies challenge the assumption that public library users will become fully engaged and empowered members of a society, or that they will enjoy economic and social goods and privileges, just because they have been given access to the latest *tools* for storing, retrieving and producing information. Libraries that simply offer classes on how to use new technologies are not doing enough. . . . If public libraries recognize that information literacy is not a neutral skill that can be 'deposited' into library patrons, they must take up this challenge as information literacy educators—to become partners with the members of their communities, pose problems, and act upon the world in order to change it. (Hall, 2010, 167)

Few public libraries have yet embraced the role of media literacy educator for adults, but many youth services librarians, particularly those offering services aimed at teens, have made strides in this direction. As Tripp (2011) explained:

> For several years, libraries have engaged in wide-ranging efforts to use digital media to enhance youth services and youth outreach efforts. Whether experimenting with gaming nights, anime clubs, digital story stations, social network pages, book blogs, or podcasting shows—to name just a few examples—many youth services librarians have been using social media and digital tools to help make sure the library continues to be a relevant space for young people. (333)

Much of the active teaching of media literacy skills has focused on teaching youth methods for protecting their online privacy and safety, and on teaching basic media creation and design. Still, these efforts vary radically from library to library in both frequency of program offerings and in depth of skills taught. Library-based media literacy programs and classes are often started and sustained by the efforts of one or two technically-inclined librarians, and they often end abruptly with staff changes or with the termination of insecure funding streams such as small local grants.

The Free Library of Philadelphia is an example of a public library that has moved into the realm of true media literacy education for youth, with a range of media-based programs that enable the "library [to] function as a platform and playground for consuming and producing media content" (Nijboer & Hammelburg, 2010, 36). As Free Library of Philadelphia youth librarian Jeff Bullard explained:

> Over the past couple of years—and even more so this past summer—[Free Library of Philadelphia] branches have been offering programs for kids and teens on photography, film making, screen writing, poetry writing, claymation, and (in some locations) using a Smartboard. We spend a lot of time teaching people how to use the computer for specific tasks; the Free Library offers computer labs and hot spots for people to learn computer skills in general. The use of PC's in the library and at home, the rise of e-readers, tablets, smartphones, and apps for everything is changing the way our public finds, and understands, information. This all falls within the need to develop "transliteracy" skills. (Bullard, 2012)

In another example of libraries working to promote media literacy, *Anythink*, "a revolution of the Rangeview Library District," is a Colorado public library system that approaches media literacy as the ability to seek, use, find, evaluate, create, and share content, and it has made great strides to incorporate an experiential service model that allows youth to learn by doing (Freas, 2012). During an interview, Lynda Freas, the *Anythink* Family Library Services Director, highlighted the system's classes for youth, which range from introductory *GarageBand* (music software) to *Robot Wars* (where participants build robots). She also emphasized that librarians, who in this system are called "guides," have had success with simply interacting with media and being available for youth in the system's facilities. She described one librarian who instead of working hidden away in an office sat in a public area of the library while adding an audio track to a video. Teens started watching him and were soon asking to participate themselves. Freas connects this with the "hanging out, messing around, and geeking out" (HOMAGO) approach (Ito, et al., 2009), used by the Chicago Public Library and the Digital Media Network in the design of the You Media Chicago digital learning environment (http://youmediachicago.org/). The HOMAGO approach discusses the various ways youth engage with media, ranging from the general participation implied in *hanging out* online; through *messing around,* with growing levels of interest forming during online play and experimentation; to *geeking out* online, which demonstrates deeply engaged participation in technology use, exploration, and creation. In *Anythink*, the HOMAGO perspective emphasizes providing teens with the ability to experience each of these levels of engagement.

One way *Anythink* staff members are ensuring that young people are able to use library services and facilities to engage with media on these multiple levels is the ongoing active pursuit of grant funding to update and build new facilities. Recently, *Anythink* has gotten funding for a Digital Learning Lab as well as a Maker Space, which will provide access to tools ranging from sewing machines to digital photography equipment, as well as a "computer guts" area where youth will be able to play with and learn about the parts of computers. In addition to their facilities, the library is also hiring age-specific guides (librarians), including youth, children, teen, and tween specialists, as well as guides specifically dedicated to technology.

Importantly, *Anythink* has also surveyed teens to learn more about what they want from the library with regard to media, including music, video, and gaming. By providing support for staff and youth, building experiences, and emphasizing creativity and hands-on experience, *Anythink* provides their visitors with media literacy development opportunities. As Freas explained, *Anythink* doesn't simply want teens to play games in the library; they want them to know something about the elements of game design and development and even how to share what they learn with their peers and the greater world. This translates into a philosophy that supports the idea of media literacy as the skills to seek, find, use, evaluate, create, and share information.

Conclusion: Media Literacy and Public Libraries—A Shared Future

Although these examples show that some U.S. public libraries are moving toward a more media literacy-based approach to providing library services, movement at this point is still limited, not yet reaching the point at which public libraries are serving as leaders in public media literary education. For the most part, larger library systems in urban areas and better-funded library systems in wealthier suburbs tend to be those that have begun to "move away from their traditional role in teaching only 'old fashioned' information skills and textual literacy to a broader competence based training and coaching in the proper use of the various media available" (Nijboer & Hammelburg, 2010, 42). Many library systems in smaller towns and rural areas, as well as library systems in less wealthy communities, are lagging behind, due largely to limited funds, limited computer and media hardware, and staff size and experience limitations.

Still, there are realistic strategies that smaller, less wealthy libraries can use to build media literacy education infrastructure. While grants may not be a feasible option for all libraries, low-cost staff development is becoming more accessible via online sources and local communities. Librarians can be encouraged and supported in participating in online communities such as *Twitter*, as well as using blogs, listservs, and other online sources for information, ideas, and support. Watching online videos can also be helpful, and there are a fair number targeted at librarians. Learning from other libraries and librarians is a great way to start the process of developing media literacy programs and supports, enabling librarians to find people who have done admirable work and to inquire about their approaches.

If librarians are looking for media-specific education, state and national conferences often offer professional development opportunities, and local community colleges usually offer low-cost media production courses. Young people themselves are another excellent source for learning about media. Teen Advisory Boards and connected teen library users may be willing to teach librarians or other teens. Librarians can even employ the HOMAGO approach of beginning to hang out with media, starting with something accessible that they already enjoy and incorporating it into library programs or services. For example, a book club that watches and critiques films based on books is one way to start and can be appropriate for almost any audience. Providing an opportunity to take and share still photographs (which can now be done on many cell phones) is another program that can encourage participants to think about how to create, edit, and share media. Even a scavenger hunt for library materials can support developing seeking skills. Above all, public librarians need to acknowledge that media literacy requires seeking, finding, using, evaluating, creating, and sharing skills. By incorporating support for these kinds of activities, public libraries can become true media literacy education leaders in their communities.

References

Aspen Institute Report of the National Leadership Conference on Media Literacy (2012). *Center for Media Literacy*. Retrieved from http://www.medialit.org/reading-room/aspen-institute-report-national-leadership-conference-media-literacy.

Aufderheide, P. (1993). Media literacy: A report of the National Leadership Conference on Media Literacy, The Aspen Institute Wye Center, Queenstown Maryland, December 7–9, 1992. Washington, DC: Aspen Institute.

Bullard, J. (September 12, 2012). [Untitled listserv posting]. Free Library of Philadelphia staff listserv.

De Rosa, C., Cantrell, J., Carlson, M., Gallagher, P., Hawk, J., Sturtz, C., Cellentani, D., Dalrymple, T., & Olszewski, L. (2010). *Perceptions of libraries 2010: Context and community*. Dublin, OH: OCLC Online Computer Library Center. Retrieved from http://www.oclc.org/reports/2010perceptions/2010perceptions_all.pdf.

Ding, S. (September 2011). The European Commission's approach to media literacy. In S. Livingstone (Ed.), *Media literacy: Ambitions, policies and measures* (5–7). London: European Cooperation in Science and Technology (COST). Retrieved from http://www.cost-transforming-audiences.eu/node/223.

Elmbord, J. K. (2011). Libraries as the spaces between us: Recognizing and valuing the third space. *Reference & User Services Quarterly, 50*, 338–350.

Forte, A., & Bruckman, A. (2009). Writing, citing, and participatory media: Wikis as learning environments in the high school classroom. *International Journal of Learning and Media, 1*(4), 23–44.

Freas, L. (2012, October 25). Telephone interview.

Hall, R. (2010). Public praxis: A vision for critical information literacy in public libraries. *Public Library Quarterly, 29*, 162–175.

Hargittai, E., & Walejko, G. (2008). The participation divide: Content creation and sharing in the digital age. *Information, Community and Society, 11*(2), 239–256.

Ito, M., Baumer, S., Bittanti, M., Cody, R., Herr-Stephenson, B., Horst, H.A., . . . Yardi, S. (2009). *Hanging out, messing around, and geeking out: Kids living and learning with new media.* Cambridge, MA: MIT Press.

Lawson, K. (2004). Libraries in the USA as traditional and virtual "third places." *New Library World, 105*(1198/1199), 125–131.

Livingstone, S. (2004). Media literacy and the challenge of new information and communication technologies. *The Communication Review, 7,* 3–14.

Livingstone, S., & Helsper, E. (2010). Balancing opportunities and risks in teenagers' use of the internet: The role of online skills and internet self-efficacy. *New Media and Society, 12,* 309–329.

Nijboer, J., & Hammelburg, E. (2010). Extending media literacy: A new direction for libraries. *New Library World, 111,* 36–45.

Oldenburg, R. (1989). *The great good place: Cafes, coffee shops, community centers, beauty parlors, general stores, bars, hangouts, and how they get you through the day.* New York: Paragon House.

Swiggum, K. (2008). Hyperworlds: The merging of generation "M," information and communication technologies, online safety, and media literacy. *PNLA Quarterly, 72*(2), 4–5, 14–18.

Tripp, L. (2011). Digital youth, libraries, and new media literacy. *The Reference Librarian, 52,* 329–341.

Widzinski, L. (2001). The evolution of media librarianship: A tangled history of change and constancy. *Studies in Media & Information Literacy Education, 1*(3). Retrieved from http://www.utpjournals.com/simile.

14

SCHOOL LIBRARIES, MEDIA LITERACY, AND THE POTENTIAL FOR CIVIC ENGAGEMENT

Gayle Bogel

Introduction

School libraries provide a formative environment for fostering the development of media literacy in K–12 schools. As an augment to classroom instruction, a co-teaching opportunity, and a doorway to authentic lifelong learning skills, media literacy can be effectively integrated by the school librarian, through multiple paths, in the daily life and learning of K–12 students.

Often physically situated as the center of a school community, the school library is a point of contact with print and digital resources for teachers and students in all disciplines. The library extends the shared learning that occurs in classrooms and encourages rich social opportunities for collaborative inquiry. As a mirror of the public spaces in the community beyond the school building walls, the school library offers the experience of shared public access and the opportunity to practice citizenship skills necessary for full participation in a democratic society.

School librarians are in a unique position to nurture critical thinking and civic engagement through existing media channels within the school and the larger community. By integrating authentic activities that provide a valuable service to the populations served, and engaging students in the design and development of those activities, school librarians are able to focus on the strengths of their role. Producing and sharing content, broadcasts, and social media contributions is a seamless introduction to media experiences that bridge the gap between school and real-world endeavors. Digital platform versions of traditional communication publications such as newspapers, yearbooks, and newsletters, are well within the reach of even minimally equipped school libraries. And as the central point for information distribution, providing information access and integration with curriculum-based goals is a powerful connection to stakeholders throughout the school building, the district, and the community.

Historical Perspective

From a historical and practical perspective, school libraries build on an accepted cultural image as a center for learning and knowledge, often being referred to as the "hub" of a school and a central point for gathering and communication. Supported by professional position statements of free speech and intellectual freedom (ALA), school librarians carry responsibility for programs and approaches that embrace civic virtues of free speech and unbiased media channels.

The encouragement and cultivation of the school community as a responsibility and charge of the school library is a direct reflection of early education reform movements' emphasis on civic interactions. Community schools in the early twentieth century recognized the value of their public spaces for dispersing ideas of public interest. Using media, primarily in printed form, to bring together school and community partners in dialogue, fostered critical thinking. (Ritzo, Nam, & Bruce, 2009) Using library spaces to encourage individual public expressions of civic viewpoints, while debating local political decisions and movements, furthered the development of committed engagement in civic duties. Early progressive reform in education—led by the philosophies of John Dewey—emphasized the value of project-based learning that results in transformed situations and embodied action. It allows students to connect their lives to the world, not just acquire knowledge or skills. (Ritzo et al., 2009)

Recent emphasis on core curriculums has acknowledged that dispositions supporting civic engagement are integral to developing critical thinking skills (ASCD, 2012). Cultivating civic engagement reaches beyond rigid definitions of student achievement. Fluency in evaluating and integrating media is a basic foundation for interacting in an interconnected society, as well as reaching core educational standards relating to skills in specific disciplines.

As media prevalence and sophistication has grown, along with ability to interact and communicate through technology, the value of providing common space for those interactions has also increased. A sense of civic responsibility and shared engagement is essential to establishing positive social behaviors in both physical and digital environments. An understanding of public responsibilities and social norms contributes to students' effectiveness as citizens who are prepared to participate in positive civic discourse. The visibility of the school library and its central location in schools emphasizes its potential to mediate community communications.

A central goal of the school library in its leadership role in current educational reform is the cultivation of civic engagement in community concerns. By using the tacit cultural understanding of the library as a public space, a platform for civil discourse that promotes the development of critical inquiry, encouraging media literacy contributes to authentic learning experiences and engagement for students and members of the larger community.

Equitable access and social inclusion are two themes with rich potential for school libraries that are preparing students to participate in evolving civic responsibilities for the twenty-first century. Both are facilitated by the effective use of media, as well as the encouragement to experiment and produce user generated content in a participatory culture. And both are tied to understandings of media production and consumption in multiple contexts.

Equitable Access

Promoting the social inclusion that is necessary for effective democratic participation is the result of providing both equitable information access and broad information content to a community. In library environments, both the technology (access) and the information (content) are made available in ways that encourage equitable approaches for all students. The cultivation of critical thinking skills to interpret and make use of access and content is an essential function of school librarians and educators. Media literacy provides a channel for developing necessary critical thinking skills that sustain equitable approaches to both content and access.

Media literacy, in practice and philosophy, is closely aligned with the core mission of the school library. The goal of promoting universal education and community empowerment through information delivery, and the guiding principle of intellectual freedom (ALA, 2008) and first amendment rights (ALA, 1989), intersect in larger discussions of community involvement.

Libraries have traditionally provided access to media of all kinds, stretching back from current iterations of social media and Internet to microfiche, printed books, illuminated manuscripts, and papyrus rolls, and have maintained the evolving forms of technology connections to access the changing media formats. School libraries have the added dimension of providing effective instruction in making use of the media and technology available to meet the explicit needs of curriculum and school reform through inquiry learning and refined versions of literacies that relate to changing information access and delivery.

Implementation of inquiry learning in multidisciplinary contexts is the hallmark of effective "literacy" frameworks—whether media literacy, information literacy, digital literacy or the umbrella term of transliteracy. Commonalities in stating the need for effectively interpreting and communicating are clarified in the goals of the multiple "literacy" definitions that are currently integrated in the school library. All describe paths to promote the formation of critical thinking necessary to effectively interpret information.

> To be *information literate*, a person must be able to recognize when information is needed and have the ability to locate, evaluate, and use effectively the needed information (ALA, 1989)

Transliteracy is the ability to read, write, and interact across a range of platforms, tools and media from signing and orality through handwriting, print, TV, radio and film, to digital social networks (Thomas, et.al, 2007)

Digital literacy is defined as how to effectively find, use, summarize, evaluate, create, and communicate information while using digital technologies (Jenkins, 2009)

Media Literacy is a twenty-first-century approach to education. It provides a framework to access, analyze, evaluate, create, and participate with messages in a variety of forms—from print to video to the Internet. Media literacy builds an understanding of the role of media in society as well as essential skills of inquiry and self-expression necessary for citizens of a democracy. (Center for Media Literacy, 2012)

School libraries have long been in the forefront as advocates for information and related literacies. Recent changes in standards for school library programs have integrated and standardized the broader view of multiple literacies (AASL, 2010). The overarching goal that echoes through definitions and approaches to interacting with media of all forms is the cultivation of civic engagement for students, variously defined as cultivating lifelong learners, digital citizens, and literate persons. All are furthered by the active role of school libraries and school librarians in helping contextualize learning in local and national community issues.

Participatory culture shifts the focus of literacy from one of individual expression to community involvement (Jenkins, 2008). Through active participation, the necessary perceptions of social connections in the shared public physical and digital spaces, and the facilitation of responsible behaviors that contribute to the common good, contribute to the development of effective democratic citizens.

Current concepts of learning commons, digital libraries, and social media interactions contribute to community change and mobilization. School library services reflect the changing needs. The emphasis on a participatory culture provides students with authentic learning experiences that capitalize on the equitable access and content available, and help them reach into the surrounding community in a socially inclusive way. In this context, the definition of media literacy is particularly relevant as a view of effective interaction with a variety of media and communication tools.

Social Inclusion

The school library has the potential to provide experiences in public interactions for students and connect with the larger community to extend those experiences in ways that do not end when students leave the school environment. Skills learned by using the emerging social and communication technologies through collaborative inquiry learning are the building blocks for encouraging "critical, socially engaged" citizens (UVM, 2002).

Historically functioning as shared public space is a privileged position for libraries of all types. For many children, checking out the first library book is often the first interaction in the public sphere. Internet access through public venues is, in many cases, the only access available to disenfranchised families—and the primary access for children in those families to participate in digital learning outside the classroom is through school or public libraries.

Perhaps the most compelling aspect of media literacy education in school libraries, a perspective that knits together the libraries' intrinsic historical value as a cultural institution and the potential for incorporating school reform efforts and advancing technologies, is promoting social inclusion through civic engagement. As a defined literacy, media literacy may have deep political consequences.

"By providing as many people as possible with a broad spectrum of media content, everybody will be included in the public media domain and will be able to establish a well-informed opinion" (Nijboer, 2010). The ongoing effect of emerging technologies that allow greater participation and deeper interactivity in the civic and political process call for educators to realize the opportunities for social inclusion that begin as students participate in the shared public and digital spaces in their schools. Fundraising, volunteering, and building sustainable community partnerships are all successful examples of using media and technologies that magnify and unite individual efforts and promote collaborative efforts and problem solving.

Standards and guidelines from diverse organizations emphasize the need for responsible and empowering use of current media channels—from the Common Core Standards for English Language Arts statement "integrate and evaluate content presented in diverse media" (CCSS, 2012) to the Association for Supervision and Curriculum Development (ASCD) Tenet 3 of the Whole Child Initiative (ASCD, 2012) "to encourage each student to be actively engaged and connected to the school and broader community." The emphasis is on creating a climate that reinforces citizenship and civic behaviors by students, family members, and staff—and includes meaningful participation in decision making through informed interactions with a variety of media.

Conclusion

School libraries function as formative environments within the school community. The multiple roles of the school librarian as instructional partner and information specialist offer the potential to prepare students as lifelong learners. School librarians contribute to the mission of K–12 schools by emphasizing media literacy as a path to civic engagement, building on the historical connections of libraries as public centers of community activity and communication. Through fostering connections that encourage volunteering, advocacy, and interactions with the larger community outside the school walls, school libraries and librarians connect initiatives and institutions through effective use of media literacy strategies.

References

American Association of School Librarians (2010). Standards for the 21st Century Learner. Retrieved from http://www.ala.org/aasl/guidelinesandstandards/learningstandards/standards.

American Library Association (1989). Presidential Committee on Information Literacy. Final Report. Retrieved from http://www.ala.org/acrl/publications/whitepapers/presidential.

American Library Association (2008). Office for Intellectual Freedom. Retrieved from http://www.ala.org/offices/oif.

Association for Supervision and Curriculum Development (ASCD) Whole Child Tenets. Retrieved from http://www.wholechildeducation.org/assets/content/mx-resources/wholechildindicators-all.pdf.

Center for Media Literacy (2012). Media Literacy: A Definition and More. Retrieved from http://www.medialit.org/media-literacy-definition-and-more.

Common Core State Standards Initiative (2012). Retrieved from http://www.corestandards.org/ELA-Literacy.

Fry, K. (2011). Media literacy education: Harnessing the technological imaginary. *Journal of Media Literacy Education, 3*(1). Retrieved from http://www.jmle.org/index.php/JMLE/article/view/172.

Jenkins, H. (2008). Confronting the challenges of participatory culture: Media education for the 21st century. MacArthur Foundation. Retrieved from http://digitallearning.macfound.org/atf/cf/%7B7E45C7E0-A3E0-4B89-AC9C-E807E1B0AE4E%7D/JENKINS_WHITE_PAPER.PDF.

Jenkins, H. (2009). *Confronting the challenges of participatory culture: Media education for the 21st century.* Cambridge, MA: MIT Press.

Nijboer, J., & Harnmelburg, E. (2010). Extending media literacy: A new direction for libraries. *New Library World, 111*(1), 36–45.

Ritzo, C., Nam, C., Bruce, B. (2009). Building a strong web: Connecting information spaces in schools and communities. *Library Trends, 58*(1), 82–94.

Thomas, S., Joseph, C., Laccetti, J., Mason, B., Mills, S., Perril, S., and Pullinger, K. (2007). Transliteracy: Crossing divides. *First Monday, 12*(3). Retrieved from http://firstmonday.org/htbin/cgiwrap/bin/ojs/index.php/fm/rt/printerFriendly/2060/1908.

University of Vermont. (2002) The John Dewey Project on Progressive Education: A Brief Overview of Progressive Education. Retrieved from http://www.uvm.edu/~dewey/articles/proged.html.

15

WHY MEDIA ARTS CURRICULUM STANDARDS COULD IMPROVE MEDIA ARTS AND CRITICAL MEDIA LITERACY IN K–12 SETTINGS

Amy Petersen Jensen

Introduction

As a long-time public school arts educator, pre-service teacher trainer, and media literacy advocate I believe in the efficacy of curriculum standards. Standards frameworks are aspirational, they drive conversations about public schooling and at their best standards can effect change in the lives and learning of the students they are intended for. Sometimes the adoption of curriculum standards provides an opportunity for new collaborations between entities that are similarly invested in student learning. I believe the adoption of National Core Arts Standards in the United States could provide an opportunity for the Media Arts Education community and Critical Media Literacy groups to collaborate to improve media arts and literacy learning in the United States.

In the spring of 2014 the United States National Coalition for Core Arts Standards (NCCAS) will publish the National Core Arts Standards, a significant revision of the national voluntary arts standards first adopted in 1994. This revision of the 1994 National Standards for Arts Education (National Association for Music Education, 1994) will include Media Arts as a fifth arts discipline. While the 1994 standards only reflected a nascent use of media within the other four art forms—dance, music, theatre, and visual arts—the 2014 standards embrace media as a stand alone art form recognizing the "growing interest in and diversity of media arts as a new mode of expression within public education" (NCCAS Media).

This interest in introducing voluntary, national media arts standards into the U.S. public school curriculum is timely. According to the College Board, fifteen other countries have also recently adopted or revised national media arts standards (College Board, 2011). Additionally, funding for Career and Technical Education Programs (CTE) is federally mandated and budgets for state CTE programs—1.2719 billion in 2010 according to the U.S. Department of Education (USDOE, 2010)—are consistently growing as career and technical education opportunities are viewed as avenues for our young adult population, including both high school and college aged individuals, to build essential literacies that can potentially address twenty-first century goals for life and work such as those described by the National Research Council which mandates that students must acquire "problem solving, critical thinking, communication, collaboration, and self-management skills" to succeed in the contemporary media and technology saturated environments (Pellegrino & Hilton, 2012, 2).

Arts educators argue that media arts learning outcomes merge the media and technology imperatives of CTE curriculum with twenty-first century learning practices and that the learning goals associated with practicing media arts processes may produce stronger technological and information literacy in young people, even furthering their career readiness in ways that other technology disciplines cannot (Snyder & Bulfin, 2007; Partnership, 2010). For example, a young media artist using tools acquired in a media arts classroom is familiar with the same technological applications that are used in career and technology education courses. However, to create as an artist within the medium of her choice she has also been introduced to artistic processes that require creative production, inquiry, and critical thinking in order to make meaning, all goals set forth by the National Research Council. The National Coalition for Core Arts Standards describes the ways that media arts standards might fortify and even improve on existing Career and Technical Education training saying, "Media arts students cultivate both artistic abilities and technological skills that include the competencies to identify and orchestrate properties of a range of distinct and hybridizing forms and genres" (NCCAS, Media).

I believe this vision of media arts standards opens the door for a new synergy between media arts educators and media literacy advocates. In the remainder of this essay I work to outline why media arts standards should matter for the media literacy community. I also acknowledge the potential obstacles for a union between media arts and critical media literacy. Finally, I argue that media arts curriculum standards infused with critical media literacy might be used to improve student learning in educational settings.

Why Media Arts Standards Should Matter for the Critical Media Literacy Community

Media arts national standards should matter for the media literacy community because media arts environments could potentially open a space where the goals of critical media literacy and the aims of media arts education converge to provide more fulfilling and useful media creation experiences for young people in school settings.

The power in this potential interchange is that media literacy advocates and media arts educators are likeminded in their desire to empower young people in media environs. For example, critical media literacy invites young people to "critically analyze relationships between media and audiences, information and power" and rouses them to "create their own messages that can challenge [commercial] media texts and narratives" (Kellner & Share, 2007a, 60). Similarly, media arts educators ask young people to engage in questions about creation that are informed by the arts processes saying, "Media Arts students should gain fluencies in the evolving languages of interfaces, mediation, codes, and conventions, as well as contingent issues of power, persuasion, and cross-cultural collaboration, thus empowering them to critically investigate and use the effects and possibilities of various media" (NCCAS, Media).

Because of this synergy in thought, critical media literacy and media arts may have the combinatory potential to help young people explore and address issues of creativity and power in media, popular culture, and new media technologies through the critical investigation of others creations and their own.

Moreover young people are better equipped than their predecessors to engage in artistic media processes and production (Goodman, 2003; Fisherkeller, 2009). Because of the growing interest in and access to media production tools both in and out of school settings, young people are better prepared to create media than youth from other generations. Unfortunately they are not yet adept enough at the critical conversation skills about their own and others' art work that lead to meaning making and agency. A union between critical media literacy and media arts curricula could provide a space where creative production and these critical conversations develop on equal footing and where observations about creation in global settings and in local settings can occur.

It is important to note that the adoption of state media arts standards in Minnesota and South Carolina, as well as standards that have been written and adopted by large school districts such as the New York City Department of Education and the Los Angeles Unified School District, are beginning to pave the way for education leaders and administrators to see media arts infused with literacy as an important subject area that is central to learning in school and not merely an enrichment activity that is relegated to after school or informal student investigation. Voluntary, national media arts standards, such as the National Core Arts Standards, provide a framework for learning that every state in the nation must consider as state education leaders develop their own arts standards. If national media arts standards are adopted or modified within states and districts there is potential that policy makers and administrators might begin to value dedicated time and space in the regular school day for media arts and media literacy curricula.

The Potential Obstacles to a New Alliance

It is a commonly held belief within the United States media literacy community that we have already participated in and failed at a union between media arts and media literacy. Media Arts has certainly been described as one of the progenitors of media literacy. As Renee Hobbs and I recount in our article, *The Past, Present and Future of Media Literacy Education* (JMLE, 2008) the media arts education movement began in the early twentieth century. As early as 1922 there is evidence that educators considered the use of media as an instructive English composition tool (Orndorff, 1921, 11, quoted in Hobbs & Jensen, 2008). Interest in the media arts education of young people grew during the "film grammar" movement of the 1960s in which students were introduced to commercial film texts and trained to read them much like they would read any other literary text. In the 1970s and 1980s, educators enamored with the potential of transportable video equipment saw important educational possibilities in video production. At that time, Worth described the equivalent importance of the art and literacy components of film education: "Making a film not only can help a child learn how films are made or why they are art, but can help him to learn how to manipulate images in his head, how to think with them, and how to communicate through them. . . . Making a film can be part of a process of teaching children how to understand and to use the visual mode in thinking and communication" (1981, 122–123).

Despite this positive view of the intersection between media arts and media literacy, a fissure began occurring between the two mindsets in the mid-1980s as represented by Len Masterman's seminal text *Teaching the Media* (1985) that encouraged educators to move away from producing media content, arguing that the inferior products produced by young people when attempting creative production would prevent them from the intents of media literacy which is to practice "critical scrutiny rather than to emulate [the media]" (23). Instead, he argued that educators should disavow the "technist trap" and should focus more intently on the "crucial activity of critical analysis" (24).

One result of this approach to teaching media was a distinct separation between media literacy and media arts. The media arts movement found a home in visual arts classrooms where artists explored film narrative, non-fiction works, and experimental and conceptual uses of film from a visual literacy perspective (McCarthy & Ondaatje, 2002). In contrast, the Media Literacy movement focused more on media effects, solidly situating its work within the fields of media and communications and building on key theories from traditional print literacy as well as cultural studies structures (Hobbs, 1998; Buckingham, 2003; Kellner & Share, 2007b) that mainly invited young people to engage intellectually with media that was produced outside of their own creative sphere. Because of this shift the contemporary Media Literacy community has grown to make connections with health literacies, news literacies, and other global communications literacies but there has been limited interest in addressing media literacies within the arts community where creative media production most frequently occurs.

Another consequence of this division between creative media production and media literacy was that neither found a sure footing in U.S. public school settings (Kubey & Baker, 1999; Kellner & Share, 2007a, 2007b). Creative media production has become the servant to other visual and performance arts mediums in schools as depicted in late twentieth-century arts standards (MENC, 1994) and in most cases media art making has been usurped by the U.S. federal government's focus on media and technology tools that grew out of the technology boom at the beginning of the twenty-first century and eventually evolved into the Career and Technology Education programs burgeoning in school systems today (Meeder & Suddreth, 2012).

Similarly, media literacy in the United States often exists within public school systems as a secondary approach to reading print texts, where the media text augments or further informs the print text. A clear demonstration of this is the descriptions of media use in the Common Core State Standards (Meeder & Suddreth, 2012), which values the integration of media use into the English Language Arts Content Standards, saying, "media skills and understandings are embedded throughout the Standards rather than treated in a separate section." But the standards never specifically describe to teachers or students how one might access, analyze, evaluate, or produce those media texts. This example demonstrates Kellner and Share's argument that "critical media literacy is not an option [in the United States] because it is not available; it is not even on the radar." They even go on to say, "Unlike educators in Canada, Great Britain, and Australia, many in the US are not informed enough about media literacy to even consider it" (2007a, 59).

To bridge this gap in preparation for substantive discussions about the value of media arts and literacy it is vitally important we realize that our cultural circumstances have dramatically changed. The democratizing effects of the technologies that surround us are now a forgone conclusion to even the most casual observer. Production of media content has become not just efficacious but culturally significant.

Media Arts Curriculum Standards Infused with Critical Media Literacy Might Be Used to Improve Student Learning in Educational Settings

Those considering what a media arts curriculum infused with critical media literacy might look like in individual states and districts should begin by investigating the district standards developed in Los Angeles Unified School District (2011) and those developed in the New York City School District (2007). These documents both demonstrate a new investment in exploring media art and media literacies within the public school system. Specifically, the New York City Schools' *Blueprint for Teaching and Learning in the Moving Image, Grades PreK–12* is a model for arts educators and media literacy advocates who hope to collaborate within school systems. The Blueprint, which was created by teachers, education leaders, and established arts advocates from the arts and cultural community overtly describes curriculum and instruction benchmarks and expectations for teachers as well as indicators of learning for young people that value both media arts and literacy. Five learning strands are dedicated to exploring media arts and include:

- Making Moving Images;
- Moving Image Literacy;
- Making Connections Through the Moving Image;
- Moving Image Community and Cultural Resources; and
- Moving Image Careers and Lifelong Learning. (*Blueprint*, 2)

Joel L. Klein, Chancellor of the New York City Department of Education describes the importance of this commitment to arts and literacies that the standards represent: "[The Blueprint] outlines clear and concise expectations for teachers and students beginning in early elementary school and continuing through a commencement level, nurturing students' creative talents and preparing them to be thoughtful and engaged audience members for these powerful [media] art forms throughout their lives" (5).

While these standards do not perfectly address every aspect of or potential for art making and literacy or even demonstrate a full understanding of critical media literacy, they do demonstrate that media artists and educators across the United States are interested in mutually beneficial integrations of arts and media literacy that improve student learning by encouraging the intersection between media art making and critical understanding of the media art form in public school classrooms.

Standards like the *New York City Blueprint for the Moving Image* demonstrate a beginning interest in making new connections between media arts making and literacy. This growing interest is indicative of the new landscape where media arts literacy is not primarily focused on a hypothetical future but on the practical present of contemporary students. The publication of the National Core Arts Standards for Media Arts should, therefore, be considered an invitation to media arts educators and media literacy advocates to develop curricula, time, and space within public schools that encourages media arts and critical media literacy learning.

References

Buckingham, D. (2003). *Media education: Literacy, learning and contemporary culture.* Cambridge, UK: Polity.

College Board for the National Coalition for Core Arts Standards (2011). *International arts education standards: A survey of the arts education standards and practices of fifteen countries and regions.* New York: Author.

Fisherkeller, J. (2009). Youth media around the world: Implications for communication and media studies. *Communication Research Trends, 28*(3), 21–25.

Goodman, S. (2003). *Teaching youth media: A critical guide to literacy, video production & social change.* New York: Teachers College Press.

Hobbs, R. (1998). The seven great debates in the media literacy movement. *Journal of Communication, 48*(2), 9–29.

Hobbs, R. & Jensen, A. (2009). The past, present and future of media literacy education. *Journal of Media Literacy Education, 1*(1), 1–11.

Kellner, D., & Share, J. (2007a). Critical media literacy is not an option in learning. *Inquiry, 1*(1), 59–69.

Kellner, D., & Share, J. (2007b). Critical media literacy, democracy, and the reconstruction of education. In D. Macedo & S.R. Steinberg (Eds.), *Media literacy: A reader* (pp. 3–23). New York: Peter Lang Publishing.

Kubey, R., & Baker, F. (1999). Has media literacy found a curricular foothold? *Education Week, 19*(9), 38–56.

McCarthy, K., & Ondaatje, E. H. (2002). *From celluloid to cyberspace: The media arts and the changing arts world.* Santa Monica, CA: RAND Corporation.

Masterman, L. (1985). *Teaching the media.* London: Comedia.

Meeder H., & Suddreth, T., with the Association for Career and Technical Education and the National Association of State Directors of Career Technical Education Consortium (2012). Common core state standards and career and technical education: Bridging the divide between college and career readiness. Washington, DC: Achieve, Inc.

Moore, D. C. (2011). Asking questions first: Navigating popular culture and transgression in an inquiry-based media literacy classroom. *Action in Teacher Education, 33*(2), 219–230.

National Association for Music Education (1994). National standards for arts education: What every young American should know and be able to do in the arts. Lanham, MD: Rowman & Littlefield Education.

National Coalition for Core Arts Standards. (2012). The Inclusion of Media Arts in the Next Generation Arts Standards. http://nccas.wikispaces.com/file/view/NCCAS_%26_Media_Arts_7–28–12+FINAL.pdf.

New York City Department of Education. (2013) Blueprint for teaching and learning in the moving image. Retrieved from http://schools.nyc.gov/offices/teachlearn/arts/Blueprints/MovingImageBP.pdf

Partnership for 21st Century Skills (2010). Arts Skills Map. Retrieved from http://www.p21.org/documents/P21_arts_map_final.pdf.

Pellegrino, J. A., & Hilton, M., eds., for the National Research Council (2012). *Education for life and work: Developing transferable knowledge and skills in the 21st century.* Washington DC: National Academies Press.

Snyder, I., & Bulfin, S. (2007). Digital literacy: What it means for arts education. In L. Bresler (Ed.), *International Handbook of Research in Arts Education* (pp. 1297–1310). New York: Springer.

U.S. Department of Education (2010). Fiscal Year 2011 Budget Summary Section III C. Career, Technical, and Adult Education. Retrieved from http://www2.ed.gov/about/overview/budget/budget11/summary/edlite-section3c.html.

Worth, S. (1981). *Studying visual communication.* Philadelphia: University of Pennsylvania Press.

PART V

CIVIC ACTIVISM

Whatever the specific design of media literacy learning programs, it can be argued that the goal of engaged citizenship is the umbrella for all media literacy activities. Whether it's healthy lifestyles, political voice, or more production skills, these are all in the context of helping enable stronger, more critical and analytical *voices*. In the Civic Activism section of this book, we read about an array of media literacy explorations that involve the notion of the active citizen as their outcome. Notions of media literacy and power are investigated, through the work of Paolo Freire and the theoretical development of activism and civic empowerment. Social movement theory is used to explore media literacy and community organizations as goal-oriented movements. The notion of social inequality is developed as a media literacy competency, with a focus on erasing inequality, closing the digital divide, shrinking the participation gap, and fostering more active civic agency. Lastly, civic activism is seen in the context of designs for civic learning, which focuses on information and out of school learning spaces that are designed through digital technologies and that foster the engagement of youth with their local communities. The argument is made that media literacy design in formal learning spaces can have an impact in local civic contexts and that this method can effectively engage young citizens in using media and critical thinking to understand and act within their local communities.

16

WHAT ARE WE REALLY TEACHING?

Outline for an Activist Media Literacy Education

Katherine G. Fry

Introduction

In late spring 2008, a still-new media literacy organization, The LAMP (Learning About Multimedia Project), embarked on an after-school workshop with college-bound high school juniors and seniors. It was a collaboration of The LAMP and the Brooklyn-based Center for the Urban Environment (CUE) at Frederick Douglass Academy in the Bedford-Stuyvesant neighborhood. The Center had been running a much longer workshop series there, and The LAMP was brought in near the end of the school year to introduce the students to visual literacy and short form documentary as another tool of expression. For months they had been working on the issue of violence, specifically creating art around that theme as a way to give voice to their experiences around their school and in the neighborhood.

It was far from a theoretical exercise. After the first session of The LAMP's documentary workshop several of the students were physically attacked as they left the school. They were jumped and robbed by a group of youths from the neighborhood who knew what time these students left the building after their program sessions. Needless to say the attack shook up the students considerably. The next week no one came back. And they didn't the week after that. Eventually a few (but not nearly all) of them, after a change of venue and much pleading on the part of their CUE lead facilitator, dribbled back for about three more sessions of media literacy/short form documentary instruction with The LAMP facilitator. The original plan had been that students would have six sessions to work in small groups, each completing a short documentary addressing an issue of violence. What was to have been six sessions turned out to be three sessions total, the last severely truncated. Clearly, three after-school sessions is very little time to choose a topic, learn basic visual language, organize, shoot, and edit a short documentary. But they did it. The outcome was three very short, very powerful documentaries about different experiences with violence. Two of the documentaries were shot entirely within the school; the third and most powerful one, *Trashing God's Living Room*, was shot in the surrounding neighborhood.

The overall goal of The LAMP media literacy portion of the workshop was to teach these older adolescents the basic grammar of visual media literacy, within the genre of documentary, to help them extend their metaphorical voices. The year-long project had a clear activist agenda, with a vision that students like these could take their knowledge and means of expression and go out and make changes in their world. The LAMP shared that agenda, adding media literacy education to the students' arsenal.

In this instance media literacy education addressed a pressing need by giving symbolic, social, and emotional power to a group who'd been at the receiving end of physical force in a socially and economically depressed neighborhood. The students needed their own kind of educational force so they could push back. The question is: should that be the purpose of *all* media literacy education? To prepare for real-world, absolute push back? Or is that the purpose of only *some* kinds of media literacy education, in some circumstances, for some people? Or, should that *never* be the purpose? Should we think of media literacy education as a shield, not a sword? For some time the field of media literacy education has been struggling with this question of overall purpose. "The Seven Great Debates in the Media Literacy Movement" in the *Journal of Communication* (1998) points to, what was at that time, a clear divide among media literacy scholars/practitioners: protectionism vs. empowerment. As Hobbs pointed out in that issue, media literacy protectionists advocated for protecting young people from potential bad effects of manipulative messages or informational bias by giving them skills to, in effect, shield themselves from bias or inherent persuasion. Media literacy educators in the empowerment camp saw media literacy more as a sword. For them media literacy education is a means to arm youth with skills in critical analysis, and to empower them to create social change through media as tools for expression and action. The protectionist camp assumed a mostly passive media recipient, while the empowerment camp assumed a mostly active audience/user.

Does the protectionist/empowerment divide still exist? Are these still the relevant concepts? Do they need to be expanded, even exploded? Who *really* needs media literacy education? And ultimately, what kind of media literacy education do we need right now, more than a decade later? These are important questions, and, while I do not offer complete answers to them, I raise and address them from my perspective as a media scholar/media literacy educator in a large, urban environment in the United States, working among constituents and stakeholders in education, community, policy, and politics. I answer the last question—What kind of media literacy education do we need now?—by outlining and explaining a five-part agenda for activist media literacy education.

Succinctly, activist media literacy education includes teaching participants to: (a) Understand the political and economic forces driving media institutions, messages, and technologies; (b) Critically analyze media content as constructions and persuasions, noting the relationship between the sender's agenda and the crafted message; (c) Recognize the characteristic biases, and very different impact, of (linear and hyper) text, versus sound, versus (still and moving) image, and how each initiates and shapes content in different ways; (d) Cultivate awareness of media environments, and specifically the ways in which digital and mobile communication technologies organize the way we live, work, form relationships, and understand the world; and (e) Building on the previous four, produce media for social and political good. Drawing inspiration from the work of educators and scholars Paolo Freire, Neil Postman, and others, I propose an activist media literacy education that advocates for teaching the potential of media as truly democratizing; that questions and pushes up against different kinds of power; and that encourages educators to turn a good deal of control over to their constituent communities, participants, students, youth, teachers, and families so that these groups can take on the responsibility of both understanding and acting on (and within) their mediated environments.

Teaching, the title of Postman and Weingartner's book (1969), is a subversive activity. The goal of education is to encourage critical awareness by raising problems and questions, not imparting static knowledge. Similarly, Macedo asserts in his forward to the 2011 edition of Freire's renowned book, *Pedagogy of the Oppressed*, "Education is a subversive force." He goes on to explain that Freire operates on the assumption that man's ontological vocation is to be a subject who acts upon and transforms his world, and in so doing moves toward ever new possibilities of a fuller and richer life individually and collectively" (32). In Freire's analysis, the goal of education is to allow people to transform the world, or at the very least show them how they can begin that process. In both views, education is neither a neutral enterprise nor a modest project. In fact, it must have an agenda for change, even radical change.

Media literacy education, too, ought to have an agenda for change, but what kind of change? How radical and subversive should it be? What needs subverting, anyway? The reasons for a clear media literacy education agenda are numerous, and the answers to these questions are complex. To address them fully is beyond the scope of this chapter. So perhaps it's best to begin with a discussion of protectionism vs. empowerment in the context of current discourse surrounding digital media and youth, which is the focus of most contemporary conversations about media awareness. As media literacy education has developed, pioneers in the field have confronted the problem of a lack of interest or recognition of necessity among educators to teach young people to take a critical position toward media messages and their own media use (Hobbs, 2004). However, the current ever-expanding menu of digital services and devices has thrust everyone into a digital milieu that seems inescapable. In this environment of mushrooming digital media use and corresponding cultural anxiety about our reliance on these media, it seems the protectionism versus empowerment divide needs re-thinking.

Does a divide between the two still exist? Are they still the relevant concepts? In short, yes they are still relevant, and yes, a divide still does exist. But those engaged in the conversation about digital media and youth don't necessarily know that they're part of a debate. The debate exists in large measure as competing discourses between those who rally around the issues salient to Internet safety and those who are aware of a larger movement to teach well-rounded critical media understanding. The larger, loosely-organized, media literacy community mostly recognizes the importance of a comparatively holistic approach to media literacy education, yet with great individual variation in motives, definition of media literacy, and desired outcomes (see Buckingham, 2009, for a more comprehensive discussion of ways media literacy can be defined and how such definitions have been employed in media regulatory policy in the U.K.). While the issues of cyberbullying, sexting, and Internet privacy need to be addressed, these issues tend to be the only issues of concern among the "safety" group, which is comprised of advocates in government, education, law enforcement, and other like organizations (Boyd & Marwick, 2009). The underlying assumption from this perspective is that media—especially the Internet—are bad, to be feared, and to be protected from. This is a very strong protectionist position. In that sense the divide appears to be alive and well in the second decade of the twenty-first century. But the field of interest has become complicated. Rapidly developing social media sites, the use of smart phones, and the growth of the Internet as a social outlet, information resource, and overall organizer of daily life means that most people are confused and somewhat fearful about what all of this means for the future, and with good reason. It's not clear yet what the long-term outcomes might be for anyone. However, young people have become scapegoats for broader social fears about changes in the digital communication landscape. Interested parties have focused these fears by scrutinizing the way youth communicate digitally, anticipating only negative consequences. They have called town meetings, produced multi-media programming, and written educational materials focused on the dangers of youth digital media use, microscopically illuminating a narrow range of youth activities—mostly cyberbullying and Internet safety—while ignoring the broader communication field and more holistic way of thinking about digital communication. It seems almost everyone is chiming in on the conversation, taking a position, and debating the best approaches to combat these problems, including school-based programs and parental controls and/or spyware. The whole thrust is very protectionist, but many of those actively working on these issues do not know about media literacy education, hence would not consider themselves media literacy educators. Certainly, they don't think about the media environment as all-encompassing. In short, this protectionist stance ignores the fact that digital media and the Internet comprise much of our public and our private communications. Furthermore, those who cultivate the deepest fear about youth engagement with digital devices are at least as reliant on them. They tend not to scrutinize their own use, and, more importantly, fail to see that there is a much larger discussion to be had about digital media as an environment.

The Digital Media Environment

Few people would argue that the media have little impact in the world. In the Hollywood hit movie *My Big Fat Greek Wedding* one of the characters explains that, in a family, the father is the head, but the mother is the neck. She's the one who turns the head—who shows him where he should be placing his attention. On our social body, our collective intelligence (conventional wisdom?) is the head, while the mainstream media are the neck. And most of the media controlling our attention are corporate-owned and networked within a tightly controlled digital infrastructure. This suggests on one hand that the patterns of content in the media do, indeed, set the agenda for what we should think about (Scheufele & Tewskbury, 2007). On the other hand, McLuhan (1964) suggested that media actually work more subtly and powerfully than that. He used the metaphor of a thief and a steak to describe the relationship between media content and media forms. According to McLuhan, the content is the steak dangled in front of us (the watchdogs) to distract us while the thief (the communication form itself) goes about his work, re-organizing and changing our lives—altering our sense ratios—practically unnoticed. Alternatively, he explained that "our technological innovations have a numbing effect, turning us into sleepwalkers blissfully unaware of the effects they are having upon us" (quoted in Strate, 2012, 466). Using these metaphors, McLuhan made the point that the medium is the message, or, more precisely, that communication technologies and the environments they create require understanding and scrutiny, lest we miss the deepest, most powerful component of our communications. Returning briefly to the *My Big Fat Greek Wedding* example, the dominant medium today (an electronic digital matrix) is the neck upon which our collective head is attached. Media literacy educators need to scrutinize media content for sure, but must be as critically mindful of media forms, and must keep both in mind (as inextricably intertwined) while they shape an educational agenda.

Media Form and Content

Because media forms shape our communications, our activities, and our understanding, we say that they create cultural environments. These environments become like the air we breathe, we are so immersed in them. This is why McLuhan made reference to their numbing effect. For our purposes here, media forms are both the media (the technologies) and the codes used within each medium. For example, the media referred to here are both mechanical and electronic: print media such as newspapers, magazines, and books; broadcast and cable television;

radio and sound recordings; and the all-encompassing Internet. Codes are the communication symbol systems—language, text, image—used within each medium. Each code has its own grammar, style, patterned arrangement, and receiver requirements. Each also has its own characteristic bias (Innis, 1951; Strate, 2012). Print, a mechanical medium, relies most heavily on language in the form of written words, and requires formal literacy, the ability to read the language in which the printed matter is written. Television, on the other hand, is an electronic medium, and it relies most heavily on moving images and sound. It does not require alphabet literacy, but does require a hardware receiver to decode the electronic content either analogically imprinted on waves or electronically digitized. The Internet in its current manifestation comprises most all of the codes. It is a purely digital medium, and requires any one of a number of different manufactured devices (laptops, smart phones, tablets, etc.) that can access the digital information infrastructure that makes up this vast de-centralized repository. All of the media forms mentioned above are still with us, because when new media come along, old media do not die out; they are re-mediated (Bolter & Grusin, 1999), which means they become content for the new medium (i.e., newspapers, television, and radio are all content on the Internet, meaning that you can access traditional radio stations, newspapers and magazines online. Most all broadcast TV stations also have an online presence and a great deal of TV programming can be accessed online). The Internet as a digital communication matrix is our newest medium and it is within that environment that we now chiefly operate.

While this is a very brief and simplistic differentiation of media technologies and corresponding codes (for a much more detailed discussion of media forms and environments, see Strate, 2012), it points out that the form, the shape, and the very medium of a message are every bit as important to examine as the message itself. To complicate matters, one must also recognize that the form, the code, will dictate what the message becomes, indeed what it can possibly be, which means that a message simply cannot be the same across different media forms. For example, a news story about a natural disaster will not be the same in the print edition of *The New York Times* as it is on *NBC Nightly News* simply because words describing any aspect of a disaster, even with accompanying still photography, cannot be compared with moving images and other analogic imagery (meaning that it cannot be broken down into discrete parts, rather must be taken in all at once) of the same disaster. That is not to say one is better than the other. It is to say they are completely different from each other. They work with different symbol systems, rely on different codes, require different tools to encode, and do not have the same capacities for information transmission. In short, they operate within vastly different communication environments. This is but one way in which to differentiate form from content, and it is essential that media literacy education teach these distinctions. A great swath of media literacy educators have focused almost exclusively on issues of content or message (Poyntz & Hoechsmann, 2009), pointing out patterns of representation, encouraging critical analyses of representations of groups of people, issues and agendas across genres, and highlighting persuasion in advertising messages, biases in news. All of this is useful and important, but must not stand alone. A deeper media literacy includes an equal understanding of form, what might be referred to as medium literacy (Meyrowitz, 1998).

Understanding form is crucial specifically to digital literacy, a deep awareness of the digital media environment. Macedo (in Freire, 2011) argues that, "Our advanced technological society is rapidly making objects of most of us and subtly programming us into conformity to the logic of its system. To the degree that this happens, we are also becoming submerged in a new culture of silence" (33). Just how are we being programmed? And what does he mean by silence? Are we not noisier than ever, spewing insights and opinions, likes and dislikes, all over the universe of *Facebook* and into the Twittersphere? Are *any* of the voices making sense? Or are most of them distractions from bigger underlying issues that need addressing at the surface?

We might be making a lot of noise, but, as objects within a system, we are silenced. We are also blinded. When we operate within a system, yet remain blind to its logic—its architecture—we are controlled, or programmed, as Rushkoff (2010) explains. In McLuhan's terminology, we are numb to its form. We are not so much subjects who are programming, but the objects of digital programmers, playing by the rules they give us, working for their (often economic) advantage. Digital web templates and social networking websites, for example, offer very narrowly-confined parameters within which to express oneself. Add to that the corporate, advertising-sponsored confines of, say, *Facebook* and *Twitter*, which keep track of personal details for target marketing, sometimes suppressing non-consumption or non-advertising friendly messages, and it becomes difficult not to recognize one's status as object. When individuals cannot use digital tools with creative freedom, but must express themselves by the rules of corporate control, they are rendered subjectively blind and mute within this digital/economic space. Simply creating awareness of these formal and economic confines is a good place for media literacy education to begin.

Media, Economics, Politics

On a micro level, media literacy education addresses issues of media form and content. On a macro level, larger socio-structural issues of power must also be addressed. An important component of media literacy education is imparting awareness of how media are paid for, who controls them, and with whom they are politically aligned. Let's begin with the very powerful economic structure. It is difficult to dispute the fact that, in the United States alone, we are experiencing an ever-widening divide between the rich and the poor. Consider the Occupy movement, which began in earnest in the fall of 2011, where the seeds of economic and political discontent were sprouting. One could say it also began, from another place on the political spectrum, with the Tea Party movement. For many reasons, the political and economic status quo isn't operating without serious public challenge anymore. Our news media report on these challenges to the status quo, with varying degrees of competence. Yet in many ways the news media themselves are party to this grave discontent. We rely on our various communication media—through information, entertainment, text, visuals, and sound—to shape what we know and say, how we understand, and how we live in an informational milieu bubbling over with discontent, obnoxious noise, and competing voices. Yet most of our media are corporations; the ad-supported corporate voice is the loudest. Meanwhile, public perception is contradicted about the economic imperatives of our media infrastructure. It seems easy to heed the dire warnings about media monopolies and the formation of giant conglomerates controlling our access to information when we rely almost solely on corporate network news outlets to inform us about our world (Bagdikian, 2004). Yet monopolies don't seem quite as gruesome when one considers the democratic potential of social media sites like *YouTube, Facebook, Twitter*, and others. There appears to be a real dispersing of centralized control when people can connect to whomever they'd like to connect, and post whatever they'd like to post. But, as outlined above, what's often overlooked is the all-seeing corporate eye, watching those posts, and collecting data to define and target users by their consumption habits. On a larger scale, what is also in danger of being overlooked is a looming threat to Internet freedom posed by the collusion of international government (via the ITU) and big business in a global effort to control the Internet for information and commerce (Pfanner, 2012). And yet, considering this, democratic potential still exists, but requires education first.

There is immense power in corporate media interest. The marriage of economic power to political interest in the corporate media realm should not escape scrutiny in media literacy education. Here, political is not equated with government, though government is certainly a key part. The fourth estate function of the press, a check on government to suppress tyranny, was to be solidified by the First Amendment to the United States Constitution. The idea was that the press remains free of political control. In the United States and many other media systems throughout the world the government cannot directly control media, but it happens that corporate money does, through advertising and through the lobbying power exerted by corporate conglomerates. Corporate economic power colludes with political power. Clearly there are a number of instances in which politics and big media money operate closely, trading people across a corporate media/politics divide which is more realistically a power bubble that excludes the average citizen-media consumer. This happens when political strategists become corporate news pundits, as, for example, when former Clinton political strategist George Stephanopolous became a journalist for *ABC News* and George W. Bush's Chief of Staff Karl Rove became a political analyst for *Fox News, Newsweek* and *The Wall Street Journal*, or when FCC chairs—from Newton Minnow to Kevin Martin—came from, and returned to, corporate media positions surrounding their media policy work with this highest-level broadcast-governing body (Chester, 2007). In a Democracy one expects that, in theory and in practice, the press remain a fourth estate, and that the broadcast airwaves, public property as mandated by the Communications Act of 1934, operate in the public interest, convenience, and necessity (Figliola, 2010). But power and money easily pollute the public interest mission, so one must ask whether democratic potential can exist in our political-economic reality. The answer remains yes, the possibility of innovative expression and democratic participation in the digital environment can exist, but such possibility begins with awareness. From there must come action.

Developing an Activist Media Literacy Agenda

Action can only come with broad awareness of power and opportunities for subverting the power inherent in media, in the political-economic structure, and in the education system. These three are not mutually exclusive territories, but are mutually reinforcing socio-cultural environments cultivated and circulated in communication. Media power specifically refers to the power exerted in media content, forms, and environments. Corporate control aside, the digital media environment is powerful in its very potential to overturn power. As Strate (2012) explains regarding the emerging digital media matrix, "Unprecedented access to information has disrupted the stability of social roles based on gender, race, ethnicity, religion, age, and socioeconomic class, and undermined authority relationships" (451). It is within this new high-access, de-centralized information milieu that the political-economic structure is adapting. An activist media literacy cohort ought to grasp this opportunity to help shape a new information political-economy for social and political good. However, what may stand in the way of this educational endeavor is the power of the education establishment itself.

What is the education power structure? It is the pure bureaucratic machinery that maintains mostly stasis in bloated systems. Departments of Education, and teacher's unions specifically, have been blamed for keeping public schools from reaching their true potential (this argument is laid out in Davis Guggenheim's recent documentary *Waiting for Superman*), but the blame cannot rest on one bureaucratic agency; public and private education systems are part of larger political-economic systems. Public education specifically, in the United States and elsewhere, struggles within an economy of privatization of social services and marketization of education (Torres & Mercado, 2006). Furthermore, there remains a tendency within the field of education at large to train teachers in a way that neither understands nor promotes learning within the whole emerging digital media environment. Torres and Mercado (2006) argue convincingly that critical media literacy education be included as core material in all teacher training on the grounds that "mass corporate media have become the most powerful instrument to reproduce and maintain dominant values and culture" (278). I would add that critical/activist media literacy education should be included in teacher training because our current digitized environment is changing us: how we learn, how we understand the world and how we form relationships. Teachers need to understand all of these parameters, and must empower their students with this understanding.

Just how can teaching empower specifically? What does empowerment look like? How is it measured? Empowerment happens when students are given a full curriculum that introduces issues of content, form, power, and potential, from the micro to the macro level. Empowerment also happens when educators learn to abdicate some of their control. All of this requires a comprehensive approach to education, including a shift in the teacher-student relationship. This whole educational thrust needs to begin within the existing media literacy education community. Those who refer to themselves formally as media literacy educators, advocates, and the like already tend toward a comprehensive approach that acknowledges the need to teach students to analyze media and to produce media messages, predicated on the assumption that media production, and not just analysis, is part of being media literate. This is a good first step toward empowerment. What needs to happen next is implementing the other components, culminating in action. On a very pragmatic level, the digital media infrastructure is an outlet to circulate student work beyond the classroom (provided classroom educators can work through the bureaucratic maze of rules and policies surrounding how the web is to be used within most schools), whatever form that student work might take. Buckingham (2003) advocates for harnessing the participatory potential of new technologies to develop student creativity. He argues that acquiring literacies promotes social action, but he doesn't necessarily see a link between media literacy, media production, and social action.

Can media literacy really be a catalyst for social change? How does one measure change? One of the toughest challenges for media literacy educators is to measure or assess whether students are indeed becoming critically literate on a number of levels. It is one thing to assess what they produce, or even what they self report. It is another thing entirely to measure a critical, activist sensibility, worldview or attitude that may have taken root and will grow. No amount of standardized testing, or even pen and paper evaluating, will get to that deeper level of consciousness. Indeed, no standardized education is fit for every population.

Many media literacy educators are experts in media literacy but not experts in being members of social classes or ethnic groups beyond their own. On the surface their motives seem correct, but they might very well be operating from an agenda that doesn't address real needs. Or that agenda could be mired in middle-class, neo-liberal assumptions about what all students/citizens need in order to operate successfully in the system, to get a job and get along, or to be good consumers (Buckingham, 2009). This attitude merely reinforces some of the weakest aspects of traditional education. These sorts of media literacy efforts, though well-intentioned, make the mistake of assuming that a set curriculum can be used in any school, no matter the geography and no matter the population. While it is a gross generalization to say that there are organizations or media literacy educators that take a completely one-size-fits-all approach to curriculum development and distribution, the point is that to cultivate a truly activist media literacy agenda, each population needs to be part of the organic development of an approach that is right for that group, tailored to that place, at that time. To further ensure that the population is part of developing the approach, the educators themselves need to give up some control—maybe a lot of control—to the students. Allowing students to define their experience, to make choices, and to have a voice as they learn the facets of media literacy and basic proficiency in production is a truly empowering experience for everyone.

To answer one of the big questions posed at the beginning of the chapter: Who really needs media literacy? The answer is everyone needs it, not only those most economically or socially disadvantaged. Postman (1979) explains best why it is so necessary.

> Every society is held together by certain modes and patterns of commu-nications which control the kind of society it is. One may call them in-formation systems, codes, message networks, or media of communication. Taken together they set and maintain the parameters of thought and learn-ing within a culture. Just as the physical environment determines what the source of food and exertions of labor shall be, the information environment gives specific direction to the kinds of ideas, social attitudes, definitions of knowledge, and intellectual capacities that will emerge. (29)

And that is the crux of it. When a society is held together by the modes and pat-terns of the communications media controlling it, then media literacy education is essential. And to the extent that there is nothing neutral in taking on the project of teaching and learning about how organized forms of communication function to maintain a society, then media literacy education must be. And it must be activ-ist. Media literacy education is education for being in the world. What's at stake? Nothing less than our understanding about who we are in relationship with each other and our environment. What's at stake is our true democratic potential.

The students at Frederick Douglass Academy in Bed-Stuy Brooklyn needed minimal intellectual guidance to help them comprehend their social and political disempowerment. What they needed most were the tools and the understanding of the power of media forms. No one had to tell them what they needed to say, but someone could guide them in ways to shape and circulate their messages. It would behoove them to have guidance in a much more comprehensive media literacy program—one that includes exploring further the economic and political disadvantages within their neighborhood and the role the digital media matrix could play in changing it. These students needed the attention of a full activist media literacy agenda, where they learned to: (a) understand the political and eco-nomic forces driving mainstream media institutions; (b) critically analyze media content as constructions; (c) recognize the characteristic biases of text, versus sound, versus image; (d) cultivate awareness of the whole mediated environment; and (e) understanding these, produce media for social and political good—for social and political change. To give them, to give everyone, that kind of media literacy is transformative.

There may always be a divide between protectionism and empowerment, but it will help if both sides are at least aware of each other. Ideally, those on both sides, and everyone in between, will see that understanding and operating within the current digital media environment requires both protection *and* empowerment, not one or the other, because one has no protection until one is empowered.

References

Bagdikian, B. (2004). *The new media monopoly*. Boston: Beacon Press.

Bolter, J., & Grusin, R. (1999). *Remediation: Understanding new media*. Cambridge, MA: MIT Press.

Boyd, D., & Marwick, A. (2009). The conundrum of visibility. *Journal of Children & Media, 3*, 410–419.

Buckingham, D. (2009). Beyond the competent consumer: The role of media literacy in the making of regulatory policy on children and food advertising in the UK. *International Journal of Cultural Policy, 15*, 217–230.

Buckingham, D. (2003). *Media education: Literacy, learning and contemporary culture*. Cambridge: Polity.

Chester, J. (2007). *Digital destiny: New media and the future of democracy*. New York: New Press.

Figliola, P. (2010). The federal communications commission: Current structure and its role in the changing telecommunications landscape. *Journal of Current Issues in Media and Telecommunications, 2*, 15–25.

Freire, P. (2011). *Pedagogy of the oppressed*. London: Continuum International Publishing Group.

Hobbs, R. (1998). The seven great debates in the media literacy movement. *Journal of Communication, 48*, 16–33.

Hobbs, R. (2004). A review of school-based initiatives in media literacy education. *American Behavioral Scientist, 48*, 42–59.

Innis, H.A. (1951). *The bias of communication*. Toronto: University of Toronto Press.

McLuhan, M. (1964). *Understanding media: The extensions of man*. New York: McGraw Hill.

Meyrowitz, J. (1998). Multiple media literacies. *Journal of Communication, 48*, 96–109.

Pfanner, E. (2012). Hidden goal is feared at web conference; warned of attempts to impose censorship, but business tops the agenda. *International Herald Tribune, Finance*, Nov. 29, p. 2.

Postman, N. (1979). *Teaching as a conserving activity*. New York: Delacorte.

Postman, N., & Weingartner, C. (1969). *Teaching as a subversive activity*. New York: Dell.

Poyntz, S., & Hoechsmann, M. (2009). *Reinventing media literacy in Canada: Embracing and transcending eclecticism*. Paper presented at the annual meeting of the International Communication Association, Chicago, IL.

Rushkoff, D. (2010). *Program or be programmed: Ten commands for a digital age*. New York: OR Books.

Scheufele, D., & Tewksbury, D. (2007). Framing, agenda setting and priming: The evolution of three media effects models. *Journal of Communication, 57,* 9–20.

Strate, L. (2008). Studying media *as* media: McLuhan and the media ecology approach. *Media Tropes, 1,* 127–142.

Strate, L. (2012). Counting electronic sheep: Understanding information in the context of media ecology. *Information, 3,* 442–471.

Torres, M., & Mercado, M. (2006). The need for critical media literacy in teacher education core curricula. *Educational Studies, 39,* 260–282.

Waiting for Superman (2010). Documentary. Guggenheim, Davis (director).

17

SHOULD I REALLY KILL MY TELEVISION? NEGOTIATING COMMON GROUND AMONG MEDIA LITERACY SCHOLARS, EDUCATORS, AND ACTIVISTS

Lori Bindig and James Castonguay

Introduction

The title of this chapter originates from a media literacy meeting attended by one of the authors in 2001, during which one of the participants performed a song telling everyone to kill their televisions.[1] In attendance that day were university faculty and graduate students from several disciplines, K–12 teachers, a pediatrician, a stay-at-home mom who also ran a non-profit, community organizers and activists, and a video artist (among others). After the song, someone asked if killing her television was a prerequisite to joining the media literacy movement, which in turn, led to a contentious yet productive debate over whether or not this anti-television stance made sense on practical, parental, pedagogical, political, and/or theoretical levels. It became clear during the discussion that those with a background in media literacy scholarship[2] were better prepared to anticipate and negotiate the wide range of explicit and implicit theoretical assumptions in the room that day.

In what follows, we summarize two general approaches to understanding media and discuss four recurring points of contention within the media literacy movement.[3] Our primary purpose is not to advocate for a particular media literacy method or political stance but to suggest instead that having a working knowledge of different theoretical perspectives and sensibilities within the media literacy movement is a useful and important prerequisite to building productive media literacy partnerships and initiatives.[4] We are confident that a firm grounding in media literacy scholarship and an awareness of longstanding debates within the movement can help to facilitate a process of participatory deliberation and consensus decision making that leads to achieving common goals.

Two Approaches

In order to illustrate the salient contested elements within the media literacy movement, we can identify two different stances or approaches in what we are calling the interventionist and cultural studies (or culturalist) frameworks. At its core, the fundamental differences between the interventionist approach and the culturalist approach occur in terms of how they conceive of the media's power and consequent effects, the perceived agency of viewers, and the motivation behind developing the viewers' critical thinking skills. Yet, as we'll see when we describe some of the recurring debates within the media literacy movement, there are points of convergence between the two frameworks.

Despite the lack of a universal definition or understanding of media literacy and its goals, several leading proponents, practitioners, and scholars have succinctly described media literacy as the ability to analyze, evaluate, and create messages across media. Within this context, five widely agreed-upon tenets, assumptions, or principles drawn from decades of research and scholarship are routinely cited with various modifications (Aufderheide, 2001). The first tenet, media are constructed and construct reality, suggests that media are not naturally occurring. Rather, each media message is carefully crafted for a specific purpose. Second, media have commercial interests, reflects the notion that many media messages are created in order to sell products or services. Third, media have ideological and political implications, suggests that media messages are encoded with taken for granted beliefs about the world. The fourth tenet, form and content are related in each medium and each medium has unique codes and conventions, explains that different forms of media have specific aesthetics and create different types of messages and impressions. Lastly, the fifth tenet, receivers negotiate meaning in media, suggests that media messages have multiple meanings and are understood differently by different audiences and individuals. These five tenets provide a touchstone for understanding the differences and similarities between today's competing media literacy frameworks.

The divergences and convergences between the interventionist and culturalist frameworks can be traced back to various communication traditions and their conceptions of media. The first tradition, the inoculation approach (Masterman, 2001), is grounded in the stimulus response (S-R) model, which is strongly associated with powerful media effects models from the early twentieth century. The S-R model conceptualizes media messages as having direct, uniform, and powerful effects on passive audiences. Also feeding into the inoculative approach is the European tradition of critical theory, most notably the Frankfurt School theorists, who viewed media as extremely powerful ideologically, and perceived the audience as a mass of passive "cultural dupes" (Adorno & Horkheimer, 2000) easily manipulated by the "culture industries" and mass media messages. Based on the S-R model and critical theory approaches, the inoculative approach can be understood as a defensive stance regarding media literacy. In other words, the inoculative approach sought to protect vulnerable audiences, particularly children, from media's corrupting influences. In addition, mass media were often dismissed on aesthetic and moral grounds as "low" culture in contrast to the timeless and positive societal values associated with "authentic" art and "high" culture.[5]

In the 1960s and 1970s, scholars at the Centre for Contemporary Cultural Studies at the University of Birmingham in England developed a different perspective regarding media culture called British Culture Studies (BCS). Instead of assuming people were passive "cultural dupes," BCS scholars believed that people do indeed have agency, but they are not always aware of it due to oppressive forces and institutions. BCS also differed from critical theory in the importance it attributed to popular culture and media. Rather than viewing "the culture industries" as mindless fodder, BCS believed that there was value in the cultural artifacts that people employed in their daily lives. However, BCS did not necessarily view these items in a celebratory manner. Rather, the value of studying these items was that they are so integrated in people's lives but they are often overlooked and taken for granted. Therefore, BCS is considered critical cultural studies not only because it looks at everyday culture critically but also because it does so in terms of ideology in order to work towards greater social justice and equality (Hall, 1999).[6] British Cultural Studies should not be confused with American Cultural Studies, as exemplified by John Fiske and more recently Henry Jenkins, which tends to examine everyday cultural artifacts in a laudatory fashion by focusing on individual pleasure and creative communities of consumers who actively resist and subvert any potential negative media influence.[7]

Here we might present this version of cultural studies as being more *optimistic* about media culture compared to the *pessimistic* media theories of the interventionists. The interventionist framework tends to ignore any possibility of positive effects audience members may experience as a result of media consumption. For the most part, interventionist scholars believe the purpose of implementing a media literacy curriculum is to intervene in between media exposure and a potentially negative effect; there would be no need to intervene against positive effects.

At its core, the cultural studies framework regards media literacy and the development of critical thinking as a source of empowerment. The cultural studies framework views media literacy as a way to challenge the status quo that is continually reinforced by the hegemonic mass media. This point of view is notably absent from the interventionist approach, which emphasizes the individual instead of the systemic. Culturalists conceptualize media and its messages as a "site of struggle" in which audiences can actively resist dominant or intended meanings. Instead of viewing media as only having negative effects on passive viewers, the cultural studies framework suggests that viewers have agency and are not as vulnerable as the interventionist framework suggests. In addition, the cultural studies framework acknowledges that media can also be a source of positive pleasure for viewers.

Recurring Debates

According to Renee Hobbs (1998), there are seven recurring points of contention within the media literacy community. These seven debates greatly impact how media literacy is conceived and implemented in both the interventionist and cultural studies frameworks. Negotiating these debates can also have great impact on the success or failure of a media literacy initiative that includes partnerships. Of the seven debates, the following (slightly modified) questions or issues are the most relevant for our purposes: (a) Do people need to be protected and inoculated from the media? (b) Should there be a production element in a media literacy program or initiative? (c) Should ideology and/or political activism be incorporated in a media literacy program? And (d) should media literacy accept funding from corporate interests? A brief overview of these four areas of contention not only better prepare one for forging productive partnerships, but also illustrate that there are convergences and divergences within and between the interventionist and cultural studies frameworks that can allow ML activists, with seemingly oppositional stances, to partner productively with each other.

Protection and Inoculation

In terms of protection from the media, it seems clear from the review of the interventionist approach that it is in favor of a protectionist stance. That said, since both cultural studies and interventionist scholars feel that media literacy is necessary, it appears that both frameworks (not just the interventionist) believe that there are dangers that result from media exposure. Although the interventionist approach may use different methods and may be more straightforward about their protectionist stance, the cultural studies paradigm also strives to protect individuals from racist, sexist, homophobic, and consumerist messages.

Media Production

Some interventionist and cultural studies proponents support the incorporation of media production because it could act as a vehicle for acquiring a variety of technical and analytical skills, provide opportunities for audiences to create their own texts, and offer non-traditional learning opportunities through application rather than theory (Alvermann, 2004; Hobbs, 1998; Singer & Singer, 1998). Other interventionist and cultural studies scholars have warned that a media production component may undermine analysis and critical thinking by merely reproducing mainstream media (Buckingham, 1998; Lewis & Jhally, 1998; Masterman, 2001).

With the proliferation of digital and online interactive media, media consumers have increasingly become media producers and content creators. Consequently, it has become increasingly difficult to ignore this component of media culture and media literacy education (De Abreu, 2011).

Ideology and Activism

A majority of those situated in the cultural studies framework feel that if media work to further ideological agendas through encoded messages within content, it is impossible for media literacy to take an apolitical stance. For those that subscribe to this approach, critical thinking involves teaching individuals to analyze the content of the messages and understand who benefits (both financially and socially) from them. Not all media educators choose to include ideological critiques and political activism into media literacy curricula. After all, as Hobbs (1998) notes, "media literacy concepts and instructional practices are attractive to people with a wide spectrum of political beliefs" (23). Consequently, some media literacy activists working toward social justice with a liberal of left-leaning political orientation may at times find themselves allied with media literacy activists motivated by conservative religious beliefs around issues like the negative effects of media violence on children or the media's sexualization and exploitation of childhood.

Corporate Funding

The issue of whether or not to accept funding from corporate interests is among the most contentious. U.S. schools and non-profits are notorious for their lack of funding; consequently, they are often forced to rely on corporate interests to provide the financial support they so desperately need. Many corporations quickly realized the growing interest in media literacy and, in turn, made available materials for schools in need. These materials risk allowing corporations to co-opt media literacy efforts and transform the movement into a public relations opportunity rather than an opportunity for reflection and critique.[8] The broader rationale for refusing corporate funding is that capitalist messages can dilute the critical impetus of media literacy while the counter-argument is that a smartly designed media literacy program can put those materials to positive uses and even use them to critique the negative aspects of profit-driven media systems and consumer culture.

Media literacy initiatives situated in the interventionist framework may not be as invested in eliminating or combating corporate influence. Greater emphasis may be placed on acquiring whatever materials best protect students from what is perceived as negative media content. One exception in this regard may be interventionist scholars approach to anti-smoking or drinking campaigns. In this instance, accepting funds or materials from tobacco or alcoholic beverage companies may be seen as an overriding conflict of interest or as a counter-productive impediment to the abstinence message. Although not always the case, most cultural studies approach proponents (particularly those aligned with BCS) are vehemently against corporate involvement in media literacy initiatives. Many culturalists seek to mitigate social inequities and injustices by challenging corporate interests and profit motives that they see as seeking to preserve the status quo.

The Future of a Movement

Although by the end of the 1990s each state in the United States had adopted some element of media literacy into its educational curriculum, as Stephanie Flores-Khoulish observed in 2004 (citing David Considine), "like other social movements, media literacy [has been] primarily 'fed at the grass-roots level by classroom teachers, not by centralized bureaucracies'" (2). Almost a decade later, we can identify two distinct yet still emerging[9] media literacy-related social movements in the United States: an educational reform movement, which seeks to increase the inclusion of media literacy within the K–12 and college curricula; and a media reform movement, which focuses on changing media policies and regulations. The former movement is represented by the organizations comprised of a significant number of educators like the National Association for Media Literacy Education and the Action Coalition for Media Education, while the latter manifests itself most prominently through the National Conference on Media Reform (NCMR) organized by Free Press, a well-funded,[10] non-profit organization that includes "movement building" as one if its main goals, and describes its members as "activists, media makers, journalists, policymakers, technologists and artists." Although some might describe both movements as being dramatic or extreme, neither movement is calling for a revolutionary break but seeking to reform the existing systems largely from within.

Even though both movements can still be categorized as emerging, each has become increasingly formalized and bureaucratized either through increased incorporation into school curricula and state standards, or through the well-funded organizations like the Free Press and its high-profile conferences. It remains to be seen what the effects of increased formal organization will be on these movements, but historically there have been costs and benefits. Formal and bureaucratic organizations tend to survive longer, but these same structures can lead to an individual interest in maintaining the status quo, "even if this means ignoring or suppressing the demands of the organization's rank and file" (Goodwin & Jasper, 2009, 192). Needless to say, this brief overview cannot do justice to any single tradition or approach or to the growing body of scholarship devoted to media literacy. Yet we hope that this essay provides a useful framework for negotiating different viewpoints and building partnerships among the "rank and file" within other disciplines, institutions, organizations, and community groups.

Notes

1. Given that media are routinely assigned significant blame for the negative things in society and given little credit for the positive (with the possible exception of social media), it is understandable why media literacy activists and educators might fight back by metaphorically killing or literally destroying their televisions. And, of course, many of the same media literacy activists who say they want to kill their televisions produce their own media, including public access television programs. The underlying argument is not the reductive media determinism implied in killing your TV but an appeal to use television differently by changing its role in society, modifying its content, and reforming its profit-driven and commercial economic model.
2. In fact, Hobbs's (1998) "great debates" essay includes a similar anecdote about a meeting she attended in 1995, which points to the continued commonality of this experience for anyone who has tried to build media literacy partnerships and coalitions.
3. Within our own institutional context of a Department of Media Studies and Communication composed of faculty trained in the humanities, arts, and social sciences, and housed in a College of Arts and Sciences, we have been involved to various degrees and with varying degrees of success with the following media literacy initiatives:

    1) Teaching media studies courses across the curriculum
    2) Offering summer media literacy courses and media literacy camps for middle school and high school students
    3) Facilitating workshops for community organizers and media literacy activists
    4) Offering media literacy courses and training for K–12 teachers
    5) Offering out-of-school time programs at area schools
    6) Partnering with area K–12 schools on developing media literacy curricula
    7) Partnering with community groups and organizations on grant applications
    8) Collaborating with other disciplines and departments at our university, including Education, Health Sciences and Biology on media literacy initiatives and grant proposals
    9) Participating in leading media education and media studies organizations like the Action Coalition for Media Education, the National Association for Media Literacy Education, the Society for Cinema and Media Studies, and the National Communication Association
    10) Publishing and presenting at national conferences on media and media literacy

4. This is not to suggest that antagonism and contentiousness cannot be deployed as strategies to achieve collective goals. For social movement theorists, this approach is exemplified by Chantal Mouffe's (1999) model of "agonistic pluralism" in opposition to Jürgen Habermas's (1994) "deliberative democracy."
5. The stress on "good taste" in the inoculative approach served as a catalyst for the development of the media as popular arts approach during the 1960s and 1970s, including film studies, which does not assume that individuals need to be protected from the negative effects of media (Considine, 2002; Masterman, 2001).
6. Both BCS and media literacy could qualify as new social movements (Staggenborg, 2011) because of their significant focus on mitigating social injustices and combating cultural inequities across boundaries of class, race, gender, and sexuality through education.

7. Jenkins's (2006) book, *Convergence Culture,* is widely cited within media literacy scholarship and is becoming increasingly influential within the media literacy movement. It is important to note in this context that regardless of whether one takes a pessimistic and negative (e.g. Adorno and Horkheimer) or optimistic and positive (e.g. John Fiske and Henry Jenkins) approach to media culture, subversive readings are only possible if an alternative image exists in an interpreter's head that she can call up at a given historical moment. In addition, if this theory of media meaning is correct, then messages could also be interpreted or negotiated in both progressive and regressive ways.

8. The National Association for Media Literacy Education (NAMLE) (co-founded by Renee Hobbs as the Alliance for a Media Literate America) accepts corporate funding. The Action Coalition for Media Education was founded as a direct response to a faction of the media literacy community that was unhappy with NAMLE's acceptance of corporate materials. According to Jeff Share (2008), "Although many media educators are members of both organizations, personal differences between some of the leaders have hindered collaboration. Media education in the U.S. is having more success on smaller levels by hard-working individuals and small organizations" (38).

9. Jeff Goodwin and James M. Jasper (2009) define a social movement as "a collective, organized, sustained, and noninstitutional challenge to authorities, power holders, or cultural beliefs and practices" (4). On the different stages or life cycles of social movements, see Staggenborg (2011).

10. All social movements need resources to sustain themselves. Within the media literacy education movement, Renee Hobbs, Patricia Aufderheide, and Henry Jenkins have received significant funding from the MacArthur Foundation for media literacy education research initiatives.

References

Adorno, T., & Horkheimer, M. (2000). The culture industry: Enlightenment as mass deception. In J.B. Schor & D.B. Holt (Eds.), *The consumer society reader* (pp. 3–19). New York: New Press.

Alvermann, D.E. (2004). Media, information communication technologies, and youth literacies: A cultural studies perspective. *American Behavioral Scientist, 48,* 78–83.

Aufderheide, P. (2001). Media literacy: From a report on the National Leadership Conference on Media Literacy. In R.W. Kubey (Ed.), *Media literacy in the information age: Current perspectives* (pp. 79–88). New Brunswick, NJ: Transaction.

Buckingham, D. (1998). Media education in the UK: Moving beyond protectionism. *Journal of Communication, 48*(1), 33–43.

Considine, D. M. (2002). Media literacy: National developments and international origins. *Journal of Popular Film & Television, 30*(1), 7–15.

Croteau, D., & Hoynes, W. (2003). *Media and Society.* Thousand Oaks, CA: Sage.

De Abreu, B.S. (2011). *Media literacy, social networking, and the Web 2.0 environment for the K–12 educator.* New York: Peter Lang.

Flores-Koulish, S.A. (2004). *Teacher education for critical consumption of mass media and popular culture.* New York: RoutledgeFalmer.

Goodwin, J., & Jasper, J.M. (2009). *The social movements reader: Cases and concepts.* Chichester, UK: Wiley-Blackwell.

Habermas, J. (1994). Three normative models of democracy. *Constellations 1*(1), 1–10.

Hall, S. (1999). Encoding/decoding. In P. Marris and S. Thornham (Eds.), *Media studies* (pp. 41–49). Edinburgh, UK: Edinburgh University Press.

Hobbs, R. (1998). The seven great debates in the media literacy movement. *Journal of Communication, 48*(1), 16–32.

Jenkins, H. (2006). *Convergence culture: Where old and new media collide.* New York: New York University Press.

Lewis, J., & Jhally, S. (1998). The struggle over media literacy. *Journal of Communication, 48*(1), 109–120.

McLuhan, M. (1964). *Understanding media: The extensions of man.* Cambridge, MA: MIT Press.

Masterman, L. (2001). A rationale for media education. In R.W. Kubey (Ed.), *Media literacy in the information age: Current perspectives* (pp. 15–68). New Brunswick, NJ: Transaction.

Mouffe, C. (1999). Deliberative democracy or agonistic pluralism? *Social Research, 66*(3), 745–758.

Piette, J. & Giroux, L. (2001). The theoretical foundations of media education programs. In R.W. Kubey (Ed.), *Media literacy in the information age: Current perspectives* (pp. 89–134). New Brunswick, NJ: Transaction.

Potter, W.J. (2004). Argument for the need for a cognitive theory of media literacy. *American Behavioral Scientist, 48*, 238–247.

Share, J. (2008). *Media literacy is elementary: Teaching youth to critically read and create media.* New York: Peter Lang.

Sholle, D., & Denski, S. (1995). Critical media literacy: Reading, remapping, rewriting. In P. McLaren, R. Hammer, D. Sholle, & S. Reilly (Eds.), *Rethinking media literacy: A critical pedagogy of representation.* New York: Peter Lang.

Singer, D.G., & Singer, J.L. (1998). Developing critical viewing skills and media literacy in children. *The annals of the American Academy of Political and Social Science, 557*, 164–180.

Staggenborg, S. (2011). *Social movements.* New York: Oxford University Press.

18

SHRINKING THE DIVIDE

Solving Social Inequalities through Media Literacy Education

Nick Pernisco

A presidential election year is an excellent time to survey the social inequalities in America that are a direct result of the digital divide. The differences between those who understand how to access, filter, interpret, and propagate ideas and those who do not becomes instantly apparent when the country is deciding on the next president. While the candidates are running to represent all citizens in the country, most people never have a one-on-one discussion with them. Instead, potential voters receive information through the media—the commercials, news reports, and online postings that are meant to substitute for human-to-human contact. Previous research has shown that those who understand and know how to use the media messages disseminated during an election are in the best position to contribute to the national debate and ultimately benefit in society (Kahne, Lee, & Feezell, 2012). Conversely, those who experience a disconnect with the mainstream dialogue, whether due to age limitations, membership in an underrepresented ethnic or racial group, low income level, disability, or language barrier, are most disengaged.

During recent elections it became clear that candidates have embraced social media as the primary way of connecting with potential voters (Hendricks & Denton, 2011). Not only does social media allow candidates and their supporters to send direct messages to the public without the filtering that occurs with publicity in newspapers and on television, but it also helps create a symbiotic relationship between candidates and the voters who support them. This is evidenced by the fact that nearly every candidate running in recent national and state-wide elections uses *Twitter* to send short messages to supporters, *YouTube* to disseminate video messages on an ongoing basis, and *Facebook* to engage in more lengthy discussions of current issues with constituents. In addition to having great control over how messages are propagated, social media also brings many cost advantages, allowing candidates to save money on television and print ads by using these free services. However, this heavy reliance on social media comes at a cost for most potential voters.

While social media has become the new standard method of direct communication between candidates and voters, it is also true that traditional media still plays a large part in helping candidates connect with a broader audience. However, television and print news outlets often repeat or otherwise retransmit news and information that first appeared in social media. Members of the television and print news audience who do not use social media are receiving second hand accounts of information first released elsewhere. In addition, because those viewers are receiving a one-way communication through the television or in a newspaper, they in no way helped shape the original message, as did perhaps someone who tweeted a direct message to the candidate with their thoughts or opinions on an issue. And since social media has become not only a method of learning about news but also of making news, those who have designated themselves only as receivers of information are often left out of the process of helping to shape policy in their communities and nationwide.

In essence, the ability to understand and use social media has become a critical factor for participation in the democratic process in America. But in order to understand and use social media, people must first have access to this online-only forum. We tend to think of the United States as a place where everybody has or should have regular access to the Internet, and so politicians, companies, and governments act in ways consistent with this notion being true. This is called the Ubiquity Myth: the common notion that 100% of Americans (or very close to 100%) have regular access to the Internet, while the real percentage is actually around 85% (Pernisco, 2011). This means that up to 15% of Americans, approximately 46 million people, lack regular Internet access (Horrigan, 2010; NCTA, 2011; International Telecommunication Union, 2011). Many of the people in this group are senior citizens, and about 17 million are people living under the poverty line. It is no wonder then that those people lacking regular Internet access and therefore access to social media are among the most disengaged of all potential voters. This disparity also keeps this group of people out of the mainstream of American culture, which carries many of its own problems.

In today's ever-increasingly Internet-connected world and with the relatively low cost of promoting a message through social media compared to traditional media, it is no wonder that all types of organizations are choosing to connect with stakeholders through new media outlets like *Facebook* and *Twitter* (Tomlin, 2011). Companies connect with customers, engaging in a mutually beneficial interaction in which customers receive news about new products and special offers, and companies receive important feedback and new ideas for products from customers. While this system seems to work well for those with regular Internet access and the means to understand the process, those without regular Internet access are falling victim to a system that increasingly favors this new form of communication. For companies that aim to reach a broad audience, it makes sense; as long as you are reaching 85% of Americans with your online message, you need not worry about the 15% of Americans you fail to reach, since reaching those other people will raise promotion costs exponentially due to the high cost of promotion through traditional media. For companies, the "other 15%" may include people who may not be able to afford or even care about the products and services anyway (Sinclair, 2009). This is why companies who promote their products online tend to skew towards a middle-income or higher audience. Those without regular Internet access learn about new products or special offers from traditional media sources such as local newspapers, radio, and broadcast television. These "offline" companies often aim to reach those with lower incomes, so using the Internet to reach a broader audience is a waste of resources. In business, this has created a two-tier system in which the 85% of consumers with regular Internet access are mostly served by a completely different group of companies than those without regular Internet access. Clearly, this aspect of the digital divide amounts to segregation in which those without regular Internet access use products and services often of superior quality than those targeted to people without regular Internet access.

Though a large percentage of the population does not have regular access to the Internet at home or work, a new trend in mobile technology is helping to bridge this divide, especially among the younger generations. Smart phones— mobile phones with high-speed access to the Internet and social media—have emerged as a potential game changer in the digital divide (Arthur, 2011). A 2009 study showed that 27% of teens used mobile phones to access the Internet, but the percentage rose to 41% for teens living in low-income homes (Brown, Campbell, & Ling, 2011). Due to its relatively low cost—one company in Los Angeles advertises unlimited phone service, texting, and Internet access for $40 per month—the technology is gaining momentum as a replacement for more costly home phone and Internet services (MetroPCS, 2011). In fact, smartphones with Internet access are quickly replacing desktop and laptop computers, due to their ability to hold data, run programs, and stay organized (Arthur, 2011). Those who have the capability to access the Internet on the small screen are more attuned to mainstream ideas and trends, which helps to narrow the digital gap that otherwise exists in poorer communities, especially among teens. The advances made possible by smartphones are promising; however, there is more that must be done to reach adoption rates of Internet services that will make a major difference to underrepresented communities.

Access to the Internet and social media alone is not enough to close the digital divide in America. A critical piece of this puzzle is ensuring that people understand the messages they are receiving. Just as attempting to read a book in a foreign language is a useless endeavor unless the reader understands the language and cultural underpinnings, attempting to understand the messages on the Internet and in social media without essential analysis skills is equally useless. Rather than letting the messages found online enter our consciousness without filtering, we should engage with these messages and think critically about their meaning. One of the basic critical thinking skills necessary for any digital citizen is understanding the concept of authorship. Experienced internet users realize that to fully understand a message, whether from a static website, from the crowd-sourced Wikipedia, or from social media like *Twitter*, appreciating the role of the message's author is critical to understanding the message itself. In contrast to traditional media, in which the author of a given work is usually known and usually clearly stated, the Internet makes it easy to obscure the original author, and therefore his/her intent with the work. The implication is that by understanding the author of a *Twitter* post or *Wikipedia* page, we can determine the credibility of that post or page and detect any biases or falsities, and then account for that when deciding to accept or reject a given message. Another aspect of online authorship is that any Internet user is also a potential author. There certainly is power in knowing that, as an Internet user, anyone can be a message consumer as well as a message creator. This gives Internet users the power to influence others and direct the dialogue on any topic.

Social media has been hailed as a way to democratize online information by allowing anyone with Internet access to both receive and disseminate messages. Although this aim is yet to be fully realized, as participation on websites like *Twitter* and *Facebook* increases, and as more people use these sites to learn about the world and share their own perspectives, a greater sense of social unity arises, the digital divide shrinks, and social underclasses rise out of poverty (Pernisco, 2011). There is no clearer case in which this fact has been illustrated than in the Middle East uprisings called the Arab Spring, which began in December 2010 and with outcomes that still reverberate globally today. While many of the protests during the uprising were censored in local state-run media outlets, protesters used *Twitter* and *Facebook* through mobile devices to rally the populous and organize protests (Huang, 2011). The use of social media during this time helped unite long-oppressed groups to fight against their oppressors. And while some governments moved to block access to the Internet within its borders, the digital organizing had already worked to connect people in person, which proves that online experiences can translate into real world outcomes.

While having access to the Internet and having the skills to analyze the messages found there are important steps towards closing the digital divide, access and rudimentary analysis alone are meaningless unless they are accompanied by broad media literacy education. After accessing and analyzing information, people need to evaluate the meaning of the information and have the ability to put it into context. This exercise of analyzing and then evaluating information is incredibly challenging, especially if the audience does not realize that the information they receive is often bias and incomplete. When our main information sources were television and newspapers, it was difficult, but not impossible, to discover the origin of a particular message; a movement, trend, or phrase could more easily be reattributed to its original author than in today's complex media landscape. Thanks to social media's key characteristic of openness, anyone can share or retweet any bit of information, making it difficult to find the origins of any given idea. This is why it is more difficult than ever to discover the origins (and therefore the intent and ultimate meaning) of movements like the Arab Spring or Occupy Wall Street (Kanalley, 2011). On a smaller scale, the average social media user could benefit from discovering the origins of a product's popularity or a popular criticism about a politician. Media literacy helps us understand that, although it may be difficult to fully understand a message's intent, knowing that we should at least be thinking critically about all messages will make us better consumers of information.

As the digital divide shrinks, more people will have access to information in social media, more people will use media literacy to help them analyze and evaluate that information, and eventually they will contribute their own ideas and help shape the discourse about any topic. Contributing feedback about information found online empowers people to shape the direction of policy, improve upon products and services, and feel more involved in mainstream society. Compared to the era before the Internet was popular with consumers, today's user of social media is viewed as highly valuable since that person has the power to start a new trend or movement in society. This happens on a large scale with political movements like Occupy Wall Street, with the help of *YouTube* and *Facebook* to spread ideology and organize supporters, and on a small scale with patrons of an ice cream store, influencing new flavor offerings by using *Yelp* and *Twitter* to communicate with the store owner and other customers. Ultimately, those who are connected to and understand the power of online media contribute to the conversation and have the power to influence changes, while those who are left out have little input into the changes in their world.

Twenty-first-century citizenship means using Internet information in every facet of life. The twenty-first-century citizen knows how to access information, understands its meaning and can put it into context, and can contribute new information for the benefit of everyone. The twenty-first-century citizen also knows how to use information to contribute to new ideas that impact society at every level. Online media and information relies on its diversity of voices and points of view to be valuable, and this cannot be fully achieved until everyone is online and contributing. This is the reason why it is so important to close the digital divide. In the United States, the digital divide is still an issue, with many groups in society underrepresented due to low income or other factors that prevent ubiquity of Internet access. However, the digital divide is shrinking in the United States, thanks to the rise of smart phones combined with low cost Internet access plans. As access to the Internet increases, it will be critical to ensure these new users understand how to use the Internet and social media in order to have a positive impact on their world.

References

Arthur, C. (2011). *How the smartphone is killing the PC.* Retrieved from http://www.guardian. co.uk/technology/2011/jun/05/smartphones-killing-pc.

Brown, K., Campbell, S., & Ling, R. (2011, March). Mobile phones bridging the digital divide for teens in the US? *Future Internet, 3*(2), 144–158.

Hendricks, J.A., & Denton, J. (2011). *Communicator-in-chief: How Barack Obama used new media technology to win the white house.* Plymouth: Lexington Books.

Horrigan, J. (2010). *Broadband adoption and use in America: Results from an FCC survey.* Federal Communications Commission. Retrieved from www.fcc.gov/DiversityFAC/032410/ consumer-survey-horrigan.pdf.

Huang, C. (2011). *Facebook and Twitter key to Arab Spring uprisings: Report.* Retrieved from http://www.thenational.ae/news/uae-news/facebook-and-twitter-key-to-arab-spring-uprisings-report.

International Telecommunication Union (2011, September 14). *Internet users per 100 inhabitants.* Retrieved from http://www.itu.int.

Kahne, J., Lee, N., & Feezell, J. (2012). Digital media literacy education and online civic and political participation. *International Journal of Communication, 6,* 1–24.

Kanalley, C. (2011, October 6). *Occupy Wall Street: Social media's role in social change.* Retrieved from http://www.huffingtonpost.com/2011/10/06/occupy-wall-street-social-media_n_999178.html.

MetroPCS (2011, August 9). *MetroPCS to launch Samsung admire for back to school.* Retrieved from http://www.prnewswire.com/news-releases/metropcs-to-launch-samsung-admire-for-back-to-school-127293268.html.

NCTA (2011, September 26). Industry data. National Cable & Telecommunications Association. Retrieved from http://www.ncta.com/Statistics.aspx

Pernisco, N. (2011, November 10). *The ubiquity myth.* Retrieved from http://understandmedia. com/journals-a-publications/44-scholarly-articles/141-the-ubiquity-myth.

Sinclair, J. (2009). Minorities, media, marketing and marginalization. *Global Media and Communication, 5*(2), 177–196.

Tomlin, G. (2011, February 20). *Companies connect with customers through social media.* Retrieved from http://www.galesburg.com/news/business/x253215290/Companies-connect-with-customers-through-social-media.

19

GAME-BASED CIVIC LEARNING IN PUBLIC PARTICIPATION PROCESSES

Eric Gordon and Steven Schirra

In the early 2000s, newspapers around the world eagerly covered the newest on-line trend in online philanthropy, said to revolutionize the way people would engage with civic issues. As one article reported:

> With a click of her mouse, Ms. Anderson donates food to starving people preserves rainforest, provides nursing care to children with AIDS and vita-mins to other needs victims. . . . Not bad for only a few minutes' work over coffee. (Ryan, 2001, E13)

Civic engagement at the click of a mouse is what Indiana-based programmer John Breen envisioned in 1999 when he created *TheHungerSite.com*, an online destination that would fuel this "click-to-donate" craze. Its participation me-chanic proved popular: Once each day, users could visit the site, click a "Donate Free Food" button, and, through corporate sponsors, provide a small donation to the United Nations World Food Programme.

Just six months after its May 1999 launch, the site logged two million clicks per week with total donations soaring to nearly $500,000 (Lewin, 2000). *The Hunger Site* became so popular that Breen, unable to keep up with its day-to-day opera-tions, sold the project to a third party. With the success of his first project behind him, Breen began working on something new. In 2007 he made more headlines after transforming a simple vocabulary-building quiz into another philanthropic goldmine—this time tackling the question: *How can we make charity more like a game?* His idea addressed a longstanding call from nonprofits to get youth more interested in civic issues through digital media, and, in particular, video games. Considering how engaged youth were with popular gaming consoles, he set out to make something that could "take a little sliver of that time and do something really beneficial with it" (Fallon, 2000, 4; Goodman, 2010).

Breen's new creation, *FreeRice.com*, provides ten grains of rice to countries with widespread starvation for each word visitors can match correctly to its definition. More popular than The Hunger Site, Free Rice generates the clicks to provide the World Food Programme with 315 million grains of rice per week—enough to feed 17,500 people. (Burak, 2011). The popular media hailed Free Rice as a success in turning players' attention away from "wasting time on computer solitaire," and toward a game "with redeeming social value" (Puente, 2008, 1D).

While *Free Rice* was a clear fundraising success, detractors complained that the game was no more than an act of *slacktivism*—described as "a pejorative portmanteau of *slacker* and *activism* used to describe pain-free do-goodery that has zero or minimal impact on the world but does give participants a deliciously self-righteous tingle" (Tom, 2009, 7). Creating an engaging word-matching game in the name of a social cause can indeed produce web traffic and generate clicks, but it does little to help players learn about the complex issue of hunger. One could easily play the game for hours and not once think critically about the issue of world hunger (in fact, one can download a "Free Rice Bot" that automates the entire gameplay process—no thought required).

Much of the attention given to civic games in the popular media has focused on them providing easy solutions to complex problems, and for some, these solutions seem a little *too easy*. But here we argue that games can produce meaningful civic learning, far beyond slacktivism. Games can create "learning that develops the skills, knowledge, and dispositions for contributing to civic life" (Ruiz, Stokes, & Watson, 2012, para. 9), and they can effectively create a context for learning within informal and public environments that are engaging, productive and conducive to subsequent learning.[1] We focus specifically on the context of public participation in urban planning where there is considerable need for quality input and increased engagement. We argue that games can provide the context to understand how civic processes are constructed so that players can act effectively within them.

The Problem of Participation

Forget my question. Never mind. I wouldn't believe the answer anyway.[2]

This is the opening comment from the floor at a public meeting about a proposed landfill in Bartlesville, Oklahoma—and it is an all too common refrain, even if not always so strikingly articulated, about civic participation. Participation can appear futile when it involves faceless bureaucracies and antiquated systems, and yet, for much of American history, the public meeting has been its most recognizable form (Sinclair, 1977). Showing up at a school gymnasium or a church recreation room to discuss local issues is too often seen as the most effective means of participating in civic life, and this is true despite rather compelling evidence that participants in these meetings tend to have very little confidence in their impact on policy outcomes.[3]

Since the Administrative Procedures Act (APA) of 1946, there has been a mandate for public participation in the decisions made by federal agencies. The APA was a product of the Great Depression, designed to mitigate the dangers of central planning in an expanding government. Public involvement was a necessary step in assuring proper regulation. Unfortunately, most of the public's involvement in real decision-making processes was nominal, at best, and there remained grave inequalities in the demographics of those choosing to get involved.

The Economic Opportunity Act of 1964 was passed partially in response to these inequalities as part of President Lyndon B. Johnson's "War on Poverty." One of its goals was to encourage outreach to underrepresented communities in the public decision-making process. It required public agencies to generate "maximum feasible participation" in planning decisions. This essentially put the onus on public officials to do outreach to low-income communities and to urge them to participate. However, the compulsory nature of public participation did not result in much creativity of form: "Maximum feasible participation" has, by and large, translated to "minimal possible effort." Many public officials continue to simply call a meeting, relegating the public process to whoever happens to show up.

While the public meeting is the lowest hanging fruit for public officials, it is often too high for participants. For many people, it is simply unrealistic to head downtown at 6 p.m. for a community meeting due to childcare concerns, work demands, or, more simply, fatigue. This is not to mention that for people to enter into a discussion with public officials and community activists requires a high level of confidence and expertise. What's more, face-to-face group conversations are affected by power differentials that cut across lines of race, class, and gender. Despite best intentions, not everyone can speak freely and openly.[4]

The Internet is opening up new avenues for participation, through online forums, civic services, communication channels to politicians, and just generally, access to information and other people. For example, the *Pew Internet and American Life Project* conducted a 2009 survey that demonstrated nearly 37% of Internet users in the United States aged 18 to 29 use blogs or social networking services (SNS) as a venue for political and/or civic involvement (Smith et al,. 2009). These same people are the least likely to attend town hall meetings or to join the Rotary Club, but they are increasingly likely to friend a politician on *Facebook* or to donate money to a charitable organization online.

Consequently, there has been a groundswell of effort on the part of public officials and planners to harness the Internet to expand the reach of civic processes.[5] From the large-scale procedures designed by organizations like America Speaks that successfully connected millions of people to the discussion of "Ground Zero" in New York, to the efforts of the 2008 Obama campaign that motivated

13 million people to provide their email addresses, new tools and new approaches are being considered in the re-imagining of the public participation process.

Digital tools are too often seen as a way of harnessing the scale of participation, but not necessarily a way of establishing contexts for learning. Many digital tools designed for civic participation seek to capture momentary attention measured in clicks. This is also true for gamified digital systems like *Free Rice*. But games, properly understood, by virtue of their structure, can create civic engagement that moves beyond slacktivism towards learning and situated actions.

A Playful Solution

As early as the 1960s, there are reports of fascinating, yet largely forgotten, efforts to experiment with game-based civic learning. The goal was not necessarily to expand participation, but to deepen it. A 1968 *Architectural Forum* article touted the possibilities of games for this purpose: "A game, which reduces the world to a comprehensible whole, and gives each player the same frame of reference, can go a long way toward giving him an understanding of his own concerns in rela-tion to the total picture" (Berkeley, 1968, 8). There were multiple examples of games, typically paper-based, which were employed within community meetings to address already apparent concerns about the inflexible form of public partici-pation. Simulation games such as *Neighborhood* and *Metropolis* let players consider the intricacies of land-use planning through role-play and problem-solving. In *Metropolis*, developed at Michigan State University and introduced in 1964, play-ers assumed the roles of administrator, politician and speculator, and were asked to make decisions about their community. A primary goal of the game was to "reduce the gap between 'plan-makers' and 'decision-makers' by letting decision-makers see the implications of 'alternative decisions chains'" (Berkeley, 1968, 9). Put another way, the aim was to transform the community meeting from a site of information download and exchange to a site for learning. Learning about unique perspectives and trade-offs in planning was conceived within these projects as a precursor to meaningful participation.

A half-decade after *Metropolis*, new efforts are underway to intervene in the routinized process of a town-hall meeting. In 2010, the game *Participatory Chi-natown* (designed by the authors of this chapter) similarly sought to do just that. Much like *Neighborhood* and *Metropolis*, *Participatory Chinatown* facilitated learning about trade-offs and possible futures in a community master planning process through perspective taking, cooperation, and competition (Gordon & Schirra, 2011). Using laptops, players guided characters through a multiplayer, virtual construction of Chinatown—all while physically sitting next to other players in a large community room. The game combined the mechanics of a scavenger hunt and card game and created an environment where players were competing against—and collaborating with—people in the same room to metaphorically represent the decision-making of the characters on matters such as jobs, hous-ing, and social space. The game was not intended to teach civics by simulating a meeting—the game was the meeting itself. Actions people took within the game were themselves civic actions, as they were shared with planners and informed the 2010 master plan of Chinatown.

One defining feature of a game, as Suits (1990) has suggested, is a series of "unnecessary obstacles" (41).[6] In baseball, for instance, it would be a lot easier to run the bases if one didn't have to hit the ball first. The elaborate set of rules in baseball is an obstacle that players impose upon themselves in order to have a meaningful context for competition and interaction. Likewise, in games played within a public meeting, players volunteer to interact with the *unnecessary* obstacles of the game so that they can be guided through the *necessary* obstacles of the meeting. When games are designed into civic processes, the player is asked to, quite literally, play with these obstacles. That is, players must think about the process of civic engagement and the various obstacles one has to overcome in order to participate.

Urban planning, neighborhood politics, national elections: These are all rule-based systems in which participation requires a relatively sophisticated understanding of the systems' function. It is rare, however, that a citizen is able to articulate how the system works and how they fit into its complex set of rules. As game designer and theorist Eric Zimmerman (2008) notes, "Being able to successfully understand, navigate, modify, and design systems will become more and more inextricably linked with how we learn, work, play, and live as engaged world citizens" (25). Playing a game puts the player into a system, forces him or her to understand the system in order to participate, and, if well designed, encourages systems thinking. While other kinds of online tools, such as discussion forums and SNS, require that users accommodate certain rules and structures, well-designed games uniquely prioritize systems and engage players in a negotiation of their boundaries. When games are applied to civic matters, they engage people by redirecting their focus from a specific issue to learning about the wider process that informs that issue. All games are about systems; games designed for civic learning are about the formal and informal systems that comprise civic life.

We are not advocating for the so-called "gamification" of civic life. Instead, we are proposing that games be considered a productive method for fostering civic learning, both within formal and informal situations. Whether trying to increase public participation in urban planning or trying to create new contexts for youth to creatively explore solutions to complex social problems, games can provide a productive framework for exploring and playing with the systems and rules of civic life. Beyond slacktivism or gamification, game-based learning is an approach to civic engagement that marries the complexity of "civic systems" with the opportunities of playful media interactions.

Notes

1. This is similar to the concept of community efficacy. For a good discussion of this, see R. Niemi and C. Chapman (1998), *The civic development of 9th- through 12th-grade students in the United States.* Washington, DC: National Center for Education Statistics. And

for more on social trust, see R. Putnam (2000), *Bowling alone* (New York: Touchstone Books).
2. Quoted in K.A. McComas (2003), Trivial pursuits: Participant views of public meetings. *Journal of Public Relations Research, 15*(2), 91–115.
3. This has been called the "paradox of participation." See P.F. Whiteley (1995) Rational choice and political participation: Evaluating the debate, Political Research Quarterly, *48*(1), 211–233.
4. There is considerable evidence that points to the positive correlation between participant confidence and quality deliberation. See S.D. Brody, D.R. Godschalk, & R.J. Burby (2003), Mandating citizen participation in plan making: Six strategic planning choices. *Journal of the American Planning Association, 69*(3), 245–264; and B. Manin (1987), On legitimacy and political deliberation. *Political Theory, 15*(3), 338–368.
5. The scope of this work on the federal level is nicely described in this report. See C. Lukensmeyer, J. Goldman, & S. Stern (2011), Assessing public participation in an open government era. IBM Center for the Business of Government. Available at http://www.businessofgovernment.org/report/assessing-public-participation-open-government-era.
6. Preceding Suits, Clark C. Abt described games as "an activity among two or more independent decision-makers seeking to achieve their objectives in some limiting context" (6). See C.C. Abt (1970), *Serious games: The art and science of games that simulate life*. New York: Viking.

References

Berkeley, E. (1968). The new gamesmanship. *Architectural Forum, 129*(5), 58–63.
Burak, A. (2011, August 9). What games have changed. *Kotaku*. Retrieved from http://kotaku.com/5829045/what-games-have-changed.
Fallon, D. (2000, August 5). Touched by the Net. *Sydney Morning Herald*, 4.
Goodman, M. (2010, July 11). Gaming Tree. *Ad Week*.
Gordon, E., & Schirra, S. (2011, June). Playing with empathy: digital role-playing games in public meetings. In *Proceedings of the 5th International Conference on Communities and Technologies* (pp. 179–185). New York: ACM.
Lewin, T. (2000, December 11). In a charitable mood? Just pick, then click. *The New York Times*, A18.
Puente, M. (2008, January 24). Learn to fight hunger, kill time all at once. *USA Today*, 1D.
Ruiz, S., Stokes, B., & Watson, J. (2012). The civic tripod for mobile and games: Activism, art and learning. *Internal Journal of Media and Learning*. Retrieved from http://civictripod.com/overview/reframing-learning-and-mobile.
Ryan, P. (2001, March 30). Charity comes to your PC. *Globe and Mail*, E13.
Sinclair, M. (1977). The public hearing as a participatory device: Evaluation of the IJC Experience. In Sewell, W.R.D., & Coppock, J.T. (Eds.), *Public Participation in Planning* (pp. 105–122). London: Wiley.
Smith, A., Schlozman, K.L., Verba, S., & Brady, H. (2009). *The Internet and civic engagement*. Pew Internet and American Life Project. Retrieved from http://www.pewinternet.org/Reports/2009/15--The-Internet-and-Civic-Engagement.aspx.
Suits, B. (1990). *Grasshopper: Games, life and utopia*. Boston: David R. Godine.
Tom, E. (2009, October 10). Slack, mouse-minded activism or realistic political action. *Weekend Australian*, 7.
Zimmerman, E. (2008). Gaming literacy: Game design as a model for literacy in the twenty-first century. In Perron, B., & Wolf, M. (Eds.), *The Video Game Theory Reader 2* (pp. 23–31). New York: Routledge.

PART VI
POLICY AND DIGITAL CITIZENSHIP

Creating media literacy policy has become an important aspect of the growth of learning in developing curriculums nationally and internationally. Along with policy has been the increased discussion on digital citizenship, Internet safety, cyberbullying, and cybersecurity, as they have become increasingly important topics both in and out of schools. In this section, we provide a voice for people working within policy arenas, and studying policy, to contribute their ideas and establish where and why media literacy education is most needed in these discussions. We read about the struggles of the European Commission to find common ground in the definition, measurement, and evaluation of media literacy across countries in the Eurozone. We explore the concept of media literacy and digital citizenship as tools to combat cyber bullying, and issues of Internet security. As inappropriate content is made more and more available with less and less filters, how we teach young people about their information habits can go a long ways toward the culture of youth and protection online. A chapter on New York City schools and their embrace of new literacies is detailed with an eye towards developing more inclusive standards and policies to reflect some of the vibrant work being done in the public school systems. Finally, a deep exploration of U.S. educational policy and the common core are conducted to show how media literacy can push effective educational measures forward to ensure Internet safety for all youth in the curriculum of the K–12 schools.

20

ON THE DIFFICULTIES OF PROMOTING MEDIA LITERACY

Sonia Livingstone and Yin-Han Wang

Introduction

All spheres of modern life—work, education, civic participation, commerce, social relations, family, and leisure—rely increasingly on an infrastructure of media,
communication, and information technologies and services. This infrastructure is
complex and opaque, embedding everyday interpersonal interaction within public and private sector provision on local, national, and global levels. People have
little choice about whether to use these media, taking their existence for granted.
While they are generally enthusiastic about the benefits, today's media environment is not one of their own making, having been largely shaped by commercial
and state interests of which users may be unaware and in relation to possibly-
misguided assumptions about those users' skills, desires, and understanding.

How effectively is the public engaging with the media and, through the media,
with the wider world? Do people know what they need to know, and what are
the costs of ignorance? Convergence and diversification in media and communications technologies and services simultaneously opens up new opportunities for
individuals and groups, yet also exposes people to new risks of exclusion, misuse,
and abuse. The pace of socio-technical change exacerbates the challenges they face:
Print literacy learned at school is relevant for a lifetime, but media education even
if obtained at school is outdated within a few years, leaving many adults unpre-
pared and without institutional support for gaining necessary media and digital literacies. We can no more send today's adults back to school than we can teach their
children what they will need to know for the media environment of tomorrow.

Knowing that other chapters in this volume will address the important issue of
children's media literacy, this chapter focuses on adults' media literacy, which we
regard as posing a particularly thorny problem. This is, first, because there is little

agreement over what adults should know about the media; second, because there is little agreement about the detriment associated with any lack of knowledge (should this centre on consumer detriment, or is there also citizen detriment at stake?); and third, because reaching the entire population in an inclusive, scalable, sustainable, and effective manner is a major policy challenge.

To explore this problem, we offer a cautionary tale from the United Kingdom. There was much optimism when the 2003 Communications Act gave the communications regulator, Ofcom (the Office of Communications), a duty to promote media literacy not just for children (usually the responsibility of education ministries and schools) but for the entire population. But reaching adults with media literacy programmes is a difficult and expensive task. In 2005 only 22% of adults had received formal lessons about digital technology and this proportion dropped to 19% in 2010 (Ofcom, 2006, 2011). To be sure, formal lessons may not be the best or only way, and many of Ofcom's initiatives took a different approach, including working with the media industry to develop mainstream programming and online resources, and working with the Government's Citizens Online centres and other bodies working locally. Yet a 2012 BBC Media Literacy report (BBC, 2012) still showed that 16% of adult Internet users (aged 15+) did not know where to start despite wanting to learn more about the Internet, and 21% felt that their Internet use was restricted due to lack of skills. More significantly, after a decade of diverse media literacy initiatives, a hard look at Ofcom's own evidence reveals only a modest benefit to the adult population.

What Happened in the United Kingdom?

In recognition of the rapidly changing media and information environment, and also as part of a wider turn to literacy policies (including political literacy, financial literacy and health literacy), Section 11 of the UK Communications Act 2003 accorded Ofcom an unprecedented duty in the history of media regulation to 'promote media literacy' among the general public (Livingstone, 2008). At the time, the United Kingdom was positioning its media and creative industries centre-stage in its plans for economic prosperity and growth, and pushing forward the national roll out of broadband so as to transfer of local and paper-based government services to become online only. Media literacy policy was incorporated into the then-New Labour government's *Digital Britain* agenda, along with the appointment of a Minister for Digital Inclusion, the development of schools' media education curriculum, and a National Plan for Digital Participation (BIS, 2010).

Initially, the requirement placed on Ofcom to promote media literacy was unclear, as the Act did not define media literacy. Adapting the widely-endorsed definition proposed by the U.S.'s 1992 National Leadership Conference on Media Literacy (that media literacy is the ability "to access, analyze, evaluate and communicate messages in a wide variety of forms" [Aufderheide, 1997]), Ofcom embarked on a decade of media literacy initiatives across the country, mobilising public and private sector (especially, media industries) as well as educators and civil society (Ofcom, n.d.). In parallel, the government sought to tackle the digital divide, later reframed as digital in/exclusion, by targeting resources (hardware, software, skills training and social support) on socially disadvantaged groups (cf. Go On Campaign,[1] Citizens Online[2]).

But despite the Act's ambitious goals, the result was a rather less ambitious approach that concentrated on fostering access to technology, functional skills, basic awareness-raising, and the provision of safety tools. Media literacy, it appeared, was valued for its potential in avoiding consumer detriment; this protectionist agenda obscured the idea of media literacy as empowering citizens seeking democratic engagement or social change for the public good. Moreover, Ofcom's evidence-based approach, generally a positive feature of its work, resulted in a highly pragmatic set of proxy measures being used to operationalize media literacy according to standards of rigour and representativeness supposedly required by the government and media industry. Little attention was paid to the claim advanced by civil society and the academy that media literacy is and should be far more than the sum of these simple measures.

Whether, ironically, Ofcom's reliance on simple measures meant that they underestimated improvement in the population's media literacy over the past decade, we cannot know. What is clear is that they found little evidence for improvement, despite a decade of concerted, if considerably underfunded effort. We illustrate this conclusion with selected findings from our recent report for the LSE Media Policy Project, where we reviewed Ofcom's successive annual media literacy reports (Ofcom, 2006, 2008, 2010, 2011, 2012, 2013), each based on nationally representative surveys of 1,800–3,300 interviews conducted at home with adults aged 16+ (Livingstone & Wang, 2013). Findings regarding access to new platforms, unsurprisingly, reveal increases in access to and use of digital technologies and platforms across the population, although social inequalities continue to mark

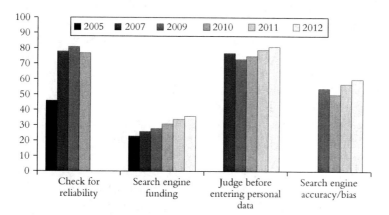

FIGURE 20.1 Understanding the Internet.

out digital inequalities in predictable ways. More interesting are findings for the more demanding dimensions of media literacy, too easily neglected by policy initiatives—namely, understanding and creating media.

People use the Internet for a variety of purposes and activities, and being able to evaluate whether a new website is reliable is an important ability that leads to being a critical user. Failure to do so may involve the risk of confusion, misinformation, or exploitation. Adults in the United Kingdom are learning, whether from direct use experience or from being guided, to perform some kind of check, such as looking for the padlock sign, to ensure the reliability of new websites. As Figure 20.1 shows, such checks rose sharply between 2005 and 2007, from 46% to 78% of adult users who reported doing so, but the rates of checking have not improved since 2007. By 2010 there were still one fifth of adults who did not perform any check when visiting a new website—particularly older people, and those from lower socioeconomic status (SES) groups.[3]

Similarly, awareness of how media are funded aids the critical evaluation of content. People generally know how broadcast media are financed—in 2012, three quarters of adults knew that programmes on BBC Television were funded mainly by license fee, and that programmes on commercial television were funded by advertising. But despite mass usage of the Internet for information and news, knowledge of its funding has risen only slowly, from 23% in 2005 to 31% in 2010. By 2012, still only 36% of adults knew that search engines were funded by advertising, and the young, the elderly, and women particularly lacked such knowledge.

More positive is the finding that many U.K. adult users have learned to make some form of judgment about a website before entering personal information, although the rise is slow (from 77% in 2007 to 81% in 2012). However, those from lower SES groups, as well as the oldest (aged 55+ years) and youngest adults (aged 16–24 years) are least likely to make any judgment, and there is some evidence that these knowledge gaps have increased over the years.[4] Similarly, even by 2012, only 60% of adult users realised that not all search results are accurate or unbiased. Again, there are notable differences by socioeconomic status, and since 2009, only the highest group has shown a steady improvement in knowledge.

In addition to knowledge about the Internet, we also examined how people are using the Internet in ways that are beneficial as these measures, also, may signal the need for promotion of media literacy so as to encourage such uses. As shown in Figure 20.2, using digital skills to participate in online debate remains low overall. Even by 2010, only 23% of Internet users (more middle than working class) reported being interested *and* confident in their ability to join in debates online or state their opinions on social or political issues, this having declined from the 26% who said this in 2007.

Another measure of participation is the weekly take-up of public or civic activities (such as finding information online about public services provided by local or national government, signing an online petition, or contacting a local councillor or MP online): of all the activities people report doing online, these are

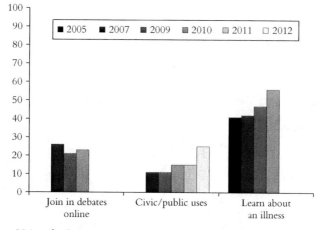

FIGURE 20.2 Using the Internet.

consistently at the bottom of the list, although a recent rise is visible from 11% of users in 2007 to 15% in 2010 and then 25% by 2012; again, these are more common among middle- than working-class adults.

Third, the Internet is an increasingly useful resource for information about health-related issues. Ofcom's evidence shows a small increase in the proportion of Internet users who have *ever* taken advantage of the Internet to look for such information, rising from 64% in 2009 to 68% in 2010. More promisingly, there was a steady rise in Internet-using adults who have sourced specific information about an illness online as and when needed. High SES adults (ABC1) are leading—rising from 44% of users in 2005 to 60% in 2010—but lower SES groups (C2DE) are catching up, rising from 36% in 2005 to 51% in 2010.

The evidence from the United Kingdom shows little improvement in media literacy among the British public, especially in relation to critical understanding and participation. And there is persistent evidence of problematically low media literacy among disadvantaged groups. It seems that early wins in raising media literacy have tailed off, either because it is the initial gains that are easiest to achieve, or because the struggle to sustain and expand media literacy initiatives has left improvements faltering. If this is the case, then considering the lack of progress in relation to critical and participatory literacy, the cuts to media literacy initiatives under the Coalition government are particularly unfortunate.

For media literacy advocates, our U.K. case has an alarming next chapter and an uncertain future. Since the formation of a Coalition government (Conservative and Liberal Democrat) in May 2010, there have been few statements in support of media literacy from Government, Ofcom, or the industry (with the exception of the BBC). Ofcom's budget for media literacy for all activities except research was cut, and the National Plan for Digital Participation is no more, although the focus on digital inclusion (i.e. on access and basic use) continues through the

Go On Campaign. At the time of writing, the United Kingdom is gearing up to
revise the Communication Act; the fate of media literacy, especially as regards the
promotion of citizens' critical understanding and creative participation with and
through digital media, hangs in the balance.

Is Europe Taking the Lead?

In Europe, support for media and digital literacy appears to be growing across
the various directorates of the European Commission and associated initiatives.
Complementing the predominant focus by media educators on children's media
literacy, the European Union's policy statements are strongly focused on adults,
recognising that media literacy is 'an important factor for active citizenship' (European Commission, n.d.) and that "it is no longer an advantage to be media literate;
rather, it is a debilitating disadvantage not to be" (EAVI, 2010, 10).[5] Significantly,
in 2009 the EC recommended that Member States "promote systematic research
through studies and projects on the different aspects and dimensions of media literacy in the digital environment and monitor and measure the progress of media
literacy levels" (Commission of the European Communities, 2009, 5), building on
the requirement in the *Audiovisual Media Services (AVMS) Directive 2007/65/EC*
for a three-yearly reporting obligation regarding the level of media literacy in all
member states (European Parliament and the Council, 2007). More recently, June
2011 saw the European Commission's Digital Agenda call for e-skills (European
Commission, 2010).

Looking more internationally, the Organisation for Economic Co-operation
and Development (OECD) identifies, through the Definition and Selection of
Competencies (DeSeCo) Project, a range of competencies organized along three
categories (PISA, 2005, 10–15), each of which is relevant to media literacy: "using
tools interactively" (including language, symbol, text, knowledge, information,
and technology); "interacting in heterogeneous groups" (including the ability to
"relate well to others," to "co-operate, work in teams," and to "manage and resolve
conflicts"); and "acting autonomously" (the ability to "act within the big picture,"
to "form and conduct life plans and personal projects," and to "defend and assert
rights, interests, limits and needs").

In parallel, UNESCO has spearheaded a range of media literacy initiatives
(Frau-Meigs, 2007), recognizing that the "information society" is essential for
building the "knowledge society," which encompasses the principles of "equal
access to quality education for all; universal access to information; cultural and
linguistic diversity; and freedom of expression" (Moeller, Joseph, Lau, & Carbo,
2011, 8). To be a literate and critical individual in the information society requires
both media literacy and information literacy—"access to information and the
evaluation and use of such information" (11), which UNESCO has converged as
Media Information Literacy (see also Livingstone et al., 2008).

Rather than the simple measures adopted by Ofcom, both UNESCO and the European Commission have embarked on a complex measurement framework to benchmark and track the effectiveness of national media and information literacy policies on a cross-national basis. Each argues for two levels of analysis. The European Association for Viewers' Interests (EAVI) was commissioned by the European Commission DG Information Society to assess the levels of media literacy in Europe 27 Member States, distinguishes (and seeks to measure) "individual competences" (namely use, as "an individual technical skill"; critical understanding, involving "fluency in comprehension and interpretation"; and the communicative ability to "establish relationships through the media" [Celot, 2011, 21]) and "environmental factors" (including "media education, media policy, media availability, roles of the Media Industry and Civil society" [22]). UNESCO, similarly, proposes to measure media information literacy first at the national and institutional level and, second, at the level of individual competencies as developed within the system of formal education (Moeller et al., 2011).

But as Moeller et al. (2011) acknowledge, these efforts at sophisticated, multilevel measurement face considerable challenges—in relation to quality criteria such as relevance, timeliness, accuracy, validity, etc., and in the process of application (differences in learning environments, consistency, cross-context applicability, cost, etc.). EAVI, similarly, has noted that the challenge of reducing changing and dynamic media-related activities to a "conclusive, universal interpretation proved unworkable" (Celot, 2011, 21). The European Commission therefore hopes not for scientific measurement but rather for reliable "indicators" and "assessment criteria" (Ding, 2011, 6). The outcome of such a revised framework is still uncertain (Bulger, 2012).

What's at Stake for Citizens and Consumers?

From the prosaic but vital tasks of locating train timetables, doing the weekly shop, or completing tax returns to more elevated, if ordinary, civic activities of finding trustworthy information or following the news, to the increasingly necessary task of updating skills ready for a fast-changing, "flexible" labour market, to familiar social pleasures of entertainment, chatting with friends, forming relationships or staying in touch with far-flung relatives to, finally, the grandest aims of speaking out and being heard in a democratic culture—all of these were once managed interpersonally or through interaction with public institutions. Now, each is increasingly mediated by commercial businesses, demanding an enhanced level of media and critical literacy from adults in their roles as consumers and citizens. Not only has research documented the benefits of having such literacy, it also documents the costs of lacking it, and these costs make themselves felt at both individual and societal levels.

It is important to recognize that mere access will not eliminate inequalities over time. Quite the contrary: gaps in media use exacerbate gaps in knowledge and participation, as the socially-advantaged keep up better with the relentless pace of socio-technical change. Indeed, if efforts are not made to close the "information and strategic skill divide," it will continue to widen, with skilled people able to take advantage of the Internet to achieve their personal goals, while the less skilled continue their struggle to locate correct information (van Deursen & van Dijk, 2009). At present in the United Kingdom, the Go On U.K. campaign finds that 16 million people aged 15+ (around one-third of the adult population) still lack such basic online skills as being able to find information, manage personal disclosure, or evaluate what is trustworthy or valuable online (Go On U.K., n.d.; see also Helsper, 2011; Grant, 2011).

Clearly, the demands on users are constantly rising—just using the Internet is no longer sufficient, adults must now gain "digital fluency" (Bartlett & Miller, 2011). This is in part because the nature of these skills depends on the complex and often opaque or even illegible information infrastructure with which people must engage (Livingstone, Papaioannou, Pérez, & Wijnen, 2012). Media design and media literacy can be considered as reverse sides of the same coin. The more complex and, especially, the more "illegible" the media environment becomes, the greater the task of media literacy. Conversely, the clearer, the easier to use, and the better designed the media environment, the less daunting the task of learning how to use it effectively. Ideally, technological innovation would embed in its very design and regulation the knowledge-based needs and practices of its users.

The costs of low media literacy include missing out on good information and instead gaining misinformation. Research evidence is growing for consumer detriment of various kinds. For example, Brown, Keller, and Stern (2009) showed that teenagers with low health and media literacy tend to use slang terms to search for sexual health information online, leading them too often to unreliable websites. The Canadian Association of Family Resource Programs (2010) showed that, while low-income, new immigrant, or female-led families strive to take advantage of the Internet to access health and product safety information, the effectiveness of such use is hindered by difficulties in comprehending, evaluating, and making good use of the complex information online. A pan-European survey found that 3 in 10 of those who disclose personal data to make purchases online feel that they have no ability to control their data online (especially compared with offline), and although people perceive personal data control to be their own responsibility, this does not always result in sufficient self-protective activities (Lusoli et al., 2006).

As the Internet becomes a more valued platform for civic engagement, digital inequalities translate into a citizen deficit also. For instance, the Hansard Society (2011) showed that although 40% of the lowest (DE) class would like to learn more about Parliament but were the least likely to use the Internet/email to source information about national political or parliamentary issues. Similarly, as Lusoli, Ward, and Gibson (2006) found that simply adding new online channels is insufficient to increase political engagement among those who do not already participate in politics via traditional methods (see also Williamson, 2010).

Meanwhile, low political efficacy and low trust account for low participation—people must believe their contribution will be responded to (Zimmerman & Rappaport, 1988; Kahne & Westheimer, 2006), although if political participation online is incorporated into media literacy education for young people, they are more likely to take part online (Kahne, Lee, & Feezell, 2010).

A standard mode of address to all is no longer considered sufficient by media literacy educators, for it is this that exacerbates knowledge gaps by providing information that permits the "rich to get richer." The teenagers, vulnerable families, less educated users, and other groups currently missing out each need a different approach that recognises cultural and local factors (Mackert, Whitten, & Garcia, 2008; Sourbati, 2009). But one-size-fits-all solutions are cheaper and easier to roll out than intensively customised approaches, especially given existing difficulties of delivering even the present offer of often-enthusiastic and creative initiatives on a sustainable basis that can encompass an entire population and be updated as often as the socio-technical infrastructure moves on. It may be these difficulties in the implementation of media literacy initiatives that account for the lack of evidence (from Ofcom and others) that media literacy initiatives are effective. As we have seen, it is also these difficulties that impede the efforts of those seeking a complex and non-reductionist approach to measuring the effectiveness of media literacy improvements.

Conclusions

Media literacy provided by schools could reach children if the political will existed, but this will still be insufficient for adults to meet the continuing demands of the fast-changing media landscape. Media literacy could be promoted to most adults through the channels of the mass media, if the commercial will existed (which it does not), but a one-size-fits-all approach risks exacerbating rather than ameliorating inequalities insofar as such resources would be disproportionately taken up by the already-knowledgeable. Commercial providers of all kinds could surely work harder to reduce the burden of media literacy, particularly in regards to complex functional, technical, contractual, and legal forms of knowledge, by improving the design and management of digital interfaces, contents, and services. New intermediaries also have a role to play—consumer organisations, most notably, can combine the necessary legal and technical expertise with a vigorous defence of ordinary people's interests, and when resources permit, they may offer a trusted source for media literacy or lead a campaign for digital environments that are sufficiently interpretable, navigable, transparent, and fair.

We have argued that, to meet the media literacy demands of the entire adult population, then, a tailored and context-appropriate approach is needed that is engaging, relevant, sustainable, and scalable. Moreover, this should encompass not merely functional skills but the full range of competences needed by consumers and citizens in a thoroughly mediated society that relies increasingly on a digital infrastructure of all of its activities. Since this is a resource intensive demand, it is likely that state action would be required to ensure that the means of delivery match up to society's aims for media literacy—to ensure sufficient provision of, first, usable, comprehensive media and information services (to minimise unnecessary media literacy burdens); second, up to date media literacy initiatives tailored to the segments of the public that most need them; and third, compensatory strategies for those who are at risk of losing out of social inclusion and civic participation in a digital age.

The media, and therefore media literacy, are no longer to be relegated to the domain of leisure and entertainment. Rather, they have become infrastructural, underpinning our work as well as family, public as well as private life, and civic as well as personal domains. Go into any household in Europe and one may find a confusion of kit and cables, incomprehensible or suboptimal contracts, confusion about what plugs into what, how things work and how to complain or get help from. Society would not accept this for the provision of water or electricity or transport. For today's complex digital media infrastructure, the same now applies, and we can no longer leave it to individuals to figure out how to cope by themselves or to bear alone the cost of getting it wrong. Yet at present, levels of media literacy do not appear to be rising—for even as people learn more, so too, there is even more to learn. Hence intervention of diverse kinds and on a substantial scale is now surely required.

Notes

1. http://www.go-on.co.uk
2. http://www.citizensonline.org.uk
3. In the United Kingdom, social research organisations often classify the population according to "social grade"—an occupation-based classification system developed by the National Readership Survey. A refers to "higher managerial, administrative and professional," B refers to "intermediate managerial, administrative and professional," C1 refers to "supervisory, clerical and junior managerial, administrative and professional," C2 refers to "skilled manual workers," D refers to "semi-skilled and unskilled manual workers," and D refers to "state pensioners, casual and lowest grade workers, unemployed with state benefits only" (National Readership Society, n.d.)
4. For example, in 2007 the difference between the highest and lowest SES groups was 17% (84% for ABs vs. 65% for DEs, but by 2011 this had widened to 25% (86% for ABs vs. 61% for DEs).
5. In its 2006 European Recommendation of Key Competences, the European Union included "digital competence" as a key competence for lifelong learning (European Parliament and the Council, 2006; Ferrari, 2012). Then media literacy has been considered by the EU Commission to be 'an essential factor [in] active citizenship, democratic participation and social cohesion' in the Information Society (Ding, 2011, 8).

References

Aufderheide, P. (1997). Media literacy: From a report of the National Leadership Conference on Media Literacy. In R. Kubey (Ed.), *Media literacy in the information age*. New York: Transaction Press.

Bartlett, J., & Miller, C. (2011). *Truth, lies and the Internet: A Report into young people's digital fluency*. London: Demos.

BBC (2012). *Media literacy: Understanding digital capabilities*. London: British Broadcasting Corporation.

BIS (Department for Business, Innovation, and Skills) (2010). *National plan for digital participation*. London: Department for Culture, Media and Sport.

Brown, J.D., Keller, S., & Stern, S. (2009). Sex, sexuality, sexting and sexed. *The Prevention Researcher, 16*(4), 12–16.

Bulger, M.E. (2012). Measuring media literacy in a national context: Challenges of definition, method and implementation. *Media Studies, 3*(6), 83–105.

Canadian Association of Family Resource Programs. (2010). *Vulnerable Families as E-Consumers: Current Attitudes, Behaviours and Barriers to E-Information*. Ottawa: Canadian Association of Family Resource Programs.

Celot, P. (2011) EAVI studies on media literacy in Europe. In S. Livingstone (Ed.), *Media literacy: Ambitions, policies and measures* (pp. 20–21). London: COST. Retrieved from: http://www.cost-transforming-audiences.eu/node/223.

Ding, S. (2011). The European Commission's approach to media literacy. In S. Livingstone (Ed.), *Media literacy: Ambitions, policies and measures* (pp. 6–8). London: COST. Retrieved from: http://www.cost-transforming-audiences.eu/node/223.

European Association for Viewers' Interests (2010). *Study on assessment criteria for media literacy levels. Final report*. Brussels: Author.

European Commission (2009). *Commission recommendation: On media literacy in the digital environment for a more competitive audiovisual and content industry and an inclusive knowledge society*. Brussels: Commission of the European Communities.

European Commission (2010). *A digital agenda for Europe*. Brussels: Author.

European Commission (n.d.). Media literacy leaflet. Brussels: European Commission. Retrieved from http://ec.europa.eu/culture/media/media-content/media-literacy/media_literacy_leaflet_en.pdf.

European Parliament and the Council (2006). Recommendation of the European Parliament and of the Council of 18 December 2006 on key competences for lifelong learning. In *Official Journal of the European Union L394*. Brussels: European Union. Retrieved from http://eur-lex.europa.eu/LexUriServ/LexUriServ.do?uri=OJ:L:2006:394:0010:0018:en:PDF.

European Parliament and the Council (2007). Directive 2007/65/EC of the European Parliament and of the Council. *Official Journal of the European Union, 332*, 27–45. Retrieved from http://eur-lex.europa.eu/LexUriServ/LexUriServ.do?uri=CELEX:32007L0065:en:NOT.

Ferrari, A. (2012). *Digital competence in practice: An analysis of frameworks*. Luxembourg: European Commission Joint Research Centre.

Frau-Meigs, D. (Ed.). (2007). *Media education: A kit for teachers, students, parents and professionals*. Paris: UNESCO Communication and Information Sector.

Grant, L. (2011). 'I'm a completely different person at home': Using digital technologies to connect learning between home and school. *Journal of Computer Assisted Learning, 27*(4), 292–301.

Hansard Society (2011). *Connecting citizens to Parliament*. London: Hansard Society. Retrieved from http://www.hansardsociety.org.uk/blogs/publications/archive/2011/09/19/connecting-citizens-to-parliament.aspx.

Helsper, E.J. (2011). *Media policy brief 3. The emergence of a digital underclass*. London: London School of Economics Media Policy Project. Retrieved from http://www2.lse.ac.uk/media@lse/pdf/MPP/LSEMPPBrief3.pdf.

Kahne, J., Lee, N. & Feezell, J.T. (2010). Digital media literacy education and online civic and political participation. *International Journal of Communication, 6,* 1–24.

Kahne, J., & Westheimer, J. (2006). The limits of efficacy: Educating citizens for a democratic society. *PS: Political Science and Politics, 39*(2), 289–296.

Livingstone, S. (2008). Engaging with media—a matter of literacy? *Communication, Culture & Critique, 1*(1), 51–62.

Livingstone, S., Papaioannou, T., Mar Grandío Pérez, M., & Wijnen, C. (2012). Critical insights in European media literacy research and policy. *Media Studies, 3*(6), 1–13.

Livingstone, S., van Couvering, E., & Thumim, N. (2008). Converging traditions of research on media and information literacies: Disciplinary, critical and methodological issues. In D.J. Leu, J. Coiro, M. Knobel, & C. Lankshear (Eds.), *Handbook of research on new literacies* (pp. 103–132). Mahwah, NJ: Lawrence Erlbaum.

Livingstone, S., & Wang, Y. (2013). *Media policy brief 2. Media literacy and the Communications Act. What has been achieved and what should be done? A 2013 update.* London: London School of Economics Media Policy Project. Retrieved from http://www2.lse.ac.uk/media@lse/documents/MPP/LSE-Media-Policy-Brief-2-Updated.pdf.

Lusoli, W., Ward, S., & Gibson, R. (2006). (Re)connecting politics? Parliament, the public and the Internet. *Parliamentary Affairs, 59*(1), 24–42.

Mackert, M., Whitten, P., & Garcia, A. (2008). Interventions for low health literate audiences. *Journal of Computer-Mediated Communication, 13,* 504–515.

Moeller, S., Joseph, A., Lau, J., & Carbo, T. (2011). Towards media and information literacy indicators. Paris: UNESCO. Available at: http://www.unesco.org/new/fileadmin/MULTIMEDIA/HQ/CI/CI/pdf/unesco_mil_indicators_background_document_2011_final_en.pdf.

National Readership Society (n.d.). What we do: Lifestyle data. Retrieved from http://www.nrs.co.uk/lifestyle-data/.

Ofcom (2006). *Media literacy audit: Report on adult media literacy,* London: Author.

Ofcom (2008). *Media literacy audit: Report on UK adults' media literacy,* London: Author.

Ofcom (2010). *UK adults' media literacy.* London: Author.

Ofcom (2011). *UK adults' media literacy.* London: Author.

Ofcom (2012). *Adults' media use and attitudes report.* London: Author.

Ofcom (2013). *Adults' media use and attitudes report.* London: Author.

Ofcom (n.d.). Media literacy. Information about Ofcom's media literacy activities. Retrieved from http://stakeholders.ofcom.org.uk/market-data-research/media-literacy/.

PISA (Programme for International Student Assessment). (2005). *The definition and selection of key competencies: Executive summary.* Paris: Organisation for Economic Co-operation and Development.

Sourbati, M. (2009). Media literacy and universal access in Europe. *The Information Society, 25*(4), 248–254.

van Deursen, A.J.A.M., & van Dijk, J.A.G.M. (2009). Improving digital skills for the use of online public information and services. *Government Information Quarterly, 26,* 333–340.

Williamson, A. (2010). Digital citizens and democratic participation. London: Hansard Society.

Zimmerman, M., & Rappaport, J. (1988). Citizen participation, perceived control, and psychological empowerment. *American Journal of Community Psychology, 16*(5), 725–750.

21

MEDIA LITERACY EDUCATION

A Requirement for Today's Digital Citizens

Frank Gallagher

In the summer of 2012, an amateurish video appeared on *YouTube*, purporting to be a trailer for a film called *The Innocence of Muslims*. By September word of its existence had spread across the globe, sparking outrage and unrest across the Muslim world. As many as 19 people were killed during demonstrations in Pakistan alone, and the death of the U.S. ambassador to Libya was initially blamed on riots against the film (Walsh, 2012).

Whether creating *The Innocence of Muslims* or videos of dancing squirrels, anyone with fairly rudimentary digital media tools and a network connection has the potential to reach a worldwide audience. Not that long ago, the only way a message could reach a mass audience was through a media company—a newspaper, TV network, publisher, or film studio. Now, using only a smart phone, you can make movies and upload them to *YouTube*, post your thoughts to *Twitter* or *Facebook* and comment on the postings of others. With a phone, computer, or game console, you can play in massively multiplayer online games like *World of Warcraft* with people from all over the world, or remix songs and videos, collaborate on science experiments or write fan-fiction that others will react to, comment on, and remix themselves.

The change from being a media consumer to a media creator has profound implications for individuals, governments, companies, societies, schools, and media literacy education. Social networking and videos shot from phones played major roles in the Arab Spring revolutions in Tunisia, Egypt, and Libya (Howard et al., 2011). In the wake of Hurricane Sandy, which slammed into the northeastern United States in November 2012, residents without power turned to *Twitter* for news, and authorities posted information about shelters, road closures, and open gas stations (Brenzel, 2012). *Facebook* pages are helping reunite residents with possessions lost in the storm surge (AP, 2012). Children have gotten into trouble for things they post but have also rallied in support of classmates in difficulty (Medina, 2012).

In these stories are several lessons that point to the importance of media literacy education, and to how it may have to change. Although news reports gave the impression that spontaneous, large demonstrations were springing up across the Muslim world in outrage over *The Innocence of Muslims*, the crowds were often thin, with few rock throwers. Most people in the Middle East never saw the trailer, and the anger was sometimes as much against local police or community issues as against the West. By focusing on the violence, media coverage of the demonstrations even provoked a certain amount of introspection in Arab countries as people realized that the protests, rather than the offending film trailer, had become the story (*The Economist*).

Ann Hornaday (2012), the film critic at *The Washington Post*, writing about the furor over *The Innocence of Muslims*, called media literacy education "as necessary a component of civic life in the 21st Century as basic literacy was in the 20th." What matters is "whether we possess the skills to make sense of what we're seeing." Do people, in the United States and around the world, have the ability to distinguish between a film and "a primitive piece of cynical agitprop?" Do they ask who is behind the video and what were they trying to achieve?

And do the creators of the thousands of hours of video uploaded to *YouTube* every day, the millions of social network posts, or photographs sent to *Flickr*, know what they're trying to convey and how they can successfully do that? Do they think about what might happen when others see what they've created? If digital technology gives anyone the reach of a global media company, it lacks the checks and balances of traditional media organizations. A newspaper or TV station has editors, fact checkers, and lawyers to make sure stories are clear, accurate, and responsible. A teenager with a smart phone has none.

With our newfound power to communicate, create, and participate comes the responsibility to use these tools and networks responsibly. Media literacy has not had to deal with the ethics and responsibilities of children as media creators before, simply because the tools only recently began to permit the easy creation and global distribution of media messages. If the technology used to help save a life may also be used to help take one, then children need to become not just savvy about production tools and techniques, but also about the ramifications of what they create.

It's hard to believe that the creator of *The Innocence of Muslims* did not know he was making a video that would upset people. Did he know people would die because of his work? Should he have anticipated that outcome?

This shift in the media ecosphere, and the power it puts in the hands of individuals, makes media literacy more important than ever, yet it is no more likely to be taught now than it has been over the past several decades. The emerging concept of digital citizenship connects media literacy with ethics and responsible use of media. Digital citizenship gives media literacy a place within a compelling framework that is gradually being adopted by schools and education leaders. Digital citizenship may be media literacy's breakthrough moment.

Vital Yet Underused

Media literacy education has been the passion of a small group of educators for many years. The Aspen Institute organized a National Leadership Conference on Media Literacy in 1992. In 1995 the first national conference for media literacy educators was held at Appalachian State University in Boone, North Carolina. Biennial conferences since have attracted hundreds of educators and the National Association for Media Literacy Education was formed as a professional body for media literacy educators. Compared to other content-area organizations, however, the number of practitioners is relatively low.

In 1999, Frank Baker and Robert Kubey surveyed state curricular standards and found that elements of media literacy were present in 48 states' frameworks. Media literacy was scattered across English, social studies, health, and media studies, but only a handful of states had a systematic approach and, just because it's on the books, doesn't mean it's actually taught. In Cable in the Classroom's 2006 research examining the state of media literacy education in the United States, 60% of educators surveyed felt that media literacy education in their school had less emphasis than it should have. Media literacy has not been part of the high-stakes tests that have defined school success for the last decade. There is no clear understanding of who "owns" it—media literacy was seen as the responsibility of individual teachers by 59% of those polled, library media specialists by 48%, and technology coordinators by 34%. Media literacy was seen as everyone's responsibility by 22%. Further, most educators (78%) learned about media literacy on their own (Cable in the Classroom & Grunwald Associates, 2006).

While the Common Core State Standards for English and Mathematics mention multimedia and contain elements that lend themselves to media literacy, there is no explicit mention of the term. At the time this was written, there was no evidence that any of the tasks in the next generation assessments being developed by the Smarter Balance or Partnership for Assessment of Readiness of College and Careers consortia will call out any specific media literacy components though some may be implied. While the implementation of the Common Core State Standards and new assessments provides ample opportunities for including media literacy in curriculum, nothing mandates it. If Baker and Kubey were to do another survey of state curricula in 2019, would they find "elements of media literacy" in state frameworks, but again, little systematic representation across the content areas? The answer may be yes, unless media literacy finds a different way to get into classrooms. That new pathway may be through digital citizenship.

Digital Citizenship

Digital citizenship is a relatively young concept. Mike Ribble and Gerald Bailey were among the first to use the term, writing about it as early as 2004. They noticed that the flood of new technologies and applications were creating novel situations that required different social, educational, and economic norms. In an effort to help create these norms, they identified nine elements of digital citizenship which Ribble (2011) has recently grouped into three categories, with media literacy implied, but not called out, in the communication and literacy topics:

Respect Your Self/Respect Others

- Etiquette
- Access
- Law

Educate Your Self/Connect with Others

- Communication
- Literacy
- Commerce

Protect Your Self/Protect Others

- Rights and Responsibility
- Safety (Security)
- Health and Welfare

There are other, similar, definitions. Internet safety expert Anne Collier (2011) talks about five components of digital citizenship and explicitly includes media literacy:

- Norms of behavior, often called "good citizenship" or "online etiquette"
- Participation or civic engagement (also seen as community, social, or political activism online)
- A sense of membership or belonging
- Three literacies: tech or digital literacy, media literacy, and social literacy
- Rights and responsibilities.

Renee Hobbs (2011, 12) talks about five essential dimensions of digital and media literacy that encompass many of the same themes of digital citizenship:

- Access—Using technology to find, share, and make sense of information.
- Analyze—Thinking critically about purpose, audience, point of view, credibility, and considering the possible consequences or effects.

- Create—Generating messages in a variety of formats, with awareness of purpose, audience, and technique.
- Reflect—Considering the impact on our own thinking, actions, and reputation.
- Act—individually or together acting to solve problems, build community, or share knowledge.

At Cable in the Classroom, we think of digital citizenship as a positive and holistic approach to teaching digital safety and security, digital literacy (which includes information and media literacy), and digital ethics and responsibility.

As more children went online and more schools were connected to the Internet, adults and policymakers became worried about potential problems children could encounter on the Internet and using digital media tools. Lurid stories about sexual predators, sexting, and cyberbullying have led to successive waves of panic about child Internet safety, what David Finkelhor (2011) calls "'Juvenoia'—an exaggerated fear about the influence of social change on children and youth" (13). Data, however, shows that the sensational stories are the exception, not the norm, and that, though there are risks, children are in more danger from neighbors and relatives in the real world than from cyber-predators. In fact, a wide variety of measures of children's risk and well-being are all trending in positive directions.

Where Ribble and Bailey asked schools to take the lead in creating digital citizens, worried policymakers required schools and libraries to install filters and block potentially objectionable content, and funded ineffective Internet safety programs based on fear and misinformation.[1]

Many educators wanted more than restrictions and prohibitions. They wanted to teach students the "how to" and not just the "don't do." As Hobbs (2011, 126) noted,

> To help students acquire the competencies of digital citizenship, we have to do more than make students sign an acceptable use policy statement or post technology usage rules in the computer lab. In addition to celebrating the most exciting ways that digital media support and enhance learning, we have to engage students in frank and authentic conversations about the problematic and challenging kinds of experiences they have online as the create and share messages.

In an early sign of a shift towards digital citizenship, the International Society for Technology in Education added digital citizenship to their standards for students, teachers, and administrators during revisions in 2007. The Consortium on School Networking recommended schools consider switching from *acceptable* use policies, defining what was allowed or prohibited, to *responsible* use policies that encourage desirable behaviors and "support the acquisition of practical skills necessary for full participation as a 21st-century citizen" (Making Progress 2011, 2). The National Association of State Boards of Education (Born in another Time, 2012) recommends that schools "address the critical areas of digital citizenship and digital literacy." The American Association of School Librarians (AASL) notes that compliance with the Children's Internet Protection Act "and some state technology standards require digital citizenship education for students." The AASL concluded by recommending that "educational technology should integrate digital citizenship education supported by well-defined responsible use policies." (Cordell, Eckhardt, Hauser, & McGriff, 2012, 4) The Kentucky Department of Education decided to deliver digital citizenship training through a "Digital Driver's License" project, based on Ribble and Bailey's nine elements, with the addition of "digital media fluency," a term sometimes used in place of media literacy (Swann & Park, 2012). In "Youth Safety on a Living Internet: Report of the Online Safety and Technology Working Group" (2010, 6), the education subcommittee recommended that the federal government "[p]romote digital citizenship in pre-K–12 education as a national priority" and "[p]romote instruction in digital media literacy and computer security in pre-K–12 education nationwide."

Digital citizenship, then, has many champions and is becoming part of instruction—sometimes as a more positive approach to mandated Internet safety instruction, sometimes as part of character development programs, sometimes in technology education and, sometimes woven throughout the curriculum. Whatever the entry point, it is beginning to take hold and provide a platform for media literacy.

Cable in the Classroom (2012) surveyed over 2,000 educators about the state of digital citizenship education in their schools and districts. About 40% felt their

TABLE 21.1 Protecting Yourself and Others by Learning Internet Safety and Security

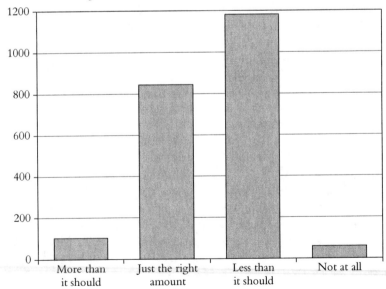

TABLE 21.2 Respecting Yourself and Others by Practicing Digital Ethics and Responsible Online Behavior

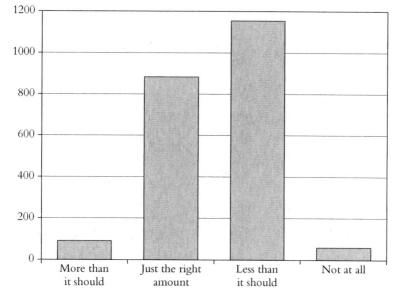

TABLE 21.3 Educating Yourself and Connecting with Others by Understanding Media and Information Literacy

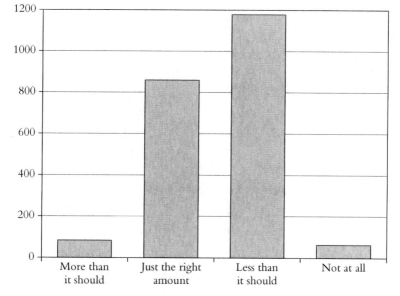

TABLE 21.4 How Well Prepared to Teach Digital Citizenship do You Feel You Are?

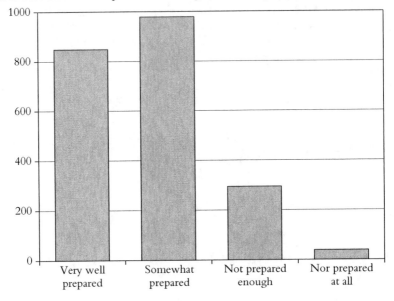

TABLE 21.5 Where do You Learn about Digital Citizenship? (Choose as many as applicable.)

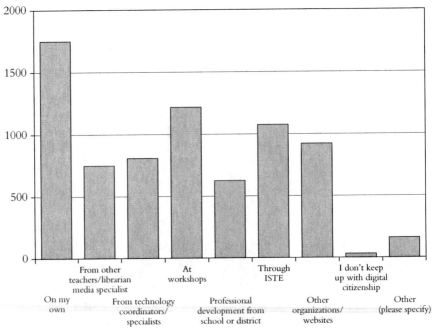

TABLE 21.6 Who at Your School/District is Responsible for Teaching Digital Citizenship? (Choose as many as applicable.)

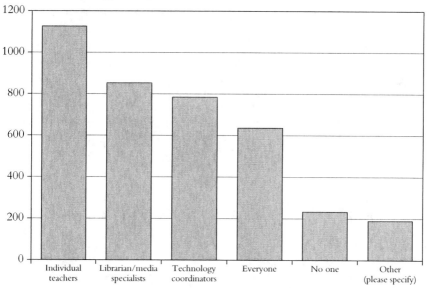

school or district emphasized the elements of digital citizenship the right amount. Although not universal, this represents substantial progress.

85% felt they were somewhat or very well prepared to teach digital citizenship.

Responsibility remains spread across a wide range of individuals, from individual teachers (52%) to volunteers (two respondents) and educators are learning about digital citizenship from a variety of sources, with many learning on their own but large numbers learning from colleagues, workshops, and professional development.

Parents, too, see the importance of digital citizenship. In a poll (Cable in the Classroom & Harris Interactive, 2012), overwhelming numbers of parents felt each of three elements of digital citizenship was important or very important for their children to learn:

Safety and security—93%
Ethics and responsibility—93%
Critical thinking/media and information literacy—87%

Parents also felt that some or a lot of the responsibility for teaching children digital citizen was theirs (97%) and their school's (89%).

There is every reason to expect that the tools and technologies used to communicate and create media will get smaller, cheaper, more powerful, and easy to use. These developments will continue to challenge and, at the same time, empower parents, educators, and children. Media literacy will remain essential to ensuring that these tools are used wisely and effectively and digital citizenship provides the necessary framework for weaving media literacy into K-12 education.

Note

1. Decades of research show that one-shot interventions, such as an assembly or single lesson, are not effective in changing behavior, nor are fear-based messages (Reaves, 2001; Understanding and Using Fear, 2000), yet many early Internet safety programs included both. In addition, the statistics used in some of these programs, such as one in five children online are approached by a predator, were the result of badly misinterpreting the actual data (Wolak, Finkelhor, & Mitchell, 2011).

References

AP (2012, November 23). Social media reuniting New Jersey victims of Superstorm Sandy with lost photos and mementos. *The Washington Post*. Retrieved from http://www.washingtonpost.com/national/social-media-reuniting-new-jersey-victims-of-superstorm-sandy-with-lost-photos-and-mementoes/2012/11/23/c1a9afb0–35ca–11e2–92f0–496af208bf23_story.html.

Aufderheide, P. (1992). *Media literacy: A report of the National Leadership Conference on Media Literacy.* Washington, DC: Communications and Society Program of the Aspen Institute.

Baker, F., & Kubey, R. (1999, October 29). Has media literacy found a curricular foothold? *Education Week*. Retrieved from http://www.frankwbaker.com/edweek.htm.

Born in another time: Ensuring educational technology meets the needs of students today—and tomorrow (2012). National Association of State Boards of Education. Retrieved from http://assess4ed.net/system/files/resources/nasbe_technology_report 2012_0.pdf.

Brenzel, K. (2012, November 12). Officials use social media during Superstorm Sandy to communicate with residents. *Lehigh Valley Express-Times*. Retrieved from http://www.lehighvalleylive.com/breaking-news/index.ssf/2012/11/officials_use_social_media_dur.html.

Cable in the Classroom (2012). The state of digital citizenship in schools. Retrieved from http://www.ciconline.org/resource/2012-survey.

Cable in the Classroom & Grunwald Associates (2006, April). *Media literacy: A vital and underserved need in schools.* Washington, DC: Author.

Cable in the Classroom & Harris Interactive (2012). The state of digital citizenship with parents. Retrieved from http://www.ciconline.org/resource/2012-survey.

Collier, A. (2011). Digital citizenship reality check: Notes from Nairobi's IGF. *Net Family News*. Retrieved from http://www.netfamilynews.org/digital-citizenship-reality-check-notes-from-nairobis-igf.

Cordell, D., Eckhardt, S., Hauser, J., & McGriff, N. (2012, October). Educational technology in schools: An AASL white paper. Chicago: American Association of School Librarians. Retrieved from http://www.ala.org/aasl/aaslissues/positionstatements/tech-white-paper.

Finkelhor, D. (2011). The Internet, youth safety and the problem of "Juvenoia." University of New Hampshire, Crimes against Children Research Center. Retrieved from http://www.unh.edu/ccrc/pdf/Juvenoia%20paper.pdf.

Hobbs, R. (2011). *Digital and media literacy: Connecting culture and classroom.* Thousand Oaks, CA: Corwin.

Hornaday, A. (2012, September 14). "Innocence of Muslims": This is not a film. (Or is it?). *The Washington Post.* Retrieved from http://www.washingtonpost.com/lifestyle/style/this-is-not-a-film-or-is-it/2012/09/14/c455a41a-fe77-11e1-b153-218509a954e1_story.html.

Howard, P., Duffy, A.; Freelon, D., Hussain, M., Mari, W., & Mazaid, M. (2011). Opening closed regimes: What was the role of social media during the Arab Spring? Project on Information Technology & Political Islam, University of Washington. Retrieved from http://dl.dropbox.com/u/12947477/publications/2011_Howard-Duffy-Freelon-Hussain-Mari-Mazaid_pITPI.pdf.

International Society for Technology in Education (n.d.). ISTE NETS: The standards for learning, leading, and teaching in the digital age. Retrieved from http://www.iste.org/standards.

Making progress: Rethinking state and district policies concerning mobile technologies and social media. (2011) Consortium on School Networking. Retrieved from http://www.cosn.org/Portals/7/docs/Web%202.0/MakingProgress_Report.pdf.

Media literacy: A position statement of National Council for the Social Studies (2009). National Council for the Social Studies. Retrieved from http://www.socialstudies.org/positions/medialiteracy1.

Medina, S. (2012, October 3). Daniel Cui, high school goalie, gets support of peers after mean prank. *Huffington Post.* Retrieved from http://www.huffingtonpost.com/2012/10/03/daniel-cui-_n_1936356.html.

Rage, but also self-criticism. (2012, September 22). *The Economist* 405(8803), 55–56.

Reaves, J. (2001, February 15). Just say no to DARE. *Time.* Retrieved from http://www.time.com/time/nation/article/0,8599,99564,00.html#ixzz1W0XkvmW1DD.

Ribble, M.S. (2011). *Digital citizenship in schools* (2nd ed.). Washington, DC: ISTE.

Ribble, M.S. (n.d.). *Digital citizenship.* Retrieved from http://www.digitalcitizenship.net/Nine_Elements.html.

Ribble, M.S., Bailey, G., & Ross, T.W. (2004, September). Digital citizenship: Addressing appropriate technology behavior. *Leading & Learning with Technology, 32*(1), 6–11.

Swann, G., & Park, M. (2012, December/2013, January). Students need a digital driver's license before they start their engines. *Learning & Leading with Technology, 40*(4), 26–28.

Understanding and using fear appeals for tobacco control. (2000, February). Health Communication Unit at the Center for Health Promotion, University of Toronto. Retrieved from http://www.thcu.ca/infoandresources/publications/fear%20appeals%20-%20web%20version.pdf.

Walsh, D. (2012, September 21). 19 Reported dead as Pakistanis protest Muhammad video. *The New York Times.* Retrieved from http://www.nytimes.com/2012/09/22/world/asia/protests-in-pakistan-over-anti-islam-film.html?pagewanted=all&_r=0.

Wolak, J., Finkelhor, D., & Mitchell, K. (2007, December). 1 in 7 youth: The statistics about online sexual solicitations. Crimes against Children Research Center, University of New Hampshire. Retrieved from http://www.unh.edu/ccrc/internet-crimes/factsheet_1in7.html.

Youth safety on a living Internet: Report of the online safety and technology working group (2010, June 4). Washington, DC: National Telecommunications and Information Administration. Retrieved from http://www.ntia.doc.gov/legacy/reports/2010/OSTWG_Final_Report_070610.pdf.

22

EMERGING FROM K–12 FUTURE SHOCK

How to Blend Digital and Media Literacy into the Common Core Standards

Rhys Daunic

"Twenty-first-century Education" is 13 years old—an era forecast to transform the way we teach and learn thanks to the democratization of limitless information and mass access to tools and channels of global communication. Amidst the global swell of digital tools and culture during this period, however, K–12 public schools in New York City (NYC) have struggled to keep up with the rest of society's immersion into the digital revolution. In fact, to date, NYC schools have no clear measures or guidelines for preparing digital and media literate citizens for an increasingly digital and mediated world. This is understandable considering that NYC schools have been absorbing an influx of mandated educational programming[1] from the federal, state, and local levels while mass digital culture outside schools has proliferated and grown in complexity.

Responding to a national paradigm shift in education, schools have been required to rethink and restructure teaching practices according to pedagogical strategies like higher order thinking, universal designs for learning, differentiation, data driven instruction and assessment, and broadening measures of teacher effectiveness (New York City Department of Education, 2012). The most recent and significant challenge has been the mandate to reconfigure entire curricula to align with the Common Core State Standards (CCSS) by 2014 (ibid.). Simultaneously, schools have also made efforts to comply with an indistinct, but consistent encouragement during this period to "integrate technology" (New York City Department of Education, 2012) (U.S. Department of Education 2004, 2010). School leaders have hustled to develop infrastructure around selecting, funding, situating, connecting, updating, repairing, and replacing a stream of rapidly obsolete resources in their often limited space. Teachers have developed strategies for organizing and managing new classroom resources and have explored methods for teaching with and about the moving target of digital tools and culture they and their students have experienced outside of school. Experimenting with these *suggested* adaptations on top of the aforementioned *mandated* school initiatives has resulted in fatigue and feels to many educators like too much too quickly.

Today's educator seems to be feeling a bit of what Alvin Toffler in 1970 would have called "Future Shock"—the state of being overwhelmed by too much change in too short a period of time (Toffler, 1970). Fortunately, the efforts of leading-edge K–12 educators and ongoing scholarship and field work by the national digital and media literacy (DML) community during this era have resulted in guidelines and models that can help simplify the adaptation of curricula to meet the exponential surge of digital tools and media that has come and is sure to continue.

The Antidote to Future Shock: Simplify

Toffler's suggested antidote to Future Shock was to "simplify the world in ways that confirm our biases," even as the world around us becomes increasingly complex (Silver, 2012). The following recommendations are an attempt at simplifying school innovation (and promoting educator sanity) in the coming years:

1. Identify your school's "pedagogical bias"—your philosophical approach to curriculum development and instructional practice.
2. Identify and internalize within your school culture broadly applicable digital skills and "media literacy" concepts necessary for twenty-first-century citizenship, identity, and the workforce.
3. Build curricula informed by the above that expands and enhances the CCSS with new tools and modes of communication that are open to continuing cultural shifts.

Applying Digital and Media Literacy (DML) to the Common Core (CCSS)

> Students need the ability to gather, comprehend, evaluate, synthesize, and report on information and ideas . . . to analyze and create a high volume and extensive range of print and nonprint texts in media forms old and new. The need to conduct research and to produce and consume media is embedded into every aspect of today's curriculum. (National Governors Association Center for Best Practices & Council of Chief State School Officers, 2010)

The CCSS have established a nationalized education policy that calls for a blending of old and new media across discipline, which implies that DML should be a fundamental element of modern curriculum development (Aspen, 2010). However, where CCSS K–12 English Language Arts standards are spelled out, skill-by-skill, year-to-year, it is left to schools to determine when, how, and what specific DML skills and concepts are taught. For example: When should students learn to type or incorporate mixed media into research or the writing process? When are students capable of determining the validity of an Internet source, identifying authorial intention in a video, or reflecting on their relationship to digital culture? Should they be introduced to programming, and where do related skills intersect with standards-based math?

To simplify the approach to answering questions like this, school leaders should refer to guidelines laid out by pioneers in digital and media literacy education (DMLE).[2] Their work has synthesized K–12 experience and research into guiding principles for developing students' (a) **digital literacy**; fundamental digital skill acquisition, and (b) **media literacy**; the extension of literacy to include "reading," "writing," and critical thinking around emerging modes of communication.[3] Informed by a strong understanding of DMLE competencies, schools can begin developing a scope and sequence of related skills and concepts into CCSS K–12 standards-based curricula.

Below I will flesh out promising practices towards these ends that I have witnessed over the past eleven years as a freelance DML curriculum developer, project designer, and collaborator in K–12 schools throughout the NYC Department of Education (NYCDOE). In doing so I will operate on the assumption that—regardless of one's bias about how new media and technological trends have affected society for better or worse—there is a consensus (Aspen, 2010) that schools must accept and adapt to changes in the nature of:

1. Citizenship: New modes of cultural exchange, commerce and the means of informing oneself, especially vital to democracy have resulted in a new "Digital Citizenship."
2. Identity: Sense of self is cultivated through a combination of interpersonal and online interaction increasingly broadcast and archived in the public sphere.
3. Work: Basic digital operational and communication skills are required throughout most levels of the modern workforce.

DMLE Success Stories, Strategies, and Common Challenges

Best practices in DMLE emerge among a range of environments, staff profiles, available resources, and student needs and backgrounds. Over the past dozen years schools have generally pushed to acquire more digital tools and connectivity, and there has been a growing national recognition of the need for student development of DML (Aspen, 2010). By reporting some lessons learned during this build-up, my intention is for curriculum developers, teachers, and school administrators to locate their schools within the array of pedagogical priorities (biases) and environments described. In doing so, they may gain insight into how their current developmental goals might intersect with DMLE basics and the CCSS and address the challenges listed below.

My Bias: Use Project-based Units to Blend DMLE with CCSS and Scaffold Basic Tech Skills

To simplify the infusion of DMLE within complex NYCDOE environments, my own bias has been towards what I call "production-based media literacy," which recommends that schools:

1. Engage new media resources ("technology"), ways of communicating, and digital literacy skills through content-driven student productions, and
2. Layer core competencies of media literacy[4] onto existing learning objectives during the production process.

Each year students arrive at schools with greater operational capacity for working with digital tools. Nonetheless, schools must develop and refine a simple scope and sequence[5] for assessing the acquisition of basic skills to lower the cost of entry for classroom digital production over time. This should be designed to minimize instructional time spent introducing and reinforcing operational skills that students will acquire fluency in through use within academic productions. The goal, in my opinion, should be to scaffold the most transferrable skills possible to allow them to eventually independently adapt to new tools as they emerge.

Common Challenges: Lack of Time and Tech Support

Even in schools most enthusiastic about DML, lack of time is an inevitable obstacle in this process. As simple and efficient as a framework for DMLE development can be, schools have to make room for additional administrative, planning and instructional time, and account for technical support issues. This will take less time as staff internalize media literacy concepts, become more fluent with digital tools (along with students), and get comfortable matching those tools and concepts with their accumulating familiarity with the CCSS. Meanwhile, schools have to account for and address the following common questions to move towards efficiency:

1. How and when will professional development occur to raise staff digital literacy to meet new and emerging digital classroom resources? Who will lead that process?
2. How and when will professional development occur to help staff layer digital and media literacy onto CCSS-curricula? Who will lead that process?
3. What is the scope and sequence for developing student digital literacy skills alongside traditional literacy skills? Who will teach those skills, how will they be assessed, and where will it fit into your program schedule?
4. Who will keep technology resources working and make purchasing decisions to enable all of the above?[6]

Promising Practice: Increase Staff DMLE Capacity by Engaging Their Professional Creativity

Molly Cutler, an Ed.D candidate in the Curriculum and Teaching program at Columbia Teachers College and former third-grade teacher, believes encouraging teachers to take creative ownership of the adaptation of their practice is key to innovative curriculum design. In 2009, Cutler used student-produced public service announcement (PSA) videos within a unit of study that bridged NYCDOE social studies content and CCSS-based persuasive writing with DMLE fundamentals. Her school environment allowed the freedom to pioneer innovative practices with the support of a DMLE consultant—opportunities Cutler feels heightened her engagement in the development of new practices. The resulting unit extended students' critical analysis of traditional texts to the deconstruction of multimedia texts, had them adapt persuasive essays into video scripts, and increased Cutler's confidence leading a production-ready classroom. The unit is now a staple of her former school's third-grade curriculum, and her students' videos and her unit plan have been shared as models for teachers nationally.[7]

Brooklyn School of Inquiry (BSI) is building DMLE capacity school wide by fostering the type of flexible and creative atmosphere throughout their staff that allowed Cutler to thrive. BSI's pedagogical bias is to encourage collaboration to create custom units of study that emphasize critical thinking, differentiation, real-world relevance, media literacy, and project-based learning "shaped by" the CCSS (Brooklyn School of Inquiry, 2012). To insure that DML is integrated in ways that resonate with instructional staff, Principal Donna Taylor and Assistant Principal Nicole Nelson have programmed bi-annual professional development (PD) workshops where teachers work with a DMLE consultant to locate where critical analysis of media and digital production can authentically extend their existing objectives. These sessions have resulted in projects or activities emerging from teacher or student interests that are then "backwards-planned" to align with the CCSS and supported by in class PD as needed from their consultant.

The BSI approach to organic parallel development of staff and student digital and media literacy is a promising practice but does not deliver immediate, comprehensive school-wide infusion of DMLE. However, over time, BSI is amassing model units of study that, like Cutler's PSA unit, layer core concepts of DMLE onto CCSS that teachers will draw from more routinely and with increasing confidence and clarity.

Promising Practice: Build Staff Digital Literacy while Serving Practical Needs

Often what stymies DMLE fluidity in schools is a lack of teacher fluency with the tools of digital production. Concurrently to their DMLE unit planning, BSI administrators are fostering a baseline of "digital literacy" among the staff by committing to school wide practical use of online tools for communication and collaboration. Streamlining existing goals for collaborative planning and home-school communication, BSI teachers plan curricula using shared cloud-based documents, and manage class websites featuring multimedia student work and resources for parents. As a result, they are not only able to access and archive their work more efficiently than before, but are also becoming better equipped to support students in digital classrooms.

Promising Practice: Spiral Interdisciplinary Classroom Goals with Student Production in DMLE "Labs"

Whether through a roaming specialist with a rolling cart of laptops, or in a designated "lab" of consolidated digital resources, some schools have programmed DML, or more commonly, "technology," as a separate program within their curriculum. This idea arrived early in the build-up to twenty-first-century education, but as emphasis on integrating new media across content areas has grown, technology resources have often been redistributed to classrooms. However, as more schools become able to digitally equip both labs and classrooms, some have developed overlapping units of study that elegantly connect DML development in the lab with enhanced core content and CCSS-based objectives in the classroom.

Spiraling DML and traditional objectives through a lab-classroom relationship requires classroom teachers to work with their lab teacher to align student digital skill and media literacy concept acquisition with parallel traditional literacy fundamentals and core content. This enables focus on expanded learning opportunities in the classroom—such as critical analysis of new and old media texts—without using up instructional time supporting technical skill development, which most teachers have not been adequately trained to do. In the lab, the digital media specialist can support critical thinking around media use and digital citizenship while working with classroom-aligned content to drive relevant productions designed to teach digital skills.

For example, DML lab teacher Garin Kaligian and fourth grade classroom teacher Elisabeth Austin-Page at P.S. 9 in Manhattan have coordinated cloud-based multimedia productions using Voicethread.com to allow students to explain problem solving strategies using pictures, numbers and words—a grade-level math objective. Students bring written work to the lab and demonstrate and reinforce mastery of math goals by making critical decisions about what digital media can be combined to help an audience understand their thinking and process. This metacognitive activity is also a great way to get students thinking about the communication value of various media in this context while also building the technical skills to wield them for an academic purpose. On both fronts, this project aligns with fourth grade CCSS ELA Standards for Speaking and Listening including: following agreed-upon rules for discussion, engaging effectively in a range of collaborative discussions on grade four topics and texts, building on others' ideas and expressing their own clearly, and adding audio recordings and visual displays to presentations when appropriate to enhance the development of main ideas or themes (National Governors Association Center for Best Practices & Council of Chief State School Officers, 2010). To solidify the coordination and academic rigor of the lab work, administrators freed up Austin-Page and her grade level colleagues to observe the production process and student performance, familiarize themselves with the software, and compare notes with Kaligian. The productions are available immediately to be replayed from the cloud and analyzed by the teacher or students in the classroom or at home for analysis or review and is archived as a model project blending DMLE and CCSS.

Creating collaborative planning time for the lab teacher to coordinate with all grade level teachers is an obstacle for this approach to school-wide DMLE. However, the potential for layering multiple CCSS standards, specific content, and DMLE objectives in an efficient interdisciplinary unit of study makes this a programming challenge worth facing.

Promising Practice: Merge DMLE with an Established School-wide Initiative

At Soundview Academy (SVA), a middle school in the South Bronx, Principal William Frackelton is leading an effort to leverage students' DML skills acquired in their Grade 6–8 filmmaking program to enhance the school-wide initiative of building "accountable talk" into students' academic interactions. Filmmaking teacher, Kevin Lopez, is piloting a model for a school-wide network of blogs that will allow students to publish multimedia "posts" and "comments" using content-specific protocols for constructing arguments and critiquing work. The goal is for teachers to observe and interact with students as digital citizens in an academic setting demonstrating an elegant blend of CCSS-based competencies (asking questions, making inferences, supporting arguments with text-based evidence), and DML critical thinking skills (critiquing effectiveness of each other's media messages, reflectively tailoring production decisions to reach authentic audiences). Frackelton's vision for the accountable talk network is to create a real world environment to leverage student enthusiasm for digital media and participatory culture, while engaging core content, assessing and polishing DML competencies, and expanding the potential of SVA academic initiatives.

SVA's logistical challenge will be to find time to train the instructional staff beyond Lopez—accommodating a range of digital literacy among them—on the effective use and moderation of these blogs. The approach will be to roll out content area blogs one academic department at a time, and train them using experienced SVA staff and students. They will start with the most technically-proficient content teams and build towards a critical mass of in-house proficiency. The potential of extending middle-school student engagement with digital communication to core content areas through this initiative makes it a worthy outlay of PD time towards further modernization of their CCSS-based curriculum.

Next Steps: Simplify your Approach, Trail Blaze, Synthesize, Transform

We can expect (or hope) that future revisions of the CCSS will more clearly situate DMLE within the scope and sequence of student development. Until then, it is left to K–12 educators, with the help of DMLE practitioners and researchers, to continue trailblazing according to their vision and values and sharing the knowledge that emerges. Perhaps by attempting to simplify criteria for DMLE inclusion in the current K–12 environment based on synthesis of best practices shared from the field,[8] we can minimize pedagogical Future Shock along the way. In doing so, we may move closer to the promise of Twenty-first-century Education: the transformation of educational practice to produce college and career ready citizens on the path to life-long learning and self-awareness that can keep up with our increasingly complex world.

Notes

1. While unpacking the federal program No Child Left Behind, followed by Race to the Top, schools also worked at absorbing and complying with updated NYCDOE City-wide Instructional Expectations.
2. I recommend schools inform their approach to DMLE through the National Association for Media Literacy Education's *Core Principles of Media Literacy Education.* Also see the Aspen Institute's *Digital and Media Literacy: A Plan of Action*, the ISTE *National Educational Technology Standards*, and the Partnership for 21st Century Education's *Route 21*.
3. The National Association for Media Literacy Education (NAMLE) defines media literacy as follows: "Within North America, media literacy is seen to consist of a series of communication competencies, including the ability to ACCESS, ANALYZE, EVALUATE, and COMMUNICATE information in a variety of forms, including print and non-print messages" (National Association for Media Literacy Education, 2012).
4. See the Aspen Institute's *Digital and Media Literacy: A Plan of Action* for a complete definition of DML and a list of DML competencies.
5. See examples of K–12 Digital Literacy Scope and Sequences at TheMediaSpot.org
6. Related to time, the total cost of ownership of computers has been wildly underestimated in the run up to digitizing schools. More digital resources in schools can bring more access to information, and thoughtful hands-on student projects if they work. Certain metrics, including the Consortium for School Networking (http://cosn.org), recommend one full time tech support person for every 60 computers—this is rarely accounted for in school budgets. Considering how basic digital tools get updated, connected, and fixed is a crucial piece of DMLE development. Part of teacher and student digital literacy empowerment will include dealing with routine operational issues, but more teacher time troubleshooting technical issues equals less development and instructional time.
7. Cutler's students' PSAs were viewed at the 2010 National Council of Teachers of English national conference. Watch the PSAs and see a breakdown of the process at TheMediaSpot.org
8. Stories of educator experiences with DMLE in K–12 and related support resources can be found on the National Association for Media Literacy Education Resource Hub (http://namle.net/resources), The Media Spot (http://themediaspot.org), and other social networks related to media literacy.

References

Aspen Institute Communications and Society Program (2010). *Digital and Media Literacy: A Plan of Action,* Washington, DC: The Aspen Institute.

Brooklyn School of Inquiry. (2010, May 28). *Curriculum.* Retrieved from http://brooklyn schoolofinquiry.org/about/curriculum/.

National Association for Media Literacy Education. (2007, November). *Core principles of media literacy education in the United States.* Retrieved from http://namle.net/wp-content/uploads/2009/09/NAMLE-CPMLE-w-questions2.pdf.

National Association for Media Literacy Education. (2010, May 28). Media literacy defined. Retrieved from http://namle.net/publications/media-literacy-definitions/.

National Governors Association Center for Best Practices & Council of Chief State School Officers (2010). *Common core state standards for English language arts and literacy in history/social studies, science, and technical subjects.* Washington, DC: Authors.

New York City Department of Education. (2010, May 28). Educational technology. Retrieved from http://schools.nyc.gov/Accountability/resources/technology/default.htm.

New York City Department of Education. (2012, June 1). Implementation guidance for the 2012–13 citywide instructional expectations. Retrieved from http://schools.nyc.gov/NR/rdonlyres/E44257E4-5975-4AAE-8B00-BACEAF219763/0/CIE_guidance.pdf.

Silver, N. (2012) *The signal and the noise: Why so many predictions fail—but some don't.* New York: Penguin.

Toffler, A. (1970). *Future shock.* New York: Random House.

U.S. Department of Education. (2010, May 28). *National education technology plan 2004: Seven major action steps and recommendations.* Retrieved from http://www2.ed.gov/about/offices/list/os/technology/plan/2004/plan_pg14.html#steps.

U.S. Department of Education. (2010, May 28). *National education technology plan 2010.* Retrieved from http://www.ed.gov/technology/netp-2010.

23

GRASPING THE COMPLEXITIES OF U.S. EDUCATIONAL POLICY AND THE CLASSROOM

How to Move Media Literacy Education Forward

Belinha S. De Abreu

State of the State

In the United States, education is in a state of transition whereby schools are beginning the implementation process of the Common Core State Standards (CCSS) in schools and districts across the country. One of the most significant aspects of this new curriculum is the realization that digital technologies must be a part of the learning process. There is an acknowledgement for the first time that educational technologies have flipped the teaching process on its ear and that as educators we must respond to this growing change in our school communities. As was stated in a report produced by the National Association of State Boards of Education,

> For educators and policymakers, one of the keys for effectively responding to this generation is remembering that educational technology is both a tool and a game changer. As digital influences expand and their effects on students' lives increases, some of students' fundamental educational experiences change as well. (National Association of State Boards of Education [NASBE], 2012)

Within the NASBE report is an acknowledgement that more will be affected than just a shift in policy, it will change the model of teaching and learning which for so long has been stagnant. Yet, the question still exists, does media literacy education fit here or are we, those who teach it, still struggling to find a place to include it in the curriculum?

As you read through the CCSS document that has been created to support language arts and math, you can see where media literacy fits in, but is not clearly stated. The term digital technologies is loosely thrown in, but not well defined. Is this a problem or an opportunity? For some, especially the more literal among us, not having a well-defined document can be problematic. For others, this may appear as the first opportunity to incorporate digital media literacy within the guidelines of their curriculum, but it also allows for there to be a stretch. One of the emphases of this new curriculum is the connection to real-world activities. The media is a part of the everyday worlds in which our students are involved.

For others, there is a conscious look at what we are seeing as an opening for exploration and for possibly providing more ways to incorporate media literacy education in the classroom. After all, what we see happening on a worldwide spectrum is this growing understanding that there needs to be much more education happening for all those involved. Both teachers and students need to learn to focus their thinking so they can better understand the world around them especially since so much of it is mediated and convoluted at times by the messages of the media.

William Kist, a professor at Kent State University in Ohio, recently wrote: "The Common Core Standards recognize that to thrive in the newly wired world, students need to master new ways of reading and writing" (Kist, 2013). In his article, Kist provides educators with bridges of ideas in the literacy component of media that can be extended from teaching students to read screen-based texts and practice in digital writing, practice in collaborative writing to discernment of informational texts (Kist, 2013). This is a huge leap from many of the print resources which are traditionally offered in schools. Further, it is asking the educator to engage students beyond just reading and also to a reinforcement of how this generation of learner engages with mediated materials that they actively use in their world.

Digital Media Literacy

The push for media literacy has grown stronger with the evolution of technology platforms in schools. With the discussion of digital citizenship and also the problems with cyberbullying, the incorporation of the term digital media literacy has become more prevalent. The challenge is with the language used to incorporate the terminology that is most effective in the classroom.

What is in a word? Searching for an expression that encompasses all of the new media technologies that have grown rapidly in our digitized worlds is certainly difficult. Applying a literacy term to this conversation creates another problem, as it places people within different literacy fields in the mix of a conversation about what "text" and "media" mean. As we look at the world we live in today, clearly the creation of the variety and spectrum of technologies has generated a need for a new form of understanding.

The digital landscape with all its new technological tools has drastically changed the world in which we educate students. There has been a recognition among educators that a more considerate, critical, and thoughtful approach is needed when implementing and using the digital devices that have become a part of the mainstream. How do we address the concept of literacy within all these formats? McDougall and Sanders (2012), in a recent article, tried to address the need for critical media literacy as applied to new digital technologies. In fact, the argument stated tries to create a balanced approach to how the issues of digital literacy have impacted what we call the field of media literacy education. Their query comes about as a means of addressing the concerns stated in part by David Buckingham, one of the leading scholars in media literacy. Buckingham states in *Media Education Journal*:

> There is now an urgent need to sharpen our arguments, and to focus our energies. There is a risk of media literacy being dispersed in a haze of digital technological rhetoric. There is a danger of it becoming far too vague and generalized and poorly defined—a matter of good intentions and warm feelings but very little actually getting done. (Buckingham, 2010)

Buckingham warns that it has become too easy to mash together terms such as media literacy and digital literacy in order to satisfy to some degree the policy-makers; policymakers who appear to have just arrived on the scene, to the work and study of media education, which has in fact been going on for more than six decades. At some level, what Buckingham is addressing is an overarching concern that the technology hype has created an opening for media literacy which may be just politically expedient, but not necessarily critical or analytical.

In the United States, these concerns have also arisen in schools of education, both in K–12 and higher education, as well as with media literacy scholars and educators who have crafted their work to be inclusive of new technologies. However, the degree of knowledge of media literacy education and its value to the educational mainstream still seems to be a puzzle. More often, when media literacy is discussed at conferences where technology is the focus, it is almost always an eye-opening experience for the attendee, as if the construction was only found in the design of media and not in its understanding: it becomes about using media to teach rather than teaching about media.

Ultimately, this argument of defining media literacy is age-old in this field. It is a conversation that happens almost every time you meet up in media literacy circles, conferences, etc. Perhaps because it is still an argument for the future; this field of thought is still being crafted and will continue to be so for the next generation of educators, policymakers, parents, and students. Buckingham states this also in the same article from the *Media Education Journal*:

> Media literacy, it seems, is a skill or a form of competency; but it is also about critical thinking, and about cultural dispositions or tastes. It is about old media and new media, about books and mobile phones. It is for young and old, for teachers and parents, for people who work in the media industries and for NGOs. It happens in schools and in homes, and indeed in the media

themselves. It is an initiative coming from the top down, but also from the bottom up. In these kinds of texts, media literacy is also often aligned with other contemporary "buzzwords" in educational and social policy. It is about creativity, citizenship, empowerment, inclusion, personalization, innovation, critical thinking . . . and the list goes on. (Buckingham, 2010)

With these ideas in mind, here is my contextual formulation of what media literacy education should be for today's digital age based upon my own experiences working with teachers, policymakers, parents, and most importantly students:

Digital media literacy education is . . .

> . . . the ability to teach and think critically about various media platforms.
> . . . an acknowledgment of the pleasure of the media to the user which is also extended to those critical conversations in the class which ask the teacher at times to extend beyond their comfort level.
> . . . about processing the changes in our digital age while listening to the student users and their knowledgeable capacity of these new realms of learning.
> . . . a voice for all students, but especially to those who do not get to speak up on how their media—their likes and dislikes, impact them personally.

Digital media literacy education . . .

> . . . engages the teacher and the learner simultaneously so that a give and take relationship can exist within the framework of the classroom, thereby becoming an equalizer of shared information.
> . . . necessitates a place in the core curriculum, because it has become an instrumental avenue for the growth of knowledge within traditional areas of learning.
> . . . extends an opportunity for outreach when dealing with issues of safety and security in today's cybersociety.
> . . . serves the wider community by being instrumental in teaching parents, law officers, and other interested parties who are invested in our school communities to access, analyze, evaluate, and produce media messages.
> . . . creates a conscious understanding of the importance of text and images as they transcend the spaces that they are housed within be it television, the Internet, social networking sites, or video games.

Digital media literacy education is . . .

> . . . a navigation tool for educators to discuss, challenge, critique, and understand how media, both traditional and new, has impact on students' beliefs, thoughts, behaviors, etc.

...a way to help students become empathetic to another person's difficulties, struggles, or concerns as it requires the participant to consider both sides of every issue.

...the opposite of censorship, because it instead seeks to address head-on the concerns and issues which arise from the technology that makes many adults fearful.

And

...a platform for ultimately creating a digital citizen that can reach beyond the scope of their medium of choice (i.e., computer or mobile devices such as the Smartphone), to be a part of the global community that is seemingly within the grasp of each individual.

These concepts are not singular but encompass a wide range of themes which are under consideration in education circles. Further, these ideas create a foundational change within teaching and learning that will directly impact education when we consider both media literacy and digital literacy moving forward.

Continuing Struggles

Even with these ideas about digital media literacy in place, there is a general dissatisfaction among educators that their voice is not heard in the policymaking arena. "In our ongoing national dialogue on school reform, there are few voices from 'the bottom' that matter. We are missing the unmediated voice of practitioners who are actually attempting reform, achieving it, failing at it, or partially achieving it and wondering why they haven't done better" (Peterson, 2002). This concern, from educators, has increased significantly as more reforms and initiatives are placed at the door of the educator with no consideration for what is actually taking place in the classroom. Sadly, when policymakers are asked why they are not involving teachers in the question of policy, they respond by saying teachers are too busy. This may be true, but teachers want to be involved at the point where policy is going to make entryway into the classroom. After all, they are the ones who are dealing with students daily and seeing the issues that are most prevalent which cannot be resolved by new standards or curriculum. As Carrie Leana (2011) writes in her article about this issue, having outsiders contribute to school reform who then dominate the ideology of school is contrary to empirical research that states the opposite. Instead, valuing the human "teacher" capital in schools is what is most important when bridging new ideas which will impact student learning in the future. Leanna states, "In the context of schools, human capital is a teacher's cumulative abilities, knowledge and skills developed through formal education and on-the-job experience."

Furthermore, there is a more vital missing link with new reform and that is an understanding of the diverse abilities of educators in using digital technologies.

Adult literacy means being able to synthesize information from a multiple online sources to write a blog post or substantive email. It means analyzing which online tools will best serve your communications purpose. It means making smart decisions about what information is useful online and how to curate and filter the endless stream of data coming in. It means reviewing your digital footprint and learning how to take some control over what information you are broadcasting to the world, from your tweets, profile pictures, and recommending links. While the common core addresses some of the above skills its guidance is far too vague, especially for teachers who are uncomfortable with technologies. (Barnwell, 2012)

This is the crux of the problem. The CCSS has left a gap without acknowledging that there are educators who are not ready for this digital journey. Instead, it allows for the possibility that educators who feel uneasy with the idea of digitizing their instruction may possibly skip what they don't know or don't exactly understand how to interpret, thus leaving the learner in their classroom at a disadvantage. Those who feel uncertain would want to travel by a roadmap that has been established, and there are many companies who produce educational materials who are willing and waiting for opportunities to distribute their wares.

Along with the massive issue of current educators who are uncomfortable with digital tools, there is also the problem with pre-service teachers who are coming into the field with limited training or understanding on how to integrate technology into lesson planning, and later implementation (Chesley & Jordan, 2012). Many young teachers are learning media integration on the job and only if the districts they are working in have access points to reach the technology. This obstruction doesn't resolve the bigger issue on how to connect with the students they will be teaching, who are already in the midst of their mediated environments. Further, the lack of technology background doesn't touch upon the literacy piece, which must also be a part of the digital instruction in education reform.

Ultimately, it will be up to educators and the state policymakers to make a significant change in the schools and incorporate digital technologies alongside media literacy education. The CCSS allows for individual states to add their own standards to the existing document, and this may be a possible solution to where media literacy constructs can be placed (Sloan, 2010). The answers for how to resolve this deficiency are not simple, but they must be a continued part of the educational dialogue if we are to have more informed electorate and citizenry now and in the future.

References

Barnwell, P. (August 22, 2012). The common core's digital-literacy gap. *Education Week*. Retrieved from http://www.edweek.org/tm/articles/2012/08/22/barnwell_digital.html.

Buckingham, D. (2010). The future of media literacy in the digital age: Same challenges for policy and practice. *Media Education Journal, 47,* 3–10.

Chesley, G., & Jordan, J. (May 2012). What's missing from teacher prep. *Educational Leadership, 69*(8), 41–45.

Harrison, D. (September 2010). The end of the virtual world. *The Journal.* Retrieved from http://thejournal.com/articles/2010/09/01/the-end-of-the-virtual-world.aspx.

Kist, W. (March 2013). New literacies and the common core. *Educational Leadership, 70*(6), 38–43.

Leana, C. (Fall 2011). The missing link in school reform. *Stanford Review.* Retrieved from http://www.ssireview.org/articles/entry/the_missing_link_in_school_reform.

McDougall, J., & Sanders, R. (2012). Critical (media) literacy and the digital: Towards sharper thinking. *Journal of Media Literacy, 58*(1), 8–21.

National Association of State Boards of Education (January 2012). Born in another time: Ensuring educational technology meets the needs of students today—and tomorrow. Retrieved from http://www.nasbe.org/study-group/technology-study-group-2012/

Peterson, A. (2002). Teacher stories: School reform's missing link. *The Voice, 7*(3), 6–8.

Sloan, W. (2010). Coming to terms with common core standards. *ASCD INFO Brief, 16*(4). Retrieved from http://www.ascd.org/publications/newsletters/policy-priorities/vol16/issue4/full/Coming-to-Terms-with-Common-Core-Standards.aspx.

PART VII
FUTURE CONNECTIONS

Finally, "Future Connections" asks us to pause and consider the "state of the field." *Media Literacy Education in Action* provides a broad palette of dispositions, viewpoints, explorations, and arguments for why media literacy is more essential to the foundations of contemporary society than ever before. In a global and digital media culture, how young people are educated to become competent citizens is core to the media literacy movement. This section takes the wide array of chapters and asks the simple question: "Where will the field go from here?" To answer this, we read from three chapters that attempt to share wisdom, experience and insight into where the field may be heading. First, we explore what is still missing from the media literacy process for students and what challenges and changes are going to be necessary for the future. Next, we look at the university as a home for a "new rhetoric" of media literacy education. This argument positions media literacy students not only for a job or career but also for an inclusive and democratic lifestyle. To do so, university educators must incorporate many strands of media literacy into their courses, program, and disciplines. Lastly, we look globally again to see a maturing discipline that has made great inroads into education across all levels. The final chapter in this section details these trends and growth patterns to provide a look into the future of a field that is growing in scope, depth, and reach.

24

MEDIA LITERACY PREPARATION IN UNDERGRADUATE TEACHER TRAINING

An American and Australian Perspective

David M. Considine and Michael M. Considine

Media Literacy in the United States

Twenty years ago, the Aspen Institute report of the National Leadership Conference on Media Literacy described the media literacy components in the undergraduate teacher preparation program at North Carolina's Appalachian State University as "perhaps the most sustained institutional effort at pre-service training within formal schooling" (Aufderheide & Firestone 1993, 4). Tellingly, it also described media literacy as "an especially difficult challenge in the United States" (2). While Australia and the United Kingdom long ago added media studies to the high school curriculum, along with externally graded state-wide exams, U.S. schools have no equivalent. In this chapter, we address one American university's experience with media literacy in undergraduate teacher preparation, and the training of Media teachers in Victoria, Australia. As such, readers should not take our discussion to be representative of approaches throughout either country as a whole.

So what can be said two decades later about the place and the purpose of media literacy within teacher preparation at Appalachian State University? Has the Reich College of Education maintained its commitment to preparing teachers to develop media literacy and, if so, is there any real evidence that when they take up teaching positions, these young professionals practice what we have preached?

The answer to the first question is, indisputably, yes. If we take the views of one recent student, that commitment remains, perhaps to the point of overkill. In the spring of 2012, a student in the middle school program, who will teach English Language Arts, wrote: "I have found the number of classes at ASU that preach the importance of media to be almost heartbreaking at some level. The idea of this literacy is so different from the world I grew up in, that at times I feel I might become frustrated when I have to use it in my classroom."

The gateway course that introduces students to media literacy is CI 2300 (Teaching and Learning in a Digital Age). It is one of a set of required core courses for all teacher education majors irrespective of the grade level or subject areas they intend to teach, which can potentially be seen as either a strength or a weakness. The course description addresses "emerging technologies . . . the implications they have for teaching and learning" and both "traditional and emerging literacies." All course instructors, irrespective of their status as tenured faculty or adjuncts, require common assignments that use common rubrics and are archived electronically where they can be accessed by administrators as part of an accountability process.

There are two major media literacy assignments in the course. The first deals with the design and creation of media for teaching and learning. As such it not only meets the production component of any traditional media literacy course but also provides the educational context by requiring that media produced is aligned with the nature and needs of different learners, state standards in the relevant subject areas, and instructional strategies that effectively engage students.

The second project focuses on media analysis and evaluation. Students are introduced to key principles of media literacy (Ontario Ministry of Education, 1989; Considine & Haley, 1999) and the T.A.P. (Text, Audience and Production) model which was developed in Scotland and then modified by Canadian media educators (Duncan, D' Ippolito, Macpherson, & Wilson, 1996). These concepts serve as the primary frameworks students utilize when evaluating media texts which may include music videos, advertising, film, TV, broadcast news, photo journalism, and more.

The course emphasis on new technologies and new literacies makes it consistent with so-called Twenty-first-century Skills, which the North Carolina Department of Public Instruction has embraced and which include Information Literacy, Media Literacy, and ICT literacy (information and communication technologies) (Trilling & Fadel, 2009). Surveys and conversations with course instructors reveal inconsistencies when it comes to providing students with an understanding of these skills. So while it is true that all sections of the course require the same major media assignments, it is not true to say that the context for requiring these assignments is consistently addressed by all instructors. The absence of this critical context in some sections of the course seems to have had an impact. As one instructor put it, he sees students after they have taken the class who say they "just watched YouTube videos in the class everyday." He added, "True or not, it's their perception of the class."

This does; however, appear to be the exception rather than the rule. For the most part in the first two years the course was offered, it proved to be popular with many students who enjoyed the hands-on, project-based approach and the opportunity to work with technologies and popular culture that they themselves are familiar and comfortable with. Comfort, however, cannot be equated with competence. Despite the fact that these students are so-called "digital natives," their exposure to media and technology outside of the classroom does not necessarily make them either media literate or thoughtful consumers or creators of media messages. Their entry level media production skills were characterized as "primitive." Nor does critically analyzing and evaluating media come naturally to them.

For one semester a doctoral student monitored two sections of the course as a learner in residence internship. He attended on campus sessions and had full access to student work posted online throughout the semester. In his final report he confirmed the weaknesses most students exhibited when initially challenged to evaluate educational media. "The analyses turned out to be mostly summaries, with little or no critical content or sense of intended audience and scant connection to relevant subject areas or standards." While recognizing that the students enjoyed using technology and were familiar with much of it, he concluded that most "are not as technically proficient as they think." "Their facility with technology," he wrote, "doesn't always translate into effective pedagogical design or presentation." These weaknesses are the very things the course seeks to help them recognize and rectify.

Achieving this is compounded by the time constraints in which the course must function. While other core courses are three credit hours, this one was reduced to just two hours. Faculty describe it as "bursting at the seams" or "butter spread over too much bread." Requiring the course for all education majors also creates problems. As one instructor wrote, "we still have resistance from students in math and science, business, physical education, and special education. It's been a struggle to convince students in these subject areas that media literacy has anything to do with their subject area." Students who appear most receptive to the course tend to be majoring in English, Social Studies, and Art.

Molly, for example, enthusiastically integrated media literacy into her Grade 6 English Language Arts class during her student teaching experience. This work included a study of propaganda and various advertising techniques. Her students had no prior experience with this material and Molly said "they absolutely loved it." The products that they created and their own speeches and advertisements to accompany these products, truly showed how well they comprehended propaganda techniques. Molly's enthusiasm about her experience is infectious but, it too, is more the exception than the rule. As a middle school major, Molly was also required to take Media and Young People, a separate course that carefully linked media literacy to National Middle School philosophy and to the developmental needs of early adolescents. In short, it reinforced her knowledge and skills by providing a critical curriculum context that focused on students and standards, not just media methods.

Without this consistent context, there seems to be too much evidence to suggest that most of the students taking 2300 will not routinely incorporate the skills and knowledge addressed in the course when they take up their first teaching position. Hart's (1999) work in the United Kingdom, for example, demonstrated that despite knowledge covered during their training, Media teachers were highly selective about what they did and did not utilize. "In practice," he wrote, "local factors, school policies, Head of Department preferences, access to resources . . . and individual commitment," all influence teachers in the decisions they make when teaching about media (70). Similarly, a United States study of Educational Technology in Teacher Education Programs (2007) found that even though colleges of education had added more courses and requirements preparing teachers with technology, on-site factors competed with, undermined and subverted the willingness or ability of novice teachers to actually practice and apply these skills. Texas Social Studies teachers, while agreeing that "media literacy was important to their curriculum," lacked confidence in their ability to analyze and evaluate media and expressed a need for more training and more resources (Stein & Prewett, 2009)

To a very real and often ignored extent, then, the culture and climate of schools will either support or subvert the willingness of young teachers to apply the new skills and knowledge addressed in teacher preparation courses. Not addressing this appears to be a major weakness in Appalachian's approach. As one instructor wrote, "The greatest weakness of the course is raising the level of expectations of these teachers with respect to their future use of media that may not be met when they become actual teachers in the real world."

One simple and significant example of potential barriers awaiting these young teachers is the inconsistent policies and guidelines related to media and technology that can differ from one county to the next. The most egregious of these is perhaps the "one size fits all" filtering policy that restricts access both students and teachers have to the Internet with scant regard for the significant differences and needs of elementary, middle, and high school teachers and their students.

Limited in the resources they are permitted to use, media literacy advocates are also sometimes hampered by administrative ignorance and the suspicion of other teachers. Too many administrators still believe that media literacy "has to do with the use of technology in the classroom," teaching **with** media and technology if you will, rather than teaching **about** media. In her study of teachers who did embrace media literacy as part of their classroom practice, De Abreu (2008) concluded that "they did not receive a lot of support from their peers, so they had to be comfortable with a kind of maverick status in their schools." In his study of Social Studies teachers in New York, Mangram (2008) noted that these concerns about what administrators and parents might think about media in the classroom, actually "restricted" teaching with media, as teachers engaged in a form of self-censorship.

So, if we actually expect teachers to apply media literacy knowledge, strategies, and skills in their own classrooms, we need to follow them into those schools after graduation to identify the variables that encourage or inhibit this. That means working with other teachers, with administrators and parents in different school districts so they come to understand and support these teachers and the legitimacy of media literacy as a necessary skill for workers and citizens in the media dominated twenty-first century. Without this support, media literacy is likely to remain marginalized, not mainstream; isolated, as British educators observed in their own country, to "the province of the enthusiasts" (Bazalgette, 1997).

Media in the State of Victoria

Despite the fact that Media has long been an accepted part of the secondary curriculum in Victoria, teacher preparation in the field is not without its problems.

The last time this writer undertook a survey of the training of Media teachers in Australia (Considine, 2005), I had been prompted by a supervisor of Media student teachers who told me bluntly, "Stop sending me duds." When I sought clarification, she explained that very few of the student teachers undertaking Media in their initial teacher training had practical experience as part of their undergraduate qualifications and in the short time available during the completion of teaching rounds, it was impractical to expect any real practical training to be completed.

This was not an isolated response. It was becoming increasingly difficult to place student or pre-service teachers as, anecdotally, more than half of schools were no longer prepared to accept them. This fact has been recognized as a significant issue by the Australian Parliament's Inquiry into Teacher Education. "Universities, as providers of teacher education courses, are obliged to offer practicum as part of their courses but there is no corresponding obligation on schools or employing authorities . . . to ensure that placements are available" (AHP, 2007).

At that time I also pointed out that in one of the major states where the teaching of Media is well established in schools, "the registration of teachers, including the determination of eligibility criteria" became the responsibility of the Victorian Institute of Education and that a federal Inquiry into Teacher Education was to be conducted by the Standing Committee on Education and Vocational Training. Before examining what, if any, impact these two initiatives may have had on the training of Media teachers, let me set out in general terms, the field of Media education and the training of Media teachers.

For this purpose I intend to use Media education in the state of Victoria as a framework for the rest of the paper. The rationale for this approach is first, after several manifestations of a National approach to curriculum matters since the 1980s, the current initiative under the auspices of the Australian Curriculum Assessment and Reporting Authority is, firstly, to include the post compulsory years of schooling (the senior Years of 11 and 12) and Media is featured throughout. Second, there is now a national focus on teacher training, and once again the issue of a shortage of school placements is receiving attention as Sian Watkins observes:

> Universities face a threat of litigation as a 12% jump in Victorian teacher-training enrollments puts further pressure on their ability to provide students with school placements. Universities faced a threat of litigation from the increasing numbers of students for whom placements are not found or are delayed. (Watkins, 2012, 11)

Background and Course Content

Media or Media Studies has been a subject within the Victorian curriculum, particularly in secondary schools, for more than 40 years. Often begun by enthusiastic teachers and based around film studies and, later, studies in television, this early Media curriculum was not limited by the constraints of state or national curriculum dictates, particularly if it was taught only in the compulsory years of schooling. My co-writer and brother David's teaching experience at Williamstown High was an early example of this model. At that time, teachers had considerable flexibility in what and how they taught. As David's experience confirmed, it was possible for young teachers, fresh out of college, to introduce and implement innovative curriculum, often offered as an elective.

As its popularity in classrooms grew, some of the more laissez-faire approaches gave way to more rigorous models of Media education and its growth as a standalone subject within the senior certificated curriculum was confirmed with its inclusion within The Arts (alongside the more traditional Art, Music, Drama, and Dance) and by 1990, as a subject worthy of study in the Victorian Certificate of Education—the two-year pre-university senior school qualification. It also has a presence in primary education as clearly espoused in The Arts Learning Area within the ACARA curriculum document mentioned earlier.

In terms of the curriculum content for Media in schools, the Victorian Essential Learning Standards (VELS) advises what should be taught at the compulsory years of schooling, (i.e. before Years 11 and 12). Media is a discipline within The Arts domain. Typical statements within the *Creating and Making* and *Exploring and Responding* dimensions provide guidance to teachers in developing their curriculum content to allow their students to understand concepts such as production techniques, media audiences, media genres, and interpretation of media texts.

A typical junior/middle school high school Media course may include animation, digital photography, and studies in advertising, television, or film. Teachers are not directed as to how they teach. The content, style, resourcing, and classroom strategies are decisions that individual, professional teachers are expected to make.

At senior level, the Victorian Curriculum and Assessment Authority (VCAA) through its *Media Study Design,* is much more proscriptive in its approach to

Media curriculum content and design. At Year 11 and Year 12, specific Areas of Study must be taught and content is designed so that students meet mandated learning outcomes. Clear advice as to how students are to be assessed is also included.

At Year 12 the semester based units and Areas of Study include, but are not limited to, the following:

> Unit 3 AOS 1 Narrative—". . . students analyze the narrative organization of fictional film, television or radio drama texts." (VCAA, 2011: 20)
>
> AOS 2 Media Production Skills—"This area of study focuses on the development of specific media production skills and technical competencies using media technologies and processes in one or more media forms." (VCAA, 2011: 22)
>
> AOS 3 Media Production Design—". . . students focus on the preparation of a production design plan for a media product designed for a specific audience in a selected media form." (VCAA, 2011: 23)
>
> AOS 2 Media Texts and Society's Values—". . . students focus on the relationship between society's values and media texts. Students undertake the study of an identified significant idea, social attitude or discourse located in a range of media texts to critically analyze its representation in the media." (VCAA, 2011: 27)

Space does not permit a more detailed description of course content. To view all the Outcome Statements, go to http://www.vcaa.vic.edu.au and navigate to the VCE tab, Media, Study Design.

Year 12 students in Media are initially graded by their teacher for 55% of their coursework. To complete their Year 12 Media assessment, students sit a final two-hour externally set formal examination, making up 45% of their assessment. These papers are graded by a panel of trained assessors. Each paper is graded a minimum of two times with neither assessor being aware of the other's grade.

While the teaching of Media has frequently been regarded with suspicion by traditionalists, who see it as an assault on literacy or a dumbing-down of the curriculum, anyone familiar with these Victorian requirements in terms of both course content and student assessment recognizes the rigor in this subject area.

Questions do remain, however, about just how well-prepared teachers are to meet these requirements, particularly when it comes to preparation for media design and production.

Training Media Teachers

Much has changed in the seven years since my initial survey in relation to how Media teachers are trained. At that time, generally, there were two common approaches in operation: (a) an initial three- to four-year non-education degree followed by a one-year Diploma of Education which included two specialist method areas, or (b) a four-year Bachelor of Education often completed as a double degree. Candidates were also required to complete a minimum of 45 days supervised teaching practice.

In many institutions a Bachelor of Teaching degree has replaced B.Eds., and, increasingly, Master of Teaching is becoming the minimum initial teacher education qualification as "Under the new National Standards, graduate entry initial teacher education programs must be a minimum of TWO years full time equivalent . . . and from 2017 Victorian higher education providers . . . will only offer two year graduate entry initial teacher education programs" (Victorian Institute of Teaching).

Eligibility to Teach Media

Who can offer to teach Media was, of course, the question underpinning my colleague's concern about the lack of any practical or production experience in the trainee Media teachers that she was assisting. What changes have occurred in the determination as to whether a candidate can undertake studies in the Method of Teaching Media? It seems that very little has changed. In its Specialist Area Guidelines, the Victorian Institute of Teaching offers the following advice for those seeking to teach Media: "A sub-major in Media Studies." If we compare this with other subjects in The Arts discipline we find:

Art: Major study in relevant area(s) of Art which includes at least one quarter of a year or practical Art content
Music: Major study in Music which includes practical music
Drama: Sub-major in Drama performance studies (Drama) or Theatre Studies, including practical Drama (VIT, 2012)

So, in the digital age of the twenty-first century there is no mandated requirement for a teacher of Media to have any form of practical or production experience in their pre-education studies. Is this necessarily a weakness? At first glance, it may appear so, especially when one considers that 35% of the final assessment for Year 12 Media in the Victorian Certificate of Education is production based. However, many teachers believe that developing the skills necessary to confidently assist students in this area can be achieved on the job and through professional development. The Australian Teachers of Media (ATOM), for instance, conducts an extensive program of professional development for new and experienced teachers of Media in both the analytical and practical aspects of the course.

Another oft stated view poses the question, "what specific aspect of practical studies would Media student teachers specialize in?" If, for instance, during their initial degree a student was to specialize in photography, how would they cope if employed by a school specializing in video production or web page design? It is a valid question as a teacher of Media can be called upon to teach, for example, advertising, television, cinema studies, and soap operas. They could also teach television news, new media, society's values, and media texts. They might also teach the influence of the media on audiences as well as the basic constructs underpinning all media studies—representation, construction, selection, distribution, and audiences. As well, they might be teaching practical studies in areas such as photography (both digital and traditional wet process), video production, radio/audio production, print, web design, etc.

Advocates suggest that it is more beneficial to specialize in what a particular school offers once the teacher is employed, ensuring that appropriate professional development is targeted. A counter argument to this point of view, however, would be that without some production experience the graduate may not be offered a position in the first place or may, in fact, lack the confidence to even apply for a Media teaching position.

As an experienced teacher of Media, a supervisor of pre-service Media teachers and an academic responsible for the teaching of Media Method studies in undergraduate and post-graduate teacher training programs, I can appreciate these different perspectives. This writer does not see the issues raised as, in any way, insurmountable. It is often expressed that "you are a teacher first, method second." Inquisitive, ambitious, young teaching professionals, particularly if they have quality mentors in the first school that employs them, will survive and thrive.

Outside the immediate school environment, ATOM is an outstanding professional association offering a wide range of support services for the novice and experienced teacher of Media. I have maintained contact with many of my graduates who have negotiated their pathway through the difficulties of being a first year teacher of Media. However, the one area that I firmly believe requires attention is the necessity for the registering body, the Victorian Institute of Teaching, to make the supervision of pre-service teachers during their practicums, a necessary part of the registration process ensuring that the mentoring obligation is shared across all systems—public, independent, and Catholic, and that a wider variety of experiences is ensured for the pre-service candidate.

References

Aufderheide, P., & Firestone, C. (1993). *Media literacy: A report of the National Leadership Conference on Media Literacy.* Queenstown, MD: Aspen Institute.

Australian Curriculum, Assessment, and Reporting Authority. (2011). *Draft shape of the Australian curriculum: The arts.* Sydney: Author.

Australian Parliament (2007). *Final report of the inquiry into teacher education.* Australian Houses of Parliament. Canberra: Author.

Bazalgette, C. (1997). Beyond the province of enthusiasts: re-establishing media education. *Metro Education, 10,* 17–21.

Considine D., & Haley G. (1999). *Visual messages: Integrating imagery into instruction.* Englewood, CO: Teacher Ideas Press.

Considine, M. (2005). Dude, where's my teaching: The education of media teachers. *Screen Education, 39,* 110–112.

De Abreu, B. (2008). *The implementation of a media literacy curriculum in the public schools: three case studies* [Doctoral dissertation]. University of Connecticut.

Duncan, B., D'Ippolitto, J., Macpherson, C., & Wilson, C. (1996). *Mass media and popular culture.* Toronto: Harcourt.

Hart, A. (1999). Teaching media in the classroom: Research and practice in Britain. *Australian screen education, 22,* 64–70.

Institute of Educational Sciences (2007). *Educational technology in teacher education programs for initial licensure.* Washington, DC: U.S. Department of Education.

Mangram, J.A. (2008). Either/or rules: Social studies teachers talk about media and popular culture. *Theory & Research in Social Education, 36*(2), 32–60.

Ontario Ministry of Education (1989). *Media literacy.* Toronto.

Stein, L., & Prewett, A. (2009). Media literacy in the social studies: Teacher perceptions and curricular challenges. *Teacher education quarterly, Winter,* 131–144.

Trilling, B., & Fadel, C. (2009). *21st century skills: Learning for life in our times.* San Francisco: Jossey-Bass.

Victorian Curriculum and Assessment Authority (2010). The arts progression point examples. *Victorian Learning Standards.* East Melbourne, Australia.

Victorian Curriculum and Assessment Authority (2011). Media study design. East Melbourne, Australia.

Victorian Curriculum and Assessment Authority. *VCE media assessment handbook* 2012–2016, East Melbourne, Australia.

Victorian Institute of Teaching (2012). Specialist area guidelines. Retrieved from www.vit.edu.au.

Watkins, S. (2012). *Student teachers with nowhere to go.* AEU News. Abbotsford; Victorian Branch, 11.

25

RHETORIC IN A NEW KEY

Media Literacy Education for the Twenty-first-century University

Gretchen Schwarz

The definition of rhetoric remains problematic from ancient Greece—Plato vs. the Sophists—to the postmodernists. Debate continues, but rhetoric as defined by Aristotle has served as a powerful notion for centuries: the faculty for discovering in the particular case all the available means of persuasion (Aristotle, 1960). Rhetoric as such was a significant subject for educational thinkers from Quintilian in the Roman Empire to Erasmus in the Renaissance and to such diverse public intellectuals as Marshall McLuhan in the twentieth century. (For a full survey of the history of rhetoric, see Smith, 2009, among others.) Rhetoric was at the core of the original medieval university curriculum which was in part comprised of rhetoric, logic, and grammar (the Trivium). Over time, rhetoric lost its centrality in the college curriculum as subjects, departments, and degree programs divided and multiplied. At the same time new subjects and disciplines emerged like media literacy, although its definition is problematic, too. However, the argument can be made that media literacy **is** rhetoric in a new key, and this new rhetoric is more important in the university curriculum than ever. At the heart of this argument are three assertions: (a) Media literacy education can be described as rhetoric for the twenty-first century; (b) The university has lost a unifying sense of purpose and needs curriculum change; and (c) Young citizens are awash in a flood of rhetoric and messages coming from the powerful new media. Changing university curriculum is difficult. However, media literacy, understood as an enlarged notion of rhetoric, has much to offer the university and its students.

Media Literacy as the New Rhetoric

Media literacy as a term has had as unsettled a history as rhetoric. In one of few studies of media literacy in the contemporary university, Mihailidis (2008) concludes:

> The analysis of programs and courses in post-secondary media literacy education reveals a term burdened by pedagogical and definitional complexities. The reported existence of media literacy does little to provide a clear picture of how it functions in the university, where it exists, and whether media literacy is achieving its intended outcomes. (7)

However, media literacy advocated as the new rhetoric, based in persuasion, has numerous strengths. First, most media literacy educators, with various disciplinary backgrounds, have some training in rhetoric, and rhetorical terms and ideas have cachet in the field. Such notions as audience, figures of speech, and ethical appeals play a role in the key questions of media literacy. Williams (2009) simply states:

> Even as literacy increasingly means the ability to choose between print, image, video, sound and all the potential combinations they could create to make a particular point with a particular audience, what will not change are the rhetorical abilities of an individual to find a purpose, correctly analyze an audience, and communicate to that audience in a tone that audience will find persuasive, engaging, and intelligent. (19)

Whether working in communication studies, English, speech, or education, some understanding of rhetoric is common among the diverse folks who "do" media literacy.

Second, the idea of media literacy as rhetoric for today is persuasive given the essential goals of many educators across the humanities: critical thinking and the creation of thoughtful messages especially within the context of a democracy. As Domine (2011) notes, the traditional definition of media literacy (the ability to access, analyze, evaluate, and create diverse media messages) has come to "focus more on understanding how students learn to think critically" (195). Crank (2005) remarks, in describing a college freshman English course including media literacy:

> Students need to begin to change the way they think as they start college, to learn to ask questions about ideology and values, and more importantly, to begin to feel comfortable dealing with cognitive dissonance, understanding that they will and should be challenged by their education. (104)

The **new** aspect of rhetoric comes through the multiple media which characterize communications. It is also acknowledged that persuasion can be found in many kinds of texts, from entertaining sitcoms that tell Americans what is normal to informational magazines that convey the centrality of consumption. Media literacy as rhetoric is just bigger than what Aristotle could have known, and even more relevant to the university.

The Value of a University Education in a Mediated Age

In *Education's End* (2007), Kronman asks the question, "Why did the question of what living is for disappear from the roster of questions our colleges and universities address in a deliberate and disciplined way?" (7). The result, whatever the causes, is "an emptiness that many people feel and a cause of anguish and yearning" (229). An increasing number of commentators worry about the diminished purposes of a university education and the reduction of a college degree to a job certificate (Lagermann & Lewis, 2011; Delbanco, 2012). In her argument for a renewed sense of purpose in university education, Nussbaum (2010) proclaims that the profit motive has taken over the university to such an extent that the arts and humanities are under attack and the "Socratic ideal . . . is under severe strain in a world bent on maximizing economic growth" (48). The absence of the Socratic ideal (the examined life) leads to a "technically trained docility that threaten[s] the very life of democracy itself" (142).

Postman (1995), a media literacy leader, says much the same thing when he declares, "Any education that is mainly about economic utility is far too limited to be useful, and in any case, so diminishes the world that it mocks one's humanity. At the very least, it diminishes the idea of what a good learner is" (31). Postman maintains that "schooling can be about how to make a life, which is quite different from how to make a living" (x). Postman advocates media literacy and technology education which is "not a technical subject. It is a branch of the humanities" (191); it questions the good and ill technology brings. This kind of education addresses the "big questions," questions often ignored now.

Moreover, today's college students do not seem to be advancing as they should be in their abilities to offer persuasive arguments, to analyze others' ideas and arguments, and to work with complex social issues in a democracy. Burbach, Flores, Harding, Matkin, and Quinn (2012) assert, "Although higher education understands the need to develop critical thinkers, it has not lived up to the task consistently" (212). College students do not all leave college with sharpened reading and writing skills. The upshot is many college students who are **not** self-reflective, **not** practiced in argumentative reasoning—whatever the medium, **not** even aware that education might have something to do with a democratic society.

At the same time that the university is having less of an intentional influence on students and their inner lives, the media have an omnipresent influence, largely an unquestioned one. Much has been written and said about digital natives. However, what professors are observing may be most arresting. Reiner (2012) observes as follows:

> One need only walk into any nook or cranny of a college campus to see the blur of fevered thumbs at work and the hypnotic glow of Facebook

walls to know what I'm talking about. In fact, new studies conducted by Reynol Junco (a researcher whose work focuses on college students and social media) suggests that American college students may spend an average of at least an hour and 40 minutes a day on Facebook and three hours a day texting. Even when they aren't texting, they are waiting, hoping, imagining that someone is trying to reach them. (B 20)

Experiments asking students to disconnect from their media have been revealing, underlining the need for media literacy at the college level. Moeller, Powers, and Roberts (2012), note, "Across the globe, many students have easy and constant access to media, yet they often receive little or no instruction about the impact of their media consumption" (45). They describe a 2010 study in which nearly 1000 students from a number of universities across five continents participated in "The World Unplugged" which asked students to withdraw from digital technology for 24 hours. A majority simply could not manage the 24 hours without their media. As the authors claim, "Students cannot learn how to fully participate in their societies as citizens and consumers, nor can they have a full appreciation for the roles of media in their lives, until they have taken a close look at their own media diet" (47). In addition, problems with plagiarism are prolific in colleges as so much information and so many publications are available online.

Professors are also concerned about students reading their e-mail or text messaging during classes. No one questions the university "deals" with corporations from Nike (clothes for athletic teams) to Target (sponsoring freshmen mixers). Students have more trouble than past students focusing on any topic for a length of time. The media are everywhere in the university, critical thinking about the media, not so much. Although media literacy educators in the United States have been preoccupied with PreK–12 education, college students deserve media literacy, too. Learning in any subject is affected by the media as are personal and societal values, and the purpose of a university education, beyond job preparation, should include critical thinking and preparation for active citizenship. Dennis (2004), who urges media literacy education for adults, notes, "If there is a consistent argument for media literacy, it is that of complexity: The media system is more complicated than ever before, it generates more content across different technological platforms, and is deemed more significant—and powerful—than at any other time in human history" (204). Even Palfrey and Gasser (2008) who demonstrate the benefits as well as the issues of the mediated world declare, "This participatory digital environment requires all of us to become more media literate" (128). Moreover, Domine (2011) who argues for media literacy as a framework in teacher education, notes that media literacy can "contextualize the pursuit of technological proficiency" (194). Technology itself needs examination. Domine's recommendations are valuable for the university as a whole.

A Possible Future

Currently media literacy education at the university level is largely non-existent, at least in any systematic way. Media literacy courses and a few programs exist here and there from communications and journalism to English, speech, education, and cultural studies. To most college faculty and students, media literacy probably remains a mystery. Still, media literacy is not entirely unknown. In a recent study, Schmidt (2012) found that permanent faculty members in the communication, English, and education departments at a four-year university in Pennsylvania "consider media literacy education to be important, yet few are involved in actually teaching about media" (13). Some see the need for media literacy although they do not feel qualified to teach it themselves.

No one answer, then, for how to include media literacy in the college curriculum exists. Colleges and universities differ greatly. Media literacy, the new rhetoric, is complicated, and the history of rhetoric in the university is sadly fractured (Mailloux, 2006). In addition, professors are not famous for their ability to play nicely with others, and the university does not encourage curriculum that transcends specializations. However, following are a few suggestions for those in the university who seek change:

- Think outside the box and seek new disciplinary arrangements. For example,

  o Renee Hobbs is now Founding Director of the Harrington School of Communication and Media at the University of Rhode Island which includes journalism, film/media, communication studies, public relations and, this is different, writing and rhetoric and a graduate program in library and information studies.
- Look for ways to connect to the other people across your university who care about media literacy. Connect, only connect!
- Do research, publishing, and presentations that support media literacy at the university level. For example, the 2012 *Journal of Media Literacy Education, 4*(3) offers an article by Ashley, Lyden, and Fasbinder, "Exploring Message Meaning: A Qualitative Media Literacy Study of College Freshmen."
- Reach out to the community. Offer a workshop through the local library or through courses for retired citizens.
- Offer professional development in media literacy, the new rhetoric, on campus. Most universities offer faculty classes through an organization such as the Institute for Teaching and Learning (Oklahoma State University) or the Academy for Teaching and Learning (Baylor University).

Media literacy as a central component of a university education, as it once was, offers many benefits: means for preparing students to be better writers, thinkers, and communicators; engaging subject matter that allows students to consider the "big" questions of purpose, ethics, and identity; critical thinking with the use of technologies; learning for engaged democratic living; opportunities for faculty to work across disciplinary boundaries; and opportunities for faculty and students to connect to community. Media literacy, as rhetoric in a new key, may prove essential in renewing the curriculum of the university. It's worth a try!

References

Aristotle (1960). *The rhetoric of Aristotle* (trans. Land Cooper). Englewood Cliffs, NJ: Prentice-Hall.

Burbach, M.E., Flores, K.L., Harding, H., Matkin, G.S., & Quinn, C.E. (2012). Deficient critical thinking skills among college graduates: Implications for leadership. *Educational Philosophy and Theory, 44*(2), 212+.

Crank, V. (2005). "Doing Disney" fosters media literacy in freshmen. *Academic Exchange Quarterly 9*(3), 100–104.

Delbanco, A. (2012). *College: What is was, is and should be*. Princeton, NJ: Princeton University.

Dennis, E.E. (2004). Out of sight and out of mind. *American Behavioral Scientist, 48*(2), 202–211. doi: 10.1177/0002764204267264

Domine, V. (2011). Building 21st century teachers: An intentional pedagogy of media literacy education. *Action in Teacher Education, 33* (2), 194–205. doi: 10.1080/0162 6620.2011.569457.

Kronman, A.T. (2007). *Education's end: Why our colleges and universities have given up on the meaning of life*. New Haven, CT: Yale University.

Lagerman, E.C., & Lewis, H. (2011). *What is college for? The public purpose of higher education*. New York: Teachers College.

Mailloux, S. (2006). *Disciplinary identities*. New York: MLA.

Mihailidis, P. (2008). Are we speaking the same language? Assessing the state of media literacy in U.S. higher education. *SIMILE, 8*(4), 1–14. doi: 10.3138/sim.8.4.001.

Moeller, S., Powers, E., & Roberts, J. (2012). "The World Unplugged" and "24 Hours without Media": Media literacy to develop self-awareness regarding media. *Communicar, 39*(20), 45–52. doi: 10.3916/C39-2012-02-04.

Nussbaum, M.C. (2010). *Not for profit*. Princeton, NJ: Princeton University.

Palfrey, J., & Gasser, U. (2008). *Born digital*. New York: Basic Books.

Postman, N. (1995). *The end of education*. New York: Knopf.

Reiner, A. (2012, September 24). Only disconnect. *The Chronicle of Higher Education*, B20.

Schmidt, H. (2012). Essential but problematic: Faculty perceptions of media literacy education at the university level. *Qualitative Research Reports in Communication, 13*(1), 10–20. doi: 10.1080/17459435.2012.719204.

Smith, C.R. (2009*). Rhetoric and human consciousness* (3rd ed.). Long Grove, IL: Waveland Press.

Williams, B.T. (2009). *Shimmering literacies*. New York: Peter Lang.

26

INTERNATIONAL MEDIA AND INFORMATIONAL LITERACY

A Conceptual Framework

Art Silverblatt, Yupa Saisanan Na Ayudhya, and Kit Jenkins

Media literacy is a critical thinking skill that is applied to the source of most of our information: the channels of mass communication. The media have become so pervasive throughout the globe that this ability to decipher messages conveyed through the media has become a twenty-first-century survival skill. Indeed, in 2011, participants in the First International Forum on Media and Information Literacy (in which the United Nations Educational, Scientific and Cultural Organization {UNESCO} is the lead partner) met in Fez, Morocco, and issued a Declaration, in which they affirmed that Media and Information Literacy is a "fundamental human right."[1] The following Conceptual Framework is designed to clarify areas of focus and provide a context for new directions and developments in the field of International Media Literacy:

Shared Areas of Consensus

Although individual countries have their own distinctive approaches to the discipline of media literacy, several points of *conceptual consensus* exist within the global media literacy community:

- *The media construct versions of reality.* According to Canada's Association for Media Literacy, "The media do not simply reflect external reality. Rather, they present carefully crafted constructions that reflect many decisions and are the result of many determining factors."[2]
- *Media literacy promotes the critical thinking skills that enable individuals to make independent choices with regard to: (a) which media programming to select, and (b) how to interpret the information that they receive through the channels of mass communication.*

- *Media content is a "text" that provides insight into contemporary cultures.* Media presentations reflect the attitudes, values, behaviors, preoccupations, patterns of thought, and myths that define a culture. And conversely, an understanding of a culture can furnish perspective into media presentations produced in that culture.
- *Media content has an impact on individuals and society.* The media have transformed the way we think about the world, each other, and ourselves. In that regard, media presentations also *reinforce* and *shape* attitudes, values, behaviors, preoccupations, and myths that define a culture.
- *Media literacy is a discipline that furnishes insight into the following types of messages:*

  o *Cumulative Messages* appear in the media with such frequency that they form new meanings, independent of individual presentations. Cumulative messages appear in media presentations with regard to gender roles, definitions of success, violence, tobacco products, and racial and cultural stereotypes.
  o *Manifest* messages are direct and clear to the audience. Ad slogans like "Don't leave home without it" (American Express) and "Just Do It" (Nike) are examples of clear manifest messages.
  o *Latent messages* are indirect and beneath the surface, and consequently, often escape the immediate attention of the audience. Latent messages may reinforce manifest messages or they may suggest entirely different meanings. For example, "G.I. Joe" commercials promote their line of war toys. However, the "G.I. Joe" ad campaign conveys latent messages glorifying war and equating violence with masculinity.

- *Media literacy offers a range of quantitative and qualitative strategies that enable individuals to decipher the information they receive through the channels of mass communications.* These critical approaches are analogous to a series of lenses, each of which provides fresh insight into media content. The effectiveness of a particular approach is dependent on the specific content, area of focus, or the culture in which the media presentation is produced. Consequently, becoming familiar with these critical approaches furnishes individuals with tools that make media content accessible and understandable.
- *The channels of mass communication are neutral.* A medium is not inherently good or evil but is simply a channel of communication. A number of factors determine whether a particular media presentation is positive or negative, including:

  o Who is producing the media presentation?
  o What is the function (or purpose) behind the production of the presentation?
  o Who is the intended audience?

- *Media literacy is apolitical.* The discipline of media literacy is not intended to promote a particular ideology. In that sense, media literacy focuses on *process* rather than *product*: media literacy doesn't tell people *what* to think, but rather, *how* to think.

- *Media literacy fosters an appreciation of media content.* Media literacy should not merely serve as an opportunity to bash the media but also provide ways to enhance the audience's enjoyment, understanding, and appreciation of media content.

Assessing National Media Literacy Programs

This area of focus examines the distinctive character of a country's Media Literacy programs. The following lines of inquiry can furnish perspective into a country's Media Literacy programs:

- Identify the media literacy concepts, principles, and analytical approaches that characterize a country's Media Literacy programs
- Identify which media literacy principles, concepts, and approaches are most effective in certain cultures.
- Consider the ways in which historical, cultural, economic and political factors influence the development of a country's media literacy programs
- Examine how a country's media system influence its media literacy programs

    - System(s) of ownership
    - Levels of digital technology
    - Media ethics
    - The history of their media systems
    - Definitions of freedom of the press, privacy, and conflicts of interest.

- Examine ways in which a country's educational philosophy and educational system affect its approach to media literacy education.
- Consider the ways in which individuals, organizations, or programs have influenced the development of a country's media literacy program
- Apply a country's preferred media literacy principles, concepts, and approaches to interpret media presentations produced in that country.
- Consider other media literacy approaches that might offer a fresh perspective into that country's media and media presentations.

Comparative Analysis

Comparative analysis focuses on what members of the media literacy community can learn from one another with regard to media literacy principles, concepts, programs, and strategies.

The following lines of inquiry examine distinctions between the media literacy programs of different countries:

- Compare the media literacy principles, concepts, and approaches that are characteristic of different cultures.
- Consider whether the approaches commonly employed in one country could be applied to the analysis of media presentations of another culture in order to provide perspective into that culture.

- Consider whether media literacy approaches employed in other countries might provide fresh insight into the media presentations of one's own country of origin.

Media Literacy and Cultural "Habits of Thought"

Psychologist Richard E. Nisbett has made the startling pronouncement that people from different cultures *think* differently. According to Nisbett, these *habits of thought* have been developed through a culture's distinctive social structures, such as a country's historical, political, economic, religious, and legal sensibilities.[3]

Nisbett's observations have several important implications with regard to the Comparative Analysis of media literacy programs. If, indeed, the thought process characteristic of people in different cultures differs dramatically, then it follows that:

- People from different cultures may construct media messages differently.
- People from different cultures may interpret media messages differently.
- Certain media literacy strategies may work more effectively in some cultures compared to others.
- Media literacy education may vary in different cultures.
- Understanding the distinctive thought pattern of a culture can provide insight into its media presentations.

  o By extension, a culture's media presentations can furnish perspective into its distinctive thought patterns.

- Analyzing the "habits of thought" in media presentations can provide insight into cultures who are transitioning from one stage of cultural sensibility to another.

International Collaborations

The Internet is an invaluable avenue for establishing global networks of media literacy scholars, producers, consumers, and students. As an example, the stated mission of the International Media Literacy Network is to "exchange knowledge, creativity, experiences, projects, research, publications, events and materials with other Media Literacy organizations around the world":

> The Media Literacy Network will . . . organize worldwide sessions, congresses and master classes to facilitate members of the network in meeting, inspiring and supporting each other. Besides the meetings the network will also initiate new Media Literacy projects to share with you.[4]

This nonprofit foundation has developed innovative media projects on a range of topics such as Safe Internet, Digital Bullying, Sexualization of the Media, the Mobile Internet, Online Privacy, and Transmedia Storytelling.

The International Media Literacy Research Forum is another organization made up of global partners: Ofcom (Great Britain), the National Association for Media Literacy Education (U.S.), CAMEO (Canada), the Australian Communications and Media Authority, the New Zealand Broadcasting Standards Authority, and the Dublin (Ireland) Institute of Technology. The mission of this organization is as follows:

> As the promotion of media literacy moves up the policy agenda there is a growing need to understand and share learning at a global level. The International Media Literacy Research Forum provides a hub for policymakers, practitioners, regulators and researchers worldwide to communicate, share ideas and promote their media literacy work. The Forum provides a platform to improve understanding of the emerging issues, promote innovative methodologies and facilitate dialogue.[5]

In addition, international media literacy organizations are now promoting collaborative media literacy scholarship. As an example, the *International Journal of Learning and Media*, a peer-reviewed journal, features articles by media literacy scholars throughout the world. For instance, Volume 3, Issue 1 (Winter, 2011) includes the following articles:

- "Blogging for Facilitating Understanding: A Study of Videogame Education" by Jose Pablo Zagal and Amy S. Bruckman;
- "The Personal and the Political: Social Networking in Manila" by Larissa Hjorth and Michael Arnold;
- "The Nirvana Effect: Tapping Video Games to Mediate Music Leaning and Interest" by Kylie Peppler, Michael Downton, Eric Lindsay, and Kenneth Hay.[6]

Finally, instructional resources for media literacy teachers are now available online. For instance, teachers from different countries are now able to share lesson plans through Internet sites such as The Media Literacy Clearinghouse and Alliance of Civilizations.

Identifying Changes in Media and Cultural Landscapes

Media literacy advocates recognize the value of sharing information as a way to anticipate changes in the media landscape. In addition, global media organizations identify ways in which the media are contributing to the evolution of a global culture. Ofcom discusses the importance of this function on its website:

> As the promotion of media literacy moves up the policy agenda, there is a growing need to maximize efforts to understand and share learning about emerging issues at a European and international level. We cooperate with

European counterparts (particularly the European Commission), providing leadership and stimulating debate with stakeholders, and contribute at conferences and events throughout the UK, in Europe and beyond.[7]

Establishing a Conceptual Framework is a significant step in the maturation of Media Literacy as an international discipline. This effort is a work in progress; we invite others to contribute to the further development of this Conceptual Framework.

Notes

1. "Declaration on Media and Information Literacy." First International Forum on Media and Information Literacy (2011). http://www.unesco.org/new/fileadmin/MULTI MEDIA/HQ/CI/CI/pdf/news/FezDeclaration.pdf.
2. Media Literacy Resource Guide (Ontario Ministry of Education) Toronto, ON. 1989.
3. Richard E. Nisbett, *The Geography of Thought* (New York, London: Free Press, 2003).
4. International Media Literacy Network (http://www.medialiteracynetwork.org).
5. The International Media Literacy Research Forum (http://www.im1rf.org).
6. *International Journal of Learning and Media*. MIT Press (http://mitpress.mit.edu).
7. Ofcom. Independent Regulator and Competition Authority for the U.K. Communications Industries (http://www.ofcom.org.uk).

LIST OF CONTRIBUTORS

Denise E. Agosto, Ph.D., is an Associate Professor in the College of Information Science & Technology at Drexel University, with research and teaching interests in young people's social media practices, children's and teens' digital information practices, and public library services. Dr. Agosto has published more than 100 items in these areas and has won numerous teaching and research awards and research grants for her work.

Neil Andersen is President of The Association for Media Literacy (Ontario). He has taught primary to post-secondary media studies for over 30 years and given keynotes and workshops across Canada, in the United States, Japan, India, China, Australia, and Europe. He has made movies and videos, authored student textbooks, journal articles, teacher resource books, and over 200 study guides, and has designed posters, interactive CDs, websites, and programs. His awards include the Jesse McCanse Award (National Telemedia Council) and The Magic Lantern Award (The Association for Media and Technology in Education).

Yupa Saisanan Na Ayudhya is currently a Fellow in Residence of Webster University in the Center for International Education (CIE). She is an advertising executive with 20 years' experience, and is the former Vice President of J. Walter Thompson Asia-Pacific (headquarters in Bangkok) and Client Service Director of JWT Europe in London. Yupa brings a wealth of international experience to the classroom, which epitomizes the academic mission of Webster University. She has global marketing communication experience working with multinational clients such as Procter & Gamble and Unilever. She works with UNESCO, NGOs, IGOs, and universities around the world to promote media and information literacy education.

Lori Bindig, Ph.D., is an Assistant Professor in the Department of Communication and Media Studies and director of the performing arts minor at Sacred Heart University. She earned her doctorate in communication from the University of Massachusetts Amherst where she was a University Fellow. Dr. Bindig has published on media literacy and eating disorders in the third edition of *Race/Gender/Class/Media,* and is the author of *Dawson's Creek: A Critical Understanding* and co-author of *The O.C.: A Critical Understanding.*

Dr. Gayle Bogel, Ph.D., is the Director of the Educational Technology Program and an Assistant Professor at Fairfield University in Fairfield, Connecticut. She has worked professionally as both a school and public librarian and is currently researching the integration of community partnerships in promoting digital equity for K–12 schools through teacher training and ongoing professional development.

James Castonguay, Ph.D., is an Associate Professor and Director of Graduate Programs in the Department of Communication and Media Studies at Sacred Heart University. He has published widely on war and media culture, and is a contributing writer to the human rights magazine, *Witness* (http://visionproject. org). Dr. Castonguay founded the Society for Cinema and Media Studies' media literacy interest group and received the 2009 Service Award from SCMS.

David M. Considine is an Australian who developed the first master's degree with a media literacy concentration at an American university. He is the author of *The Cinema of Adolescence, Visual Messages: Integrating Imagery into Instruction,* and dozens of scholarly chapters and articles that articulate the role of media literacy in education, particularly for the middle school years. He convened and chaired the first National Media Literacy Conference in the United States at North Carolina's Appalachian State University in September 1995. He worked as a media literacy consultant for the Office of National Drug Control Policy. Dr. Considine retired in 2012.

Michael M. Considine has taught for more than 25 years in high schools, colleges of technical and further education (TAFE), and universities in Melbourne, Australia. His passion is the training of media teachers and he is currently tutoring in the M.Teach./B.Ed. program at Deakin University. He provides mentoring for pre-service teachers in the senior secondary media classes he conducts at RMIT University. He is a life member of the Australian Teachers of Media having served as its chairman and extension education officer. He has published widely and his latest article explores discourses of teenagers, family, and school in *Daria, Dawson's Creek, Buffy the Vampire Slayer,* and a Britney Spears video clip (*Screen Education* No. 70, forthcoming).

Rhys Daunic is the Founder and Director of The Media Spot. Rhys works with educators to develop production-based media literacy curricula. Throughout his career, he has produced process-focused, behind-the-scenes films and other open media literacy resources for themediaspot.org. He is a member of the board of directors of the National Association for Media Literacy Education and teaches a course on K–12 Media Literacy at Teachers College, Columbia University.

Belinha S. De Abreu, Ph.D., is a Media Literacy Educator and Assistant Professor in the Department of Educational Technology at Fairfield University. Her research interests include media literacy education, new media, visual and information literacy, global perspectives, critical thinking, young adults, and teacher training. Dr. De Abreu's focus is on the impact of learning as a result of media and technology consumed by K–12 students; providing students with viable, real-life opportunities for engaging in various technological environments while in turn encouraging students to be creative and conscious users of technology and media. Dr. De Abreu's work has been featured in *Cable in the Classroom* and *The Journal of Media Literacy*. She is the author of *Media Literacy, Social Networking and the Web 2.0 World for the K–12 Educator* (Peter Lang Publishers, 2011). She currently serves as the Vice President for the National Telemedia Council.

Dr Michael Dezuanni is a Senior Lecturer and researcher in the field of digital cultures and education, which includes film and media education, digital literacies and arts education. He is the Deputy Director of Queensland University of Technology's Children and Youth Research Centre and is a co-appointment of the Faculty of Education and Creative Industries Faculty at QUT. The aim of both his teaching and research is to explore the most effective, productive, and meaningful ways for individuals to gain knowledge and understanding of the media and technologies in their lives.

Katherine G. Fry, Ph.D., is Professor of Media Studies in the Department of Television and Radio at Brooklyn College, CUNY, and co-founder and Education Director of The LAMP, a grass-roots media literacy organization based in New York City. Fry's research interests are in news and advertising criticism, media ecology, and media literacy. In addition to scholarly articles and book chapters, she is author of *Constructing the Heartland: Television News and Natural Disaster* (2003) and *Identities in Context: Media, Myth, Religion in Space and Time* (2008).

Frank Gallagher is Executive Director of Cable in the Classroom (CIC), the education foundation of the cable telecommunications industry and is the 2012–2013 chair of the Partnership for 21st Century Skills. He is a graduate of the University of Arizona, received a master's degree from the University of Maryland and taught in Maryland middle schools. He is a specialist in the areas of media literacy, digital citizenship, and the impact of media on children and was the recipient of a 2011 Family Online Safety Institute Award for Outstanding Achievement.

Eric Gordon is a Fellow at the Berkman Center for Internet and Society at Harvard University where he studies mediated civic engagement, location-based media, and serious games. He is also an Associate Professor in the department of Visual and Media Arts at Emerson College where he is the founding director of the Engagement Game Lab, which focuses on the design and research of digital games and playful systems that foster civic engagement. In addition to numerous articles and chapters, he is the author of two books: *Net Locality: Why Location Matters in a Networked World* (with Adriana de Souza e Silva, 2011) and *The Urban Spectator: American Concept Cities from Kodak to Google* (2010). He received his Ph.D. in 2003 from the School of Cinematic Arts at the University of Southern California.

Margaret Carmody Hagood is Associate Professor of Literacy Education at the College of Charleston. She teaches undergraduate and graduate courses in the connections between foundational and new/digital literacies and in research methodologies. She's the co-editor of the *Journal of Adolescent & Adult Literacy*.

Kit Jenkins, ABC, serves as Interim Associate Dean and member of the fulltime faculty for the School of Communications (SOC), emphasizing international perspectives in the curriculum. From 2003 to 2007, she served as Director of Webster University, Thailand, an extended site of Webster University in St. Louis. In that capacity, she was responsible for all academic issues, campus operations, institutional marketing and recruitment, and governmental relations for the Asian campus. Previous to her assignment in Thailand, Jenkins headed the Public Relations program in the SOC for 13 years. She is also currently a professor for the online communications program and oversees the undergraduate Media Literacy major.

Amy Petersen Jensen, Ph.D., is the Department Chair in the Theatre and Media Arts Department at Brigham Young University. Recent book publications include *Theatre in a Media Culture: Production, Performance and Perception Since 1970* (Mcfarland, 2007) and the Co-edited volume *(Re) imagining Literacies for Content-area Classrooms* (Teachers College Press, 2010). Amy has served as the first Vice President of the National Association for Media Literacy Education, Co-editor of the Journal of Media Literacy Education and currently serves as the editor for the American Alliance for Theater in Education's *Youth Theatre Journal*. Amy is on the leadership team for the National Coalition for Core Arts Standards where she is responsible for the development of national standards for Media Arts and Theatre.

Tessa Jolls is President and CEO of the Center for Media Literacy (CML), a position she has held since 1999. During that time, she has restructured CML to focus, grow, and change, preparing to meet the demand for an expanded vision of literacy for the twenty-first century. Her primary focus is on providing models and resources for implementing media literacy in school and community settings. CML's research-based framework, Questions/TIPS (Q/TIPS) serves as the basis for CML's curricula and professional development packages, including the recently published Trilogy of Toolkits called *Media Literacy: A System for Learning AnyTime, AnyWhere*.

William Kist (http://twitter.com/williamkist) has been researching classroom uses of new media across disciplines and grade levels for nearly 20 years. His profiles of teachers who are broadening our conception of literacy have been included in his books *New Literacies in Action* and *The Socially Networked Classroom*. Building upon this work, Dr. Kist's most recent book, *The Global School*, describes teachers who are using new media to collaborate with students and teachers across the world. A former high school English teacher and curriculum supervisor and currently an Associate Professor at Kent State University, Bill has presented nationally and internationally with over 50 articles and book chapters to his credit. A member of the National Book Critics Circle, he reviews books for the *Cleveland Plain Dealer* and remains active as a filmmaker and musician himself, having earned a regional Emmy nomination for Outstanding Music Composition.

Dr. Marcus Leaning is Head of the School of Media and Film at the University of Winchester in the United Kingdom. He is an active researcher in Media Education and has published numerous books, articles, and chapters on the topic. Recent books include *Issues in Information and Media Literacy, Volumes 1 and 2* (Informing Science Press, 2009), *The Internet Power and Society: Rethinking the Power of the Internet to Change Lives* (Chandos, 2009) and *Exploring Collaborative Learning in Media Education* (Higher Education Academy, 2013).

Dr. Alice Y.L. Lee is an Associate Professor at the Department of Journalism, Hong Kong Baptist University. Her research interests include media education, online news media, media and information literacy (MIL), and Net Generation. She is currently a member of the Committee on Home-School Co-operation at the Education Bureau, Hong Kong SAR Government. She is also the vice chairperson of the Hong Kong Association of Media Education.

Sonia Livingstone is Professor of Social Psychology, Department of Media and Communications at LSE, and author or editor of seventeen books and many academic articles and chapters. Recent books include *Meanings of Audiences* (with Richard Butsch, 2013), *Media Regulation* (with Peter Lunt, 2012), *Children and the Internet* (2009), and *The Handbook of New Media* (with Leah Lievrouw, 2006). She has held visiting professor positions at the Universities of Bergen, Copenhagen, Harvard, Illinois, Milan, Paris II, and Stockholm, and is on the editorial board of several leading journals. She was President of the International Communication Association in 2007–2008.

Per Lundgren is the Senior Advisor to the Nordic Council of Ministers, Media and Culture and a member of the board of directors of the World Summit on Media for Children Foundation. For the City of Karlstad and Karlstad University in Sweden, he is the co-founder of The Alliance of Civilizations Media Literacy Education Clearinghouse. He is the author of the 2002 survey in the Scandinavian countries on media literacy for the European Commission. He is a member of the second expert group of UNESCO's Media and Information Literacy Curriculum for Teachers and the past director of the Sixth World Summit on Media for Children and Youth in Karlstad Sweden, 2010.

Rachel M. Magee is a doctoral candidate at the iSchool at Drexel University. As a youth advocate, she is interested in developing research that works to improve the lives of young people. Her dissertation, informed by her background as a teen services librarian, is focused on teens' everyday life technology experiences and differing levels of technology use. Previously, she received her M.A. in Information Resources and Library Science from the University of Arizona, as well as a B.A. in English and a B.S. in Radio-Television-Film from the University of Texas at Austin.

Dr. Julian McDougall is Associate Professor in the Centre for Excellence in Media Practice at Bournemouth University. He is co-editor of the *Media Education Research Journal* and author of *After the Media: Culture and Identity in the 21st Century, The Media Teacher's Book, Barthes Mythologies Today: Readings of Contemporary Culture, Studying Videogames*, and *Media Studies: The Basics*. He has published a range of research into media literacies, textual practices, and pedagogy. At CEMP, he is Programme Leader for the Educational Doctorate in Creative & Media Education and is currently supervising doctoral research into digital ethnography as a pedagogic approach.

Jad P. Melki, Ph.D., is the Director of Media Studies and an Assistant Professor of journalism and media studies at the American University of Beirut. He is chair of the Media and Digital Literacy Academy of Beirut, a visiting faculty at the Salzburg Academy on Media and Global Change, and an affiliated research director at the International Center for Media and the Public Agenda at the University of Maryland, College Park, where he received his Ph.D. Contact: jad.melki@aub.edu.lb.

Paul Mihailidis, Ph.D., is an Assistant Professor in Media Studies the school of communication at Emerson College in Boston, where he teaches media literacy and interactive media. His research focuses on the nexus of media, education, and civic voices. His most recent books are *Media Literacy and the Emerging Citizen: Youth Participation and Engagement in the Digital Age* (Peter Lang, 2014) and *News Literacy: Global Perspectives for the Newsroom and the Classroom* (Peter Lang, 2011).

Mihailidis directs the new global engagement lab at Emerson College, and the Salzburg Academy on Media and Global Change. He sits on the board of directors for the National Association of Media Literacy Education.

Deirdre J. Morgenthaler, holds a master's degree in Communication and is currently pursuing her doctorate in Educational Studies and Research at the University of Colorado Denver.

Nick Pernisco is an Associate Instructor in the Media Studies department at Santa Monica College, where he teaches courses on media literacy, race, and gender in journalism, and radio and television production. He is also founder of www.UnderstandMedia.com, a media literacy website containing original articles, podcasts, videos, lesson plans, discussion forums, and a blog. Nick also produces educational videos about media literacy, and edits the *Student Journal of Media Literacy Education*. He currently splits his time between Los Angeles and Seattle.

Erin Reilly is Creative Director and Research Fellow for Annenberg Innovation Lab at USC's Annenberg School for Communications & Journalism. Her research focus is children, youth, and media and the interdisciplinary, creative learning experiences that occur through social and cultural participation with emergent technologies. She is a board member of the National Association for Media Literacy Educators and serves on advisory boards, such as PBS Emmy-award winning Sci Girls, Gulf of Maine Research Institute's Educational Advisory Group, and National Assessment of Educational Progress where she is helping to develop the first technology and engineering literacy assessment.

Steven Schirra received his S.M. in Comparative Media Studies from the Massachusetts Institute of Technology. His research interests include serious games, social television, and human-computer interaction. As a games researcher, he has worked with the Engagement Game Lab, the MIT Game Lab, and The Education Arcade. In 2011, his research team at the Engagement Game Lab was awarded Best Direct-Impact Game by Games for Change.

Gretchen Schwarz teaches media literacy education and other graduate courses in the Department of Curriculum and Instruction at Baylor University. She began studying media literacy while at Oklahoma State University. Schwarz also taught high school English and German for 13 years in New Mexico and Texas. A special research interest is graphic novels.

Art Silverblatt is Professor of Communications and Journalism at Webster University in St. Louis, Missouri. He earned his Ph.D. in 1980 from Michigan State University. He is the author of numerous books and articles, including *Media Literacy: Keys to Interpreting Media Messages*, (Praeger Publications, ABC-Clio, 2007,

2014), *The Dictionary of Media Literacy* (Greenwood Press, 1997), *Approaches to Media Literacy* (M.E. Sharpe, 1999, 2008), *International Communications: A Media Literacy Approach* (M.E. Sharpe, 2004), *Approaches to Genre Study* (M.E. Sharpe, 2006), and *Handbook of Media Literacy* (ABC-Clio, 2013). He is currently Vice President of the Gateway Media Literacy Partners (GMLP), a regional media literacy consortium.

Barbara J. Walkosz is a Senior Scientist at Klein Buendel, Inc. in Golden, Colorado. Her background is in media education, health communication, and social marketing. She is interested in media literacy as a means to promoting critical thinking about how the media impacts our health. Her current work focuses on the development and implementation of health communication campaigns to promote healthy behavior and institutional policy change.

Yin-Han Wang holds a Ph.D. in Media and Communications from the London School of Economics and Political Science. Prior to joining LSE, she studied MSc Advertising at the University of Illinois, Urbana-Champaign. Her research interests are identity and media consumption, gender and issues of representation, media literacies, and young people's social and civic uses of the Internet. She is currently an independent researcher.

Annette Woods is an Associate Professor in the Faculty of Education at Queensland University of Technology. She teaches and researches in the fields of literacy, social justice, and curriculum and pedagogy. Her most recent research includes a large-scale evaluation of a school reform project aimed at improving school outcomes for indigenous students, an investigation of teachers' use of the official curriculum, and a school reform project that has investigated the links between engagement in media arts and digital texts on teacher and student capacity in teaching and learning literacy in primary schools.

INDEX

FreeRice.com 154
Free Rice online project 56
Free Rice project 56, 154, 156
Freire, Paolo 123, 127
future shock of K–12 education, antidote
  for: DML success stories, strategies,
  common challenges 186; New York
  City challenges 184–5; simplification
  solution 185

Gaines, Eliot 33
game-based learning in public
  participation processes 153–7; names
  and types 156–7; origins and goals 156;
  participation problems 154–6; types of
  learning created 154
Gasser, U. 216
Gauntlett, D. 5–6
Getting Started in Media Education
  (Pungente) 25
Gibson, R. 168
Golay, Jean-Pierre 19
Goodreads website 56
Google: copyright issues vs. authors xxvii;
  doc application 53; information truth
  issues 31; search engine 31, 46
Google Earth application 54
Google Nexus 7 (tablet) 57
Go On Campaign (UK) 166
Government's Citizens Online centres
  (UK) 162

Habermas, Jurgen 144
Habermasian model of public sphere
  communication 5
Hagood, Margaret xvi–xvii
Hall, S. 105
Hansard Society 168
Harding, H. 215
Harris, Jonathan 47
Hart, A. 206
Hibr Lubnani (Lebanese Ink) digital
  literacy training 79–80
Hobbs, Renee: on attractiveness of media
  literacy concepts 142; co-founding of
  Alliance for a Media Literate America
  145; on connecting media literacy
  studies 16; on five essential dimensions
  of digital and media literacy 176; "great
  debates" essay 144; on helping students
  acquire digital citizenship competencies
  177; on history of media arts education
  movement 119; on media literacy
  protectionism for young people 126;

on partnership development 17; role
  at University of Rhode Island 217; on
  seven recurring points of contention in
  media literacy community 141
HOMAGO ("hanging out, messing
  around, and geeking out") library
  strategy 106, 108
Hong Kong media education: iPads
  usage 88–90; MARS MEDIA
  Community Project 90–1; old vs.
  new paradigm 91, 92; participation of
  Net Geners 88–92; primary school
  program efforts 88–90; program
  goals 91; *21st Century Skills Learning:
  Creative Information Technology Education
  Project* 89; Web 2.0, digital technology
  integration 59, 79, 91–2
The Hunger Site 153–4

Information and Communications
  Technology (ICT) literacy 99
information literacy: call for, in Hong
  Kong 92; goal of teaching xxix;
  integration with media literacy xvii, 62,
  92, 97–101; Nordic concerns for xvii,
  59, 62; role of libraries 112; UNESCO
  training program 62, 66
"In my language" *YouTube* video (Baggs)
  37–8, 40, 43
Inquiry into Teacher Education (Australia)
  207
Inside Plato's Cave on-line course for
  teachers (Pungente) 7
International Journal of Learning and Media
  223
international media and information
  literacy 219–24
International Media Literacy Network 222
International Media Literacy Research
  Forum 223
Internet: access issues 148; age of users
  xxiv; Children's Internet Protection
  Act 178; collective intelligence fostered
  by 47; as a digital communication
  matrix 130; global reach enabled by
  54; governmental efforts at control of
  132; graphs for understanding 163, 165;
  impact on the 2008 U.S. presidential
  election xxvi; and information
  credibility 11; initial celebrations about
  xxiv–xxv; international collaboration
  projects 222–3; open and free use
  xxiv–xxv; reasons for using 164–5; role
  in helping deal with social inequalities